You Gotta Eat Here Too!

John Catucci
and Michael Vlessides

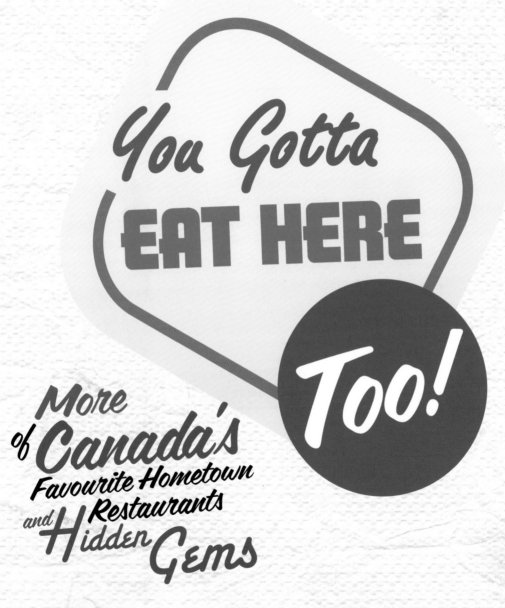

You Gotta
EAT HERE
Too!

More
of Canada's
Favourite Hometown
and Restaurants
Hidden Gems

Collins

You Gotta Eat Here Too!
Text and photographs copyright © 2014 by Lone Eagle Entertainment Ltd.
All rights reserved.

Published by Collins,
an imprint of HarperCollins Publishers Ltd

First edition

The authors and publisher are grateful to the restaurants featured in *You Gotta Eat Here Too!*,
which have provided all the recipes in this book. Recipes may differ from those presented on the
television show *You Gotta Eat Here!* Where necessary, chefs have modified recipes to suit the
needs of home cooks. On behalf of all the chefs and restaurants, we hope you enjoy!

HarperCollins books may be purchased for educational, business, or sales promotional
use through our Special Markets Department.

HarperCollins Publishers Ltd
2 Bloor Street East, 20th Floor
Toronto, Ontario, Canada
M4W 1A8

www.harpercollins.ca

Library and Archives Canada Cataloguing in Publication
information is available upon request.

ISBN 978-1-44342-948-1

Researcher: Sarah Hewitt
Photographs by Josh Henderson except for studio photos by Geoff George

Printed and bound in Canada
TC 9 8 7 6 5 4 3 2 1

Contents

WESTERN CANADA

NORTHERN CANADA

Introduction

HAPPENS EVERY TIME.

No matter where I go in this great country of ours, people stop me on the street and ask me the same thing: *John, what's your favourite restaurant?*

Having eaten at hundreds of amazing joints, it's not as easy a question to answer as you might think. Sure, I could rattle off my all-time Top 5 or Top 10 without breaking too much of a sweat, but picking The One isn't quite so easy. I mean, where do I even start?

Of course, the food is hugely important, but you might be surprised to know that it's not just about the food for me. It's never just about the food. In fact, I've eaten in restaurants that served up some of the most amazing dishes I've ever put in my mouth, but they wouldn't even scratch the surface of my list. Why? No heart.

You see, heart is the secret ingredient that separates the great restaurants from all the rest. Yes, I *love* a good meal. But great restaurants not only serve up great food, they do it while making an emotional connection with their customers, too. And the restaurants I love the most are the ones where I feel that connection.

For me, sitting down to a meal isn't just about feeding my body (OK, so I'll jam a burger in my piehole just as soon as the next guy), but feeding my soul, too. The best places do that with seemingly little effort. You know the joints I'm talking about, the ones where you feel as though you've dropped into a friend's house unexpectedly and they ask you to stay for dinner. The meal feels like a continuation of your own traditions; the staff is like family.

For a guy who's on the road more than at home, that means a lot. I appreciate the warmth, the comfort, and the love I feel from these strangers when I can't be with my own family. These are the places that make me forget I'm working. The food is great, the conversation flows, the love is all around, and the hugs don't stop when the cameras do.

The beauty of the restaurants we feature in *You Gotta Eat Here Too!* is that they're not chains. These aren't multinational corporations whose goal is to create the same experience no matter where in the world you might be. These are one-of-a-kind treasures, mom-and-pop shops (or mom-and-mom shops . . . or pop-and-pop shops) that strive to do things differently from everyone else.

After all, it takes commitment to be a part of the *You Gotta Eat Here!* family. We take our cameras, lights, and sound equipment and barge into people's very livelihoods. They have to close their doors for a couple of days, send their eager (and sometimes disappointed!) customers away, and try to teach an Italian guy the secrets of their success. Each restaurant is grateful for the opportunity, some make it easy, and many reach that magic place where food, fun, and family all come together in perfect harmony.

Interestingly, that magic seems to happen when the owner is heavily involved in the business. Walk into some restaurants, and you can tell there's very little connection between the people who sign the cheques and the people who receive them. These joints are a dime a dozen and don't leave you with much more than a full stomach. But the places I love are the ones where the owner's passion is palpable. He or she is proud to introduce you to every single employee on the staff, whether they're cleaning the floor or cooking your meal. These are the owners that eagerly watch you take that first bite and offer you more when you finish the last.

And while my tastes definitely push me toward the Italian side of the culinary spectrum, in the end it doesn't really matter what kind of food I'm being served. From Mexican to Polish, poutine to pizza, if there's love on the menu, I'm diggin' it.

So what's my all-time, number-one, hands-down favourite restaurant? I'm not saying. At least not now, that is. In the meantime, you're going to have to do your own research. And when you visit a joint that dishes out the love as freely as it dishes out the food, drop us a line at tips@yougottaeathere.ca.

Massive Meals Across the Country

Canada's a big country, right? After a day of mushing our dog team across the frozen tundra or paddling a canoeful of beaver pelts down the St. Lawrence, we Canucks can work up an appetite every bit as big as our home and native land. Don't feel bad about it, friends. Dig in! With meals like this peppered across this great country of ours, you won't have to go far to satisfy your craving for XXL.

MAMMOTH BURGER
Bernie & The Boys Bistro,
Drumheller, AB

*One and a half pounds
of bun. One and a
half pounds of beef. A
mountain of fixings. Any
questions?*

FURIOUS CANNUCKER PIE
Pie, Barrie, ON

*A three-pizza stack topped
with a pound of poutine.
Defibrillator optional.*

BURRITO GUADALAJARA
Fiesta Mexicana
Restaurantey Cantina,
Kamloops, BC

*Tons of fillings on a
burrito so big it must be
custom-made.*

PANCAKE STACKER
The Early Bird, London, ON

*Four pancakes are just the
beginning . . .*

ELVIS PLATTER
Big T's BBQ &
Smokehouse, Calgary, AB

*Six different kinds of
smoked meat paired with
six sides . . . king-sized!*

THE ITALIAN JOB
That Italian Place,
Brampton, ON

*A 2-foot long stromboli.
'Nuf said.*

INDIAN TACO
Burger Barn,
Ohsweken, ON

*Only a foundation of
bannock can stand
up to the mountain of
meaty chili, cheese, and
veggies that comes next!*

Eastern Canada

Chafe's Landing

EST. 2008
11 MAIN ROAD, PETTY HARBOUR
ST. JOHN'S, NL · A0A 3H0
709-747-0802
WWW.CHAFESLANDING.COM

I f you've never been to Newfoundland, you're missing something. The people here are the salt of the earth—the happiest, most laid-back and fun-loving I've ever met. Well, if you take all that goodness and wrap it up into a neat little restaurant, you've got Chafe's Landing: a place that's as traditional as Newfoundland itself, a warm, comforting joint that serves up the best that The Rock has to offer, both on and off the plate.

Visiting Chafe's Landing is like taking a trip back home, an experience that has a lot to do with the fact that the restaurant is . . . well . . . a house. The building dates back to 1878, when it was constructed by Edward Chafe. Now, generations later, husband-and-wife team Todd and Angela Chafe serve a mix of local seafood and game that harkens back to their ancestors. And if you're wondering whether the food is fresh, don't bother: Todd comes from a long line of fishermen, and starts his work day at 3:00 a.m., when he hits the boat to secure the day's catch. After he docks later in the afternoon, he and Angela work their magic in the kitchen, leaving people all across this gorgeous little town—and nearby St. John's—smiling as a result.

Few things made me happier at Chafe's than the Pulled Moose Roll, where classic sandwich meets Newfoundlander twist. The sandwich is built upon a heap of moose meat (did you know there are more than 100,000 moose in Newfoundland?) that gets slow-roasted until succulent, then pulled and cooked in its own gravy. Then it's onto a gorgeous ciabatta bun, along with sautéed mushrooms and onions, and a pile of shredded mozzarella and Cheddar cheese. Melted in the oven and served piping hot, the sandwich tastes like a little bit of paradise. The roll is served with the best Newfoundlander side dish you'll find this side of the Grand Banks: fries topped with dressing

That boy knows his cod! Mark Saunders is one of the geniuses behind the down-home delights at Chafe's, though his culinary repertoire extends well beyond Newfoundland's fave fish.

and moose gravy. The dressing's unique flavour comes from loads of Newfoundland savory, which locals claim is the world's finest.

Todd and Angela's Fish and Chips come highly recommended and are the most popular item on the menu. The Lobster Club is a triple-decker behemoth, with lobsters that go from boat to pot in the same day. Crab Rolls are sweet and buttery, served on a New England hot dog bun. Other menu faves are the overflowing platter of fried seafood known as the Captain's Plate, and the Surf and Turf Burger (beef burger topped with beer-battered onion rings and crispy popcorn shrimp). No wonder this place is a *You Gotta Eat Here!* Fan Favourite!

As they say here in Petty Harbour, the food is toothsome, bai. And that, my friends, is the truth.

Moose is a staple of the Newfoundland diet, and Chafe's Landing is no different; here the moose becomes several dishes, including the comforting Pulled Moose Roll.

If you like your fish on the cheesy side, Chafe's Cod au Gratin is your answer. This ooey, gooey mess features poached fish baked in a creamy white sauce and buried under mounds of shredded Cheddar cheese.

Codfish Cakes

Makes: 12 to 15 cakes

Cod is a Newfoundland staple that gets lots of play at Chafe's Landing. The Codfish Cakes start as giant slabs of salted cod, which are rehydrated, desalinated, and boiled until deliciously tender. The cod hunks are blended with sautéed onions, mashed potatoes, and savory, then pan-fried for a crispy finish. As locals will tell you, the cakes are the perfect balance between fish and bodados (that's *potatoes* to you), made even better by the side of vegetable pickle they're served with.

1 pound salt cod
6 potatoes
2 tablespoons margarine
1 onion, finely chopped
½ teaspoon black pepper
1 tablespoon dried savory
Vegetable pickle (optional)

Soak the salt cod in water in the fridge overnight.

Drain the salt cod and rinse well under cold running water. Place the cod in a saucepan and cover with fresh water. Bring to a boil, reduce heat to low, and simmer for 5 to 10 minutes, until the fish starts to flake apart. Drain well and transfer to a large bowl. Using a fork, flake cod. Set aside.

Peel and quarter the potatoes. Place in a large saucepan and add enough cold water to just cover the potatoes. Bring to a boil over medium heat and cook until tender. Drain potatoes, then mash. Set aside.

In a skillet over medium heat, melt margarine. Add onions and cook until soft and translucent. Stir the onions into the mashed potatoes, then add the potato mixture to the flaked cod. Season with pepper and savory and stir until well combined. Scoop mixture into 12 to 15 ice-cream-scoop sized cakes, and flatten them with your hands.

In a greased skillet over medium heat, fry cakes for 3 minutes per side, until golden brown.

Serve with a garden salad and vegetable pickle, if using.

CheeseCurds Gourmet Burgers and Poutinerie

EST. 2012
380 PLEASANT STREET
DARTMOUTH, NS · B2Y 3S5
902-444-3446
WWW.CHEESECURDSBURGERS.COM

Four words: Best. Onion. Rings. Ever.

Not what you'd expect from a place that calls itself CheeseCurds, right? Well, surprises are the name of the game at this neo-classic burger joint, where a seasoned navy veteran and accomplished chef whips up some of the most ingenious burger creations this side of the Continental Divide. As for poutine, they've got that, too, in equally inventive machinations!

The heart and soul of CheeseCurds is Bill Pratt, whose extensive culinary resumé boasts a host of far-flung accolades, like serving as personal chef for Prince Charles and Princess Diana aboard the royal yacht *Britannia*. But after decades of bouncing around the world, Bill and his family moved back to Halifax, where Bill decided to create a whimsical-yet-efficient eatery that offers its customers the best in Canadian comfort food: burgers, poutine, and onion rings.

Onions rings? Yes! Onion rings! Remember when you were a kid and you pulled the onion out just to eat the crust? Well that's *not* these rings, my friends. Bill soaks the Spanish onion slices in buttermilk for about

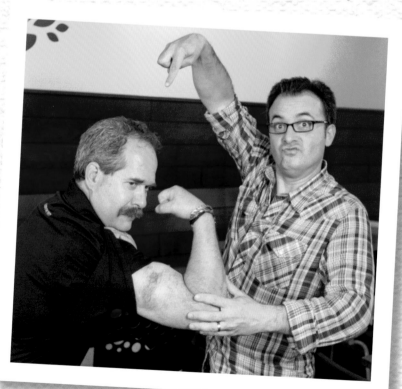

Look at dem guns! CheeseCurds chef and owner Bill Pratt has had his share of wild experiences, and also makes the best onion rings on the planet. He will beat half of human-kind in an arm wrestle to boot!

135 years before coating them with panko and deep-frying. The result is a perfect little halo of goodness, the best ring I've ever popped into my greedy little mouth.

Bill's onion rings make a cameo appearance on his Legendary CC Porker, a triple-decker behemoth that features two 6-ounce Black Angus beef patties (sourced from local ranchers), each of which is topped with two strips of bacon and a mound of cheese curds. (Hey, Bill never claimed his food was healthy . . . just yummy!) Add some of CheeseCurds' cheesy-and-garlicky CC Sauce, a mountain of fixings, and crown it all with a couple of angelic onion rings, and the result, *mon peeps,* is down-home goodness.

If you're beginning to pick up what I'm putting down, you know you won't find just any ol' meat-and-bun fabrications at CheeseCurds, a *You Gotta Eat Here!* Fan Favourite. CheeseCurds offers exciting burger creations for every possible preference, of which the Pork Schnitzel Burger is one of the most popular. This stroke of culinary brilliance consists of a crispy pork schnitzel topped with Cheddar cheese and peameal bacon, blanketed with Bill's homemade caramelized onion jam. Pair it with some luxurious Brandy Peppercorn Poutine and you've arrived, baby. Other CheeseCurds highlights are the Monster Mozza Crunch Burger (fried cheese topped with bacon and chipotle mayo), Thai Chicken Burger, Honolulu Burger (complete with a slice of caramelized pineapple), and Spicy Veggie Lentil and Bean Burger (with hints of Asia in every bite). The Sweet Potato Curry Poutine features a homemade curry sauce inspired by

well-known chef Vikram Vij, and the Triple Bacon CC Cheese Dog is a jumbo dog fried with two strips of bacon and topped with fried onions and cheese curds. *Yowza!*

My advice? Do like the locals do and go back again and again, and try something different every time. Except the onion rings. Order those every time. And tell 'em John sent ya.

Maybe they should just call the Pork Schnitzel Burger the Fave Burger, since it's one of the most sought-after items on the Curds menu. It features one of Bill's favorite toppings, his homemade caramelized onion jam. I'll fave it!

Lamb Burger

Makes: 8 servings

A flavour bomb if ever there was one. And if the flavour of the lamb isn't enough, Bill goes hard-core Mediterranean by surrounding it with piles, heaps, and mounds of grilled onions, peppers, and zucchini, fresh bruschetta topping, crumbled feta cheese, hummus, and arugula on a bun.

Burger

½ cup finely diced onion
1 tablespoon minced garlic
½ cup panko bread crumbs
2 tablespoons chopped fresh mint
2 tablespoons chopped fresh cilantro
¼ cup grainy Dijon mustard
2 teaspoons salt
1 teaspoon black pepper
Zest and juice of 1 lemon
3 eggs
2½ pounds ground fresh lamb

Grilled Vegetables

1 red onion, thickly sliced
1 sweet red pepper, cut into 1-inch-wide strips
1 large zucchini, cut into ¼-inch-thick coins
Extra virgin olive oil
Salt and pepper

Bruschetta

2 medium Roma tomatoes, cut into ½-inch dice
1 tablespoon minced yellow onion
1 large basil leaf, sliced very thinly
1 tablespoon extra virgin olive oil
1 teaspoon balsamic vinegar
Pinch of sea salt
Pinch of freshly cracked black pepper

Assembly

8 hamburger or ciabatta buns brushed with garlic butter
8 ounces feta cheese, crumbled
1 cup arugula
1 cup hummus

Burger

In a large bowl, thoroughly combine all of the ingredients except the lamb. Add the lamb and stir or mix with your hands just until incorporated (be careful not to over-mix or the texture of the burger will be too tough).

Divide burger mixture into 8 patties. Arrange patties about 4 inches apart on a sheet of parchment paper and cover with another sheet of parchment (plastic wrap also works well). Use the largest can in your pantry to flatten each patty to about ¼ inch thick. Refrigerate the patties until ready to use.

Grilled Vegetables

Preheat barbeque or oven to 375°F. Brush the prepared vegetables with oil and season with salt and pepper. Grill the vegetables on the barbeque or in the oven until both sides just start to wilt. Transfer the grilled veggies to a plate and set aside.

Bruschetta

In a small bowl, combine all of the ingredients. Refrigerate until ready to use.

Assembly

Heat a griddle or barbeque to medium. (CheeseCurds prefers griddle cooking so that the meat can cook in its own fat.) Cook the burgers for 4 to 6 minutes on the first side. Flip, then return vegetables to the grill to reheat. Continue cooking for 4 to 6 minutes.

When the burger is almost cooked, split your buns and toast them on the barbeque or grill until slightly browned.

To assemble the burgers, divide the grilled veggies among the bottom halves of the buns and top with the grilled burger patties. Sprinkle each patty with about one-eighth of the feta, then dollop with 1 heaping tablespoon of bruschetta topping. Place a few leaves of arugula on top. Spread hummus on the top halves of the buns and cover burgers. Enjoy!

The Churchill Arms

EST. 2003
75 QUEEN STREET
CHARLOTTETOWN, PEI · C1A 4A8
902-367-3450
WWW.CHURCHILLARMS.CA

How do you know a restaurant is worth visiting? When everyone you bump into on the street tells you to go there! That's the Churchill Arms, Charlottetown's answer to merry old England, where classic pub grub goes hand in hand with the curries that Brits adore. Here you'll find the welcoming pub spirit alive and well, as people from all walks of life sit down to a delicious meal, share a pint, and spend some time with friends and family.

And that's exactly how Francine wants it. Francine Thorpe is the Churchill's high-energy owner, a British expat who emigrated to PEI more than two decades ago. Her recipes—most of which are inspired by her grandmother's home cooking—come from the heart, and the kitchen is her playground.

Curries are big at the Churchill, and a highlight for me was Francine's Butter Chicken. One of the mellower curries at the Churchill, the Butter Chicken was a great warm-up (call me a wimp and I'll hit you with a meatball). Francine marinates chicken breast chunks overnight before frying them in heaps of butter. Then she adds a hefty portion of her "master" curry sauce, spiked with a shot of cream. Rich, tender, and exotic, this is a curry rookie's dream.

Francine's recipes are all traditional, having been passed down through generations.

The Butter Chicken is served alongside a warm piece of naan bread and either basmati rice or thick-cut french fries. If you're planning on staying a while (as in, like, falling asleep at your table), go big and order the Onion Bhaji, piles of onion slices bathed in a spiced chickpea batter before hitting the deep-fryer. Messy fingers and all, they're tasty enough on their own, but are also a great way to soak up the extra Butter Chicken sauce on your plate, too.

Perfect for curry newbies, the Churchill's Butter Chicken is a mellow groove that'll fill your belly as much as it tickles your taste buds.

There's lots more curry where that came from. Climbing slightly up the spice scale is the infinitely popular Chicken Tikka Masala, which features chicken that's been marinated overnight then roasted on skewers and doused in a creamy tikka sauce. Served with naan bread and your choice of basmati rice or french fries, the deep orange dish leaves your belly and your mouth warm and happy. Francine will even currify your fries for you: her Curry Chips are topped with Cheddar cheese and served with a choice of madras, tikka, or korma sauce. Indian poutine!

And now you'll have to excuse me. I need to start walking the streets of Charlottetown so I can tell people where to go. To the Churchill Arms, that is.

The Churchill Arms is a local fave, playing host to people from the full spectrum of Charlottetown's cultural rainbow, whether they're enjoying a pint after work or warming their bellies at lunch.

Steak and Stout Pie

Makes: 4 servings

Traditional British pub food plays a part in Francine's menu, but none tickled my proverbial fancy more than the Steak and Stout Pie, a rich and steamy beef stew highlighted by the savoury taste of stout. What makes this meal truly unique is the potato bread crust that covers the crock when it arrives at your table, a thick and hearty way to soak up the juices waiting underneath. Customers say it's the perfect comfort food on a rainy day. I say it tastes like love.

Filling

2 tablespoons vegetable or canola oil
2 pounds stewing beef
3 tablespoons all-purpose flour
1 cup sliced carrots (cut into coins)
1 cup thinly sliced mushrooms
1 onion, finely chopped
2 cups beef stock
2 cups stout (dark ale)
3 bay leaves

2 tablespoons Worcestershire sauce
1 tablespoon dried basil
1 to 2 tablespoons cornstarch (to thicken as desired)

Crust

6 to 8 potatoes (or 4 cups, mashed)
1 cup all-purpose flour
2 tablespoons butter
oregano (optional)

Filling

In a pot over medium heat, heat the oil.

In a large bowl, toss the stewing beef with the flour. Add the floured beef to the pot and sear until browned on all sides, about 2 minutes. Add the carrots, mushrooms, and onion and stir to combine. Add the stock and stout and stir well. Stir in the bay leaves, Worcestershire, and basil. Bring to a boil, reduce heat, and simmer for 2 to 3 hours, until the beef is tender and cooked through. Stir in the cornstarch and cook until mixture is desired consistency.

Mashed Potatoes

Peel potatoes and boil until tender. Drain and mash until smooth, adding butter and cream if desired.

Crust

In a large bowl, combine the mashed potatoes and flour. Using your hands, divide the potato and flour mixture into 4 even balls. Flatten each ball with the palm of your hands.

In a skillet over medium heat, melt the butter. Add the potato cakes and fry until golden brown, flipping once.

Assembly

Divide the pie filling among 4 serving bowls. Top each with 1 piece of hot potato crust. Sprinkle with oregano if desired.

Colette's Place

EST. 1982
201 BROOKSIDE STREET
GLACE BAY, NS · B1A 1L6
902-849-8430

Nova Scotia's Cape Breton Island is one of the warmest places in the world. Not on the thermometer, mind you, but in the heart. This is a place where total strangers feel like family after a few short minutes, and the conversation flows as freely as the love. And smack in the middle of all that positive energy is Colette's Place, a family affair that has its priorities straight: people first, profits later.

Yet Colette's wasn't always Colette's. Back in 1982, Judy McKinnon started Judy's Place, a family restaurant dedicated to simple, homemade meals at a fair price. Fast-forward 22 years, and Judy's daughter Colette takes over, changing little about the place but the name. Now Colette's husband, Frankie Martin, is on cooking duty while Colette serves as general manager, but customers know they can still count on getting the heart-warming comfort food they've come to know and love over the past three decades. As for Judy, she's still an important part of this family's recipe, filling in for Frankie in the kitchen on his days off.

Standing the test of time on Colette's menu is the signature BBQ Sausage Dinner, a dish conceived by Judy when she first opened the restaurant. The secret to the dish is the approach: Judy knew that her local pork sausages are less fatty when boiled first, after which they are fried on the flattop for texture. After frying, the sausages are baked in a tray swimming with homemade barbeque sauce. The sausages are only ready when they're piping hot, which is when they're served alongside mashed potatoes and seasonal vegetables. This is a down-home, warm-your-heart meal that will leave you looking for a recliner and a nap afterwards.

Frankie Martin is not only Colette's husband, he's also the driving force behind the comfort classics served here daily. . . and one heck of a nice guy, to boot.

Warm hearts are a specialty at Colette's, and you can feel the love in every bite of the Roast Turkey Dinner, a little bit of holiday comfort no matter what the calendar says. The Bay Boy Belter Sandwich is a grilled cheese on steroids, spiking the original with batter-fried bread and slices of oven-roasted beef, along with three slices of bacon.

Dessert is another homemade undertaking at Colette's, this time the exclusive preserve of Karen Bran, a grandmother of seven who has come out of retirement, to Frankie and Colette's delight. Karen loves her work so much, she does it for nothing, but her creations taste like a million bucks. The Carrot Cake is both topped *and* stuffed with sweet cream-cheese icing, a classic small-town-diner dessert that has grown to legendary proportions in the area. Karen's Butterscotch Pie is a sweet and sticky delight topped with whipped cream, and it's in high demand.

And if you're embarrassed by the butterscotch on your face, don't be. It won't be long before someone else in the place walks over and wipes your mug clean. Sure, they'll probably make fun of you afterwards, but isn't that just what you'd expect from family?

One slice . . . or the whole dang thing? Karen Bran's Carrot Cake is *not* a low-cal offering, but that may not stop you from, er, *overindulging.*

Scottish Toast

Makes: 4 servings

Scottish Toast is a breakfast menu item that's ordered regardless of the hour: French toast topped with warm oatmeal and warm maple syrup.

8 eggs
2 cups old-fashioned rolled oats
1 cup loosely packed brown sugar
8 thick slices bread

In a small bowl, whisk the eggs until frothy.

In another small bowl, combine the oats and brown sugar.

Working with one slice of bread at a time, dip the bread into the egg mixture, coating both sides. Dip the egg-drenched bread into the oat mixture, coating both sides.

Fry coated slices in a greased skillet over medium-high heat for 5 minutes per side, or until golden.

Serve with warm maple syrup and a side of bacon, ham, or sausage.

Famous Festive Poutine

Makes: 4 or more servings

Both Frankie and Judy love stuffing their customers to the max, and nothing gets the job done quite like the Famous Festive Poutine. It starts with a bed of crispy fries, but this is where any resemblance between the original and this version ends. The Festive is then topped with a thick layer of homemade stuffing: a hearty fusion of bread chunks, butter, and bacon. Next is a layer of succulent, slow-cooked turkey. Turkey gravy plus a mound of mozzarella blankets the entire proceeding, making the dish taste like Christmas on a plate . . . only with fries and cheese, too.

Poutine

1 boneless, skinless turkey breast (4 ounces)
Salt and pepper
12 medium potatoes (6 for fries, 6 for stuffing)
16 to 24 ounces shredded mozzarella cheese

Gravy

1 cup all-purpose flour
1 tablespoon onion powder
1 teaspoon poultry seasoning
Pinch of dried sage
Pinch of salt and pepper

Stuffing

1 small loaf bread, torn into 1-inch pieces
1 cup chicken stock
½ cup butter, room temperature
6 slices uncooked bacon
1 tablespoon poultry seasoning
1 tablespoon dried sage
1 tablespoon onion powder
1 teaspoon salt
1 teaspoon black pepper

Poutine

Preheat oven to 350°F.

Place the turkey breast skin-side up in a roasting pan. Season with salt and pepper and cover pan with aluminum foil. Roast for about 1½ hours, or until juices run clear when pierced with a fork. Transfer the turkey breast to a plate to rest for 10 to 15 minutes, then cut turkey into slices, reserving the pan drippings.

Meanwhile, peel and quarter 6 potatoes. Place in a large saucepan and add enough cold water to just cover. Bring to a boil over medium heat and cook until tender. Drain potatoes, then mash. Set aside.

Gravy

Heat a medium saucepan over medium heat. Add the reserved pan drippings and an equal amount of water to the saucepan and bring to a boil.

In a small bowl, whisk together 1 cup cold water and flour. Add 2 tablespoons of the flour water to the saucepan and stir to combine. Cook for 1 to 2 minutes, until the gravy thickens, adding more of the flour water as needed to reach desired consistency. Stir in the onion powder, poultry seasoning, sage, salt, and pepper. Set aside.

Stuffing

Preheat oven to 375°F.

Heat a small pan over medium heat. Cook 6 slices of bacon until crisp, flipping once. Chop into small pieces.

Place the bread in a roasting pan. Add 5 cups of the mashed potatoes and the chicken stock and stir to combine. Stir in the butter and crispy bacon. Add the poultry seasoning, sage, onion powder, salt, and pepper and stir well. Cover and bake in preheated oven for 30 minutes.

Assembly

Cut the remaining 6 potatoes into french fries. Deep-fry or oven-bake until golden brown.

Divide the fries evenly among serving plates (deep dishes or boats work well). Top with sliced turkey breast, stuffing, gravy, and mozzarella cheese. (Optional: Top with cranberry sauce as well.)

Flavor 19

EST. 2011
1225 GRAND LAKE ROAD
LINGAN GOLF COURSE
SYDNEY, NS · B1M 1A2
905-562-2233
WWW.CBFLAVOR.COM/NINETEEN

'm no golfer. In fact, I'd have a hard time telling the difference between a golf club and a billy club. But show me a golf-course restaurant serving up delicious salads, ingenious burgers and sandwiches, and a raft of homemade entrées, and I'll buy a pair of knickers and start wearing polo shirts instead of plaid. The good news is that Flavor 19—situated on the grounds of the Lingan Golf & Country Club—takes all comers . . . even duffers like me!

Once the site of the Lingan Golf Course Restaurant, Flavor 19 took over in 2011 and has been making a splash in Sydney's dining scene ever since. That's all because of owner and chef Scott Morrison, a native of Cape Breton Island who knows what people like to eat. I'm a big fan of Scott's fun-loving personality and his willingness to dream big when it comes to food.

Big dreams come in many forms at Flavor 19, but perhaps none more grandiose than the Fat Cat Burger, a mammoth creation that tickles your taste buds from every angle. The linchpin of the burger is a 1-pound patty of charbroiled AAA Canadian Black Angus beef, but Scott's just getting warmed up.

Sure, laugh now. Just wait until you've dug into Flavor 19's massive Fat Cat Burger, which boasts enough calories to keep you going for that extra round.

The patty is laid atop two deep-fried mozzarella sticks sandwiched around a pile of fries, then topped with more mozzarella cheese and a pile of Scott's sweet and crunchy double-dipped onion rings. Smear some smoked chili mayonnaise on the bun and you've got a burger that's nothing less than divine.

Another heavenly burger experience comes in Flavor 19's Mac and Cheese Burger, a comforting combination you won't soon forget. That memory may well come from the residue on your clothes (this bad boy is MESSY), but it's worth the dry-cleaning bill. Scott starts with a ½ pound of charbroiled beef goodness on a sourdough bun, then piles on creamy mac and cheese that's been spiked with just enough hot sauce to wake you up.

Getting messy is a recurring theme at Flavor 19, and Scott's signature chicken wings continue the trend. The deep-fried wings are available in 19 flavours, but my fave is the Root Beer Wings, with the taste of chipotle barbeque and sweet, sticky root beer. The Spiced Rum & Cola Wings are equally inventive. Indian Butter Curry adds a South Asian flair to your meal. If it's old-fashioned goodness you crave, don't miss the Mac and Cheese with Buttermilk Fried Chicken, a nostalgic trip to the Deep South.

So if you're wondering why everyone at Flavor 19 seems so darned happy, it might not be because of their success on the links. Heck, they might not even be golfers at all. And that's just fine with me (though I bought myself a pair of knickers anyway).

Chicken meets pop meets deep-fried heaven in Flavor 19's signature Root Beer Wings.

Atlantic Lobster
Burger

Makes: 4 to 6 servings

I wouldn't be doing my job if I didn't brag about chef Scott Morrison's Atlantic Lobster Burger, which is as hefty as it is delicious. Scott covers the lobster patty in his signature mango salsa and serves it on a sourdough bun smeared with sweet chipotle mayo. I've had lots of lobster sandwiches in my travels, but never anything quite like this. Stupid good, my friends!

4 tablespoons sea salt
2 live Atlantic lobsters (1½ pounds each)
1 pound Yukon Gold potatoes, peeled and quartered
3 green onions, chopped
1 sweet red pepper, diced
Juice of 1 lemon
½ cup sour cream
Salt and pepper
¼ cup all-purpose flour
3 eggs, beaten
2 cups panko bread crumbs
5 tablespoons olive oil
Fresh sourdough or soft white buns
Mayonnaise seasoned with chipotle powder
Lettuce
Tomatoes
Mango salsa (or other favourite salsa)

Add the sea salt to a large pot of water and bring to a boil. Plunge the lobsters headfirst into the boiling water and cook for 12 minutes. Drain and set the lobsters aside to cool. Once cooled, extract the lobster meat and discard shells.

In a large saucepan of boiling salted water, cook the potatoes until tender. Drain and mash the potatoes. Add the green onions, red pepper, lemon juice, and sour cream and stir to combine. Add the lobster meat and season with salt and pepper. Stir well. Using your hands, form mixture into 6 even patties.

Preheat oven to 400°F. Line a baking sheet with parchment paper.

Prepare your breading station: in three separate shallow dishes, place the flour, eggs, and panko.

Working with one patty at a time, dredge the patty in flour, then dip in eggs, then panko, coating both sides. Transfer to a plate, cover, and refrigerate for about 2 hours.

In a skillet, heat the oil over medium-high heat. Sauté the lobster patties for 4 to 5 minutes, until golden brown on each side. Transfer to prepared baking sheet and bake for 10 minutes or until golden brown.

To serve, place each patty on a toasted bun and top with mango salsa, or, alternatively, mayonnaise, lettuce, and tomato.

Rocket Bakery and Fresh Food

EST. 2011
272 WATER STREET
ST. JOHN'S, NL · A1C 1B7
709-738-2011
WWW.ROCKETFOOD.CA

Newfoundland is a special place. This is where life seems to slow down, where people recognize that happiness is tallied by more than just numbers in a bank account. It's this kind of attitude that brought Kelly and Mark Mansell to The Rock. After years in the hubbub of Toronto, the couple heard from friends in St. John's about a bakery in a heritage building that was shutting its doors forever. One love-at-first-sight visit later, the couple had moved themselves and their two teenage boys to their new life, and the friendly light of St. John's shone just a little brighter.

Warm, inviting, and incredibly popular, Rocket Bakery is a local's delight. Its high ceiling and huge windows make the space incredibly bright, perfect for the communal tables that bring people together inside. The space features many of the 120-year-old building's original details and fixtures, giving it a cool vintage vibe that only adds to the culinary experience. And if you happen to walk by on a Tuesday, don't be alarmed by the sounds coming from inside. That's when the Rocket hosts a kitchen party, a traditional Newfoundlander jam session where the tunes play into the wee hours of the morning.

One of my favourite Rocket meals is the Sausage Rolls. Checking in on the hand-held delight scale, they're nothing like those store-

A hub of community activity, Rocket Bakery is the perfect place for locals and tourists to cozy up with some delicious food and fine company.

bought versions I'll never go back to. The basis is homemade sausage, a tasty blend of pork, tons of garlic, veggies, and spices. This savoury interior is then wrapped in homemade puff pastry, a decadent blanket spiked with butter, butter, and . . . um . . . more butter! Filled with the sausage mix, brushed with an egg wash, and baked, these are the sausage rolls that all sausages want to be when they grow up: flaky, tasty, and full of love. In other words, pork fat + butter = yum!

You'd have to be a Viking to eat Rocket's Stout Pie by hand, but I've seen worse. And hell, you'd be crazy to let something as simple as a lack of cutlery get between you and this savoury delight. The dish is a mélange of ground lamb, veggies, and potatoes, but it's the stout that adds a depth of flavour that's hard to match. Combine that with the flaky, buttery pie crust, and you've got beauty on a plate.

There's enough variety at the Rocket to satisfy the pickiest tastes, from sweet to spicy, local to continental. Salt Cod Cakes are traditional Newfoundland discs of fresh-baked golden goodness; the Mushroom, Asparagus and Goat Cheese Tarts are creamy squares of vegetarian complexity. Rocket Bakery also does its own version of flatbread pizza (with homemade crust, of course). The Baked French Toast is reminiscent of a bread pudding, only this time made fresh from croissant bits with egg, whipping cream, and sugar, and covered with a drizzling of maple syrup and a heaping dollop of homemade whipped cream.

Like Newfoundland itself, Rocket Bakery is a special place. Devoted customers say it's like coming home. I say this is what love is supposed to feel like.

The combination of dense, delicious filling and homemade flaky pie crust makes the Rocket's Stout Pie a must-eat item. Even better, it's edible beer!

Chicken & Chorizo
Empanada

Makes: 4 to 6 servings

These portable treats use pie crust (hey, more butter!) as their foundation, stuffed to overflowing with a medley of tender chicken and chorizo sausage that's been mixed with onion, garlic, raisins, green olives, and spices. Baked until golden brown and served with a side of cooling sour cream, this empanada is perfect when paired with a heap of Rocket's delightful quinoa salad.

1 tablespoon oil
1 pound boneless, skinless chicken thighs, diced
3 garlic cloves, minced
1 large onion, diced
½ cup white wine
1 pound chorizo sausage, diced
1 cup chicken stock
1 tablespoon chili powder
½ tablespoon ground cumin
½ teaspoon cayenne pepper
A pinch of salt and pepper
¼ cup pitted and sliced green olives
¼ cup raisins
1 egg
1 pound pie dough

In a large skillet over medium-high heat, heat the oil. Sauté the chicken until nicely browned on all sides. Add the garlic and onion and cook for 5 to 6 minutes, stirring occasionally, until the onion is translucent. Add the white wine and continue to cook for 10 minutes or until the sauce thickens, stirring with a wooden spoon to loosen any brown bits on the bottom of the pan. Add the chorizo, chicken stock, chili powder, cumin, cayenne, and salt and pepper and stir to combine. Simmer until the liquid has been reduced by one-quarter. Remove from heat, stir in the olives and raisins, and set aside to cool completely.

Preheat oven to 375°F. Line a baking sheet with parchment paper.

In a small bowl, whisk together the egg and 1 tablespoon of water to make an egg wash. Set aside.

Roll out the pie dough to ⅛ inch thickness and cut into six 6-inch rounds.

Divide the cooled empanada filling into 6 even portions. Place each portion in the centre of a pastry round. Brush the edges of each pastry round with the prepared egg wash, fold pastry in half over the filling, and crimp edges with a fork. Transfer to prepared baking sheet. Bake in preheated oven for 30 to 35 minutes or until pastry is golden brown.

Tess

EST. 2009
5687 CHARLES STREET
HALIFAX, NS · B3K 1K5
902-406-3133
WWW.CHEZTESS.CA

Unusual unions often result in the unexpected, but when it comes to Tess, they also result in the extraordinary. That's extraordinary as in flavours, friends. How else can you explain the endless array of culinary delights that come from a French restaurant inspired by the Maritimes and owned by a New Yorker? *C'est délicieux!*

Hidden romantically in the north end of Halifax, Tess is a quiet respite from the business of the city's downtown core. Committed to its cuisine and dedicated to serving ridiculously tasty fare to happy locals and visitors alike, Tess has earned its reputation on the back of talented (and super fun!) chef Michael Cullen, who once considered a career as a jazz musician. Washing dishes in his spare time, Michael fell in love with the restaurant world, and hasn't looked back. Now he's a chef, and his dedication to his craft shines through with every dish he creates.

Take, for example, Tess's Croque Madame Waffle. This savoury innovation starts with homemade waffles spiked with tons of house-cured ham and Swiss cheese. Once cooked, the waffle is cut into quarters and served under a fried egg and a blanket of Michael's Dijon cream sauce with a sprinkle of cheese. Some might call it the most exotic grilled cheese they've ever seen, but for me it was high-caloric deliciousness.

Michael's penchant for cream and butter (hey, this is a French place, after all) is evident in his Coquilles St. Jacques Crêpe, a complex creation that pays tribute to local seafood offerings. Michael starts by searing wild scallops in butter, to which he adds mushrooms and

He's a wild and crazy guy, that chef Michael Cullen! In fact, this dude loves his job so much, he can't wait to get to work.

spinach, followed by creamy Emmental cheese sauce. While this is cooking, Michael expertly spins a buckwheat crêpe, which, when done, he twists and fills with the creamy scallop mélange. I agree with the locals: Nova Scotia may be known for its scallops, but it should be known for this dish! Three words: So. Much. Cream!

Should you be lucky enough to visit Tess on multiple occasions (most people do!), make sure you sample some of Michael's other creamy creations, including The Roscoff (a slow-roasted chicken and glazed ham sandwich topped with sliced green apple, asparagus, and Emmental cheese sauce); the Apple, Bacon, and Raisin Belgian Waffle (drizzled in maple syrup and . . . butter!); and the Seafood Pot Pie (local haddock, shrimp, scallops, and salmon in a sherry cream sauce and topped with a puff pastry crust). Crêpes come in many shapes and sizes, including the Sausage and Eggs Crêpe (with caramelized apples!), Crêpe Cordon Bleu (packed with roasted chicken, ham, cherry tomatoes, and Swiss cheese), and, for dessert lovers, Crêpe Suzette (flambéed orange segments with butter, sugar, and orange liqueur).

In the end, Tess is a reflection of the personalities that make this restaurant tick: traditional yet daring; fun yet quiet. And creamy. Oh so creamy.

Luxury meets East Coast seafood freshness in the Coquilles St. Jacques Crêpe, which erupts with a lava flow of creamy cheese sauce when you cut into it.

Unlike traditional versions, this quiche deviates from the norm by using—as the name suggests—potatoes as the crust. The crust is baked on its own before being filled with mushrooms, Swiss cheese, egg, and cream. After baking, the filling becomes light, fluffy, and stupidly cheesy, and the crust makes it seem like you're finishing each mouthful with a potato pancake. And that's a good thing in my book!

Special equipment: 10-inch springform pan

Crust

1 tablespoon butter
3 cups grated potatoes
Juice of ½ lemon
¼ teaspoon salt
½ teaspoon black pepper

Filling

1 tablespoon butter
1 cup sliced cremini mushrooms
½ teaspoon salt
9 eggs
1 cup half and half (10%) cream
2 cups heavy or whipping (35%) cream
⅛ teaspoon ground nutmeg
1 cup shredded Swiss cheese

Crust
Preheat oven to 375°F. Butter a 10-inch springform pan.
Wrap the grated potatoes in a clean kitchen towel and squeeze dry. In a large bowl, combine the potatoes, lemon juice, and salt and pepper. Press evenly into the bottom of prepared springform pan. Bake in preheated oven for 20 minutes, or until golden around the edges.

Filling
In a skillet over medium heat, melt the butter. Add the cremini mushrooms, season with salt and cook for 6 to 8 minutes, stirring occasionally, until slightly underdone. Set aside to cool.
In a medium bowl, whisk together the eggs, both creams, and nutmeg. Stir in the mushrooms and cheese.

Assembly
Preheat oven to 375°F. Pour the egg mixture into prepared crust. Bake in preheated oven until quiche is set, about 45 minutes.

Sweet Treats That'll Keep You Coming Back for More

Dessert . . . it's not just for dinner anymore. In fact, have one taste of these sweet delights and you might just skip dinner (or lunch . . . or breakfast) and head straight for the meal-ender.

BAKLAVA

Sofra, Edmonton, AB

A classic Mediterranean dessert meets ethereal perfection at the hands of chef Yuksel Gultekin. Hey, is that honey dripping down your face?

FAT ELVIS SHAKE

Boogie's Burgers, Calgary, AB

Can a drink be a dessert? When it's filled with vanilla ice cream, peanut butter, banana, and chopped bacon, you're damn right it can be!

FLAPPER PIE

Hilltop Diner Café, Langley, BC

A Prairie classic that will send your tongue singing a happy tune: graham crumb crust, custard, meringue, and graham crumbles.

IT'S-A-SMORE

Kawaii Crepe, Winnipeg, MB

Crispy crêpe overflowing with toasted marshmallows, chocolate-hazelnut spread, and graham cracker chunks. Just like camping, without the bugs.

TERI-VANI ICE-CREAM WAFFLE

Miura Waffle Milk Bar, Vancouver, BC

Homemade waffle topped with homemade vanilla ice cream topped with homemade teriyaki sauce, followed by a mound of whipped cream. Teriyaki sauce? Yes, captain . . . teriyaki sauce!

CARROT CAKE

Colette's Place, Glace Bay, NS

Like cream cheese icing? Granny Karen Bran tops and stuffs her massive carrot cake with it. And the world, my friends, is happy.

CINNAMON BUNS

Highlevel Diner, Edmonton, AB

Eight-plus ounces of steaming dough love doused in butter. Big enough to share with a friend, but why would you?

MONKEY BREAD

Earth to Table Bread Bar, Hamilton, ON

Is it a doughnut or a cinnamon bun? I'm not sure and, frankly, I don't care. Once you taste it, you won't either.

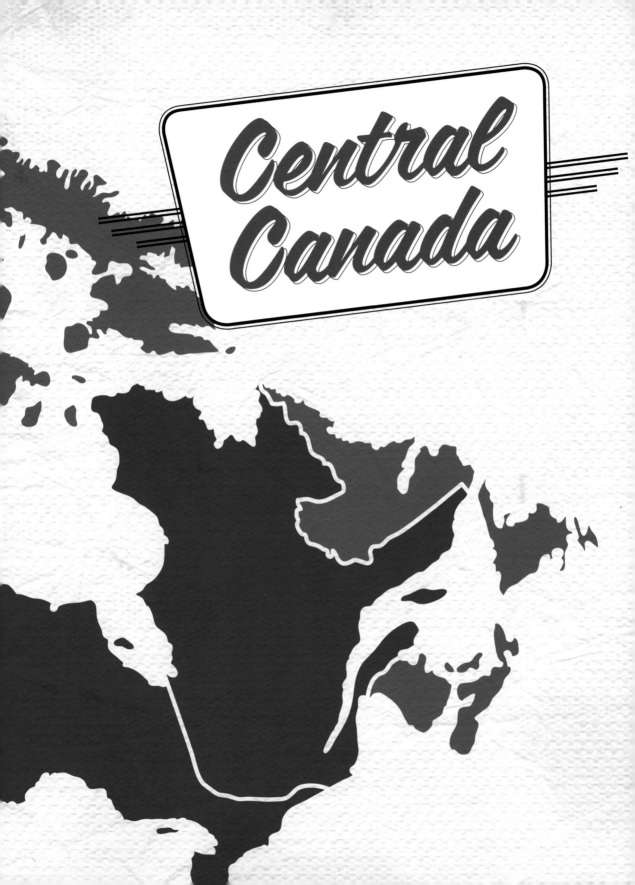

Central Canada

The Argyle Street Grill

EST. 2010
345 ARGYLE STREET SOUTH
CALEDONIA, ON · N3W 1K7
905-765-9622
WWW.THEARGYLESTREETGRILL.COM

Small towns sometimes get a bad rap. Sure, you know everybody by name, but the food options are sometimes limited. Well, the Argyle Street Grill turns this theory on its head. This is the place where you get the hands-on service that only a small town can offer . . . with big-city culinary creativity.

Chef Wade Taylor is proud of what he creates, and his Rotisserie Chicken and Ribs—an Argyle Street fave—is one of his masterpieces.

Just make sure you're on the lookout, because you may drive right by it. Tucked away in a strip mall, the Argyle's unassuming exterior doesn't do justice to the chic, funky vibe inside. Whether you're comfortably inside a booth or chowing down at the communal table, owners Wade and Kevin have something to appeal to every taste and style. From boisterous families to awkward teens on a first date to hockey teams celebrating their latest victory, there's something for everyone at the Argyle.

As for me, please pass the ribs . . . the 7.65 Braised Beef Short Ribs, to be exact. Why 7.65? It's not only Caledonia's telephone prefix, it's the number of hours these tasty ribs take to cook. That's 4 hours in the marinade, quickly seared at high temperature to give the meat its signature texture, then baked for 3.65 hours in Wade's hearty homemade stock. The Argyle is one of those places that gives vegetarians pause to reconsider, and its Rotisserie Chicken and Ribs is one of the primary culprits. Using local meat (Wade and Kevin believe strongly in supporting local suppliers), the dish starts with pork ribs coated in a secret dry rub, then left alone for 24 hours before being slow-cooked over a tray of beer for as long as 5 hours. The chicken also undergoes the rub-and-sit phenomenon before hitting the rotisserie for a crisp, juicy finish. When it's time for serving, both are generously basted with Argyle's BBQ Sauce. Served with a mound of fresh-cut fries and homemade coleslaw, this dish tastes as good as it smells . . . and it smells like heaven, my friends.

If you're a poutine lover, you've gotta try the Two Way Grand Poutine, a sinfully substantial marriage of crispy fries and local cheese curds (squeak!) topped with gravy-washed pulled short ribs on one side and rotisserie chicken on the other. Shepherd's Pie sees piles of ground chuck simmered in a rich stew of peas, carrots, corn, onions, and celery, topped with a generous layer of creamy buttermilk-mashed potatoes and a sprinkling of nippy Parmesan cheese.

Pass on the red meat and there's still loads of variety at the Argyle, including the Farmer's Market Flatbread: a fire-grilled marriage of market-fresh veggies, mozzarella, and feta. Fish and Chips features flaky North Atlantic haddock, while the Molten Marble Cheese Planks are Wade's ingenious and local take on the (typically frozen) mozzarella stick. Nachos are equally inventive, with homemade tortilla chips topped with olive tapenade, chopped green onions, mixed cheeses, hot banana peppers, and fresh diced tomatoes.

It's these kinds of offerings that have quickly carved out a niche for the Argyle, where daily doses of delicious food are converting the big-city naysayers into believers, one by one. And yeah, this boy may be from Toronto, but I know I'll be making the trip!

Don't be surprised if Wade serves this up to you with a sincere "good luck."
Argyle's Two Way Grand Poutine is decadent, delicious, and . . . um . . . sizeable!

Braised Beef Short Ribs

Makes: 4 to 6 servings

If you're thinking that a dish called "short ribs" is small, you're in for a rude awakening, my friend. The Argyle's short ribs are as massive as they are tender, and complemented perfectly by the fluffy mound of mashed potatoes the restaurant serves alongside.

Timing note: ribs need to marinate for 4 hours and braise for 3 hours

Marinade

½ cup olive oil

⅓ cup red wine vinegar

¼ cup red wine

2 tablespoons Worcestershire sauce

2 tablespoons steak sauce (preferably HP sauce)

2 tablespoons whole-grain mustard

1½ tablespoons minced garlic

1 tablespoon fresh thyme

1 tablespoon sea salt

1 tablespoon black pepper

Beef Short Ribs

1 rack of ribs with 4 bones

⅓ cup canola oil

5 medium carrots, chopped

½ cup chopped celery

2½ cups chopped onion

½ 13-ounce can tomato paste

8 garlic cloves, chopped

1 bottle (750 mL) red wine (Merlot)

3 sprigs fresh thyme

8 cups beef stock

1 cup beef gravy

1 bay leaf

A pinch of salt and pepper

⅓ cup cornstarch

⅓ cup water

Marinade

In a large bowl, combine all of the ingredients. Set aside.

Beef Short Ribs

Using a sharp knife, carefully cut the short ribs between the bones into individual portions. Transfer the short ribs to a resealable bag, add the prepared marinade, seal bag, and turn to coat. Refrigerate for 4 hours.

Preheat oven to 300°F.

In a braising pot over medium-high heat, heat the oil until sizzling. Remove the ribs from the marinade (discard marinade) and, being mindful of the sizzling oil, carefully place the ribs in the pot. Sear the meat until well browned on all sides. Transfer the ribs to a plate and set aside.

Reduce heat to medium and, to the same pot, add the carrots, celery, and onions and cook, stirring frequently to prevent burning, for about 5 minutes, until lightly browned. Stir in the tomato paste and garlic. Cook, stirring constantly, for another 3 minutes. Add the wine, stirring with a wooden spoon to scrape up any browned bits from the bottom of the pot. Stir in the thyme, stock, gravy, bay leaf, and salt and pepper and bring to a boil. Turn off the heat and return the reserved ribs to the pot. Cover pot with aluminum foil and cook in preheated oven for 3 hours, until meat easily falls off the bone when pulled with a fork.

Remove the pot from the oven. Using cooking tongs, gently transfer the ribs to a plate and set aside. Allow the liquid in the pot to cool for 15 to 20 minutes, or until room temperature. As the liquid cools, a layer of fat will form on the top. Using a spoon, carefully skim off the layer of fat and discard.

Using a fine-mesh sieve, carefully strain the liquid into a large saucepan (discard any solids). Bring liquid just to a simmer over medium heat.

In a small bowl, whisk together the cornstarch and water. Pour into the saucepan and cook, whisking constantly, until thickened.

Transfer the ribs to the pan with the sauce and heat until warmed through.

Serve with mashed potatoes.

Barque Smokehouse

EST. 2011
299 RONCESVALLES AVENUE
TORONTO, ON · M6R 2M3
416-532-7700
WWW.BARQUE.CA

When most of us get tired of our jobs, we go on vacation. For some people, though, a couple of weeks in Florida or Mexico just isn't enough. Take long-time friends David Neinstein and Jonathan Persofsky, for example. When David and Jonathan tired of corporate life, they decided to open a smokehouse. Crazy? Maybe. But Barque—the product of their simultaneous career shift—now has one of the fastest-growing and most dedicated followings in Canada's biggest city, where people line up every weekend for a coveted table.

But *You Gotta Eat Here!* Fan Favourite Barque is a travel story, too. To help make the transition from office to kitchen, David hit the road for the States, of all places. Here, over a span of six months, he ate at over 100 different barbeque restaurants, which provided the inspiration for Barque's recipes. Knowing their expertise was more in *eating* food than *preparing* it, David and Jonathan's next challenge was to find a man to make their vision a culinary reality. Enter chef Bryan Birch, who helped develop the menu that has made Barque a darling of Toronto's vibrant brunch scene.

Of the many options Barque's menu throws at you, none speaks to its ingenuity and daring like the Barque Benedict. The only "traditional" thing about this benny is the poached eggs, which sit atop a mound of smoked beef brisket and homemade cornbread. Covering

Yeah, Bryan Birch and I look serious in this picture. Damn serious. Then again, injecting beef brisket with a secret blend of beef jus and apple juice is no laughing matter.

this delightfully smoky mess is a Barbeque Hollandaise Sauce, which only deepens the richness of the brisket. So if you're looking for a wonderfully different take on a breakfast classic, look no further.

Though Barque is appropriately known for its brunch, lunches and dinners here are equally ridiculous. The Fried Chicken Sandwich takes everyone's favourite southern-fried heart-stopper and puts it on a soft bun slathered with special in-house "baconnaise" (mayo made with bacon fat!), then tops it with pickled fennel, tomatoes, and Gruyère cheese. Sesame-Crusted Pork Tacos and Sushi Rice Krispy Balls are popular appetizers, and as a main, the Barque Brisket Sandwich teams smoked brisket with red cabbage coleslaw, fried onions, and horseradish mayo on a soft bun. Hell, Barque even hosts a family night every Sunday, when your table is weighted with nine different salad-to-dessert dishes, with lots of smoked goodness in between!

And who knows? You might be so inspired by your visit to Barque that you run to the office on Monday morning and tell your boss to take his job and shove it. Of course, you might soon find yourself on the road, but if a restaurant like Barque is the product of your journey, I'm good with that.

One taste of Bryan's Barque Benedict and you'll see why everyone is raving about Barque, which was named one of Toronto's best new restaurants of 2012 by *Toronto Life* magazine.

Smoked Duck Pancakes

Makes: 4 servings

When you top three fluffy pancakes with homemade blueberry compote, a pile of smoked duck, and a creamy dollop of whipped goat cheese, you've got flapjacks like momma *never* made. This mélange of flavours works so well together, you may never go back to a traditional pancake breakfast.

Special equipment: smoker (optional)

Smoked Duck

1 teaspoon white sugar
1 teaspoon raw sugar
1 teaspoon kosher salt
1 teaspoon black pepper
1 teaspoon garlic powder
1 teaspoon onion powder (or preferably 1 teaspoon granulated onion)
1 teaspoon dried thyme
1 teaspoon dried rosemary
2 duck legs (6 to 7 ounces each)

Whipped Chèvre

⅔ cup chèvre (goat cheese), room temperature
2 tablespoons whipping (35%) cream

Blueberry Compote

1 pint fresh blueberries
¼ cup orange juice (preferably freshly squeezed)
½ cup white sugar

Pancakes

1 cup all-purpose flour
¼ cup white sugar
1 teaspoon baking soda
1 teaspoon baking powder

1 large egg
½ cup buttermilk
½ cup 2% milk
3 tablespoons butter, melted
1 tablespoon vegetable oil

Smoked Duck

Preheat smoker to 225°F or oven to 325°F.

In a small bowl, combine everything but the duck legs to make a rub. Massage rub into duck legs.

Place the legs bone-side down in the smoker for 4 hours or place duck legs in a medium baking dish, pierce skin with a fork, and bake for 2 hours or until the temperature on a meat thermometer registers 165°F (if you twist the leg, it should turn freely).

Remove the duck from the smoker or oven and set aside for 30 minutes to cool.

Remove the skin from the duck, saving any crispy parts. Using a fork, pull the meat into strips. Set aside. Chop the crispy skin and reserve with the pulled meat.

Whipped Chèvre

In a bowl, combine the chèvre and cream. Whisk until fluffy. Set aside in the fridge.

Blueberry Compote

In a saucepan over medium heat, combine the blueberries, orange juice, and sugar. Bring to a boil, stirring frequently. Reduce heat and simmer for 30 minutes. (Note: If substituting frozen for fresh blueberries, reduce cooking time to 15 minutes.)

Pancakes

In a large bowl, sift together the flour, sugar, baking soda, and baking powder.

In a separate bowl, whisk together the egg, buttermilk, milk, and butter. Slowly add the wet ingredients to the dry ingredients, stirring until even in consistency.

In a large skillet over medium heat, heat the oil. For each pancake, pour ¼ cup of the mixture into the hot pan. Cook for 1 to 2 minutes, or until the edges start to bubble. Flip and cook the second side for another 2 minutes. The cooked pancakes should be golden brown on both sides (you may need to slightly adjust the heat so that all the pancakes cook evenly). Transfer cooked pancakes to a plate and keep warm.

Assembly

Place 3 pancakes on each serving plate. Top with 1 tablespoon of blueberry compote, a small handful of smoked duck and 1 tablespoon of whipped chèvre. Maple syrup is optional. Enjoy.

Black Forest Inn

EST. 1967
255 KING STREET EAST
HAMILTON, ON · L8N 1B9
905-528-3538
WWW.BLACKFORESTINN.CA

think I must have been Bavarian in a former life. Sure, the Italian in me craves pasta on a regular basis, but on a blustery winter day, nothing warms and comforts me like a warm plate of schnitzel. And judging by the success of Hamilton's Black Forest Inn, I'm not the only one. This Canadian legend has been comforting visitors from near and far with old-world, stick-to-your-ribs classics since Lester B. Pearson was prime minister.

Like every good Bavarian restaurant, the Black Forest Inn is a family affair with a storied history. It was founded by Fred and Rosa Oberreiter back in 1967. Son Wolfgang Schoen and wife Gabi took over in 1986 and haven't skipped a beat. The Black Forest serves up the same dishes it always has, just how its loyal patrons like it.

And of the Black Forest's varied offerings, none says tradition quite as clearly as its schnitzel, which comes in 13 varieties and represents six countries. The Vienna Schnitzel is gorgeous in its simplicity: a butterflied and pounded piece of pork tenderloin fried to golden brown. I love how crispy and light the schnitzel tastes, and the squeeze of fresh lemon adds a brightness that hugs me from the inside.

I was also lucky enough to sample the Schnitzel Cordon Bleu, a pork loin topped with Black Forest ham (pork on pork!) and Emmental cheese before being folded, pounded shut, breaded, and fried. Why do I love it? It combines my two favourite food groups: crispy and

Behind these storied walls lie almost 50 years of tradition. The Black Forest Inn's décor pays homage to old-world Germany and Austria, and strives to give its customers a real European experience.

gooey! The Jaeger Schnitzel is a Black Forest favourite, topped in a rich, homemade mushroom sauce. The Schnitzel Husar gets covered with a creamy paprika sauce then smothered in bacon and hot peppers, while the Schnitzel à la Holstein is braised in a demi-glace and topped with a fried egg, caviar, and smoked salmon. *Jawohl!*

If you want to buck the schnitzel trend, Wolfgang's menu boasts a host of other Bavarian delights. Meataholics crave the Black Forest Plate (Schwarzwaldhaus Platte), a one- or two-person platter comprising a Vienna Schnitzel, a grilled Vienna Sausage, and a Kassler Rippchen (smoked pork loin), with potatoes and sauerkraut. The Farmer's Feast (Bauernschmaus) features roast pork, smoked ham, and grilled sausage served alongside gravy-covered dumplings and potatoes.

Wolfgang Schoen is the fun-loving owner of the Black Forest Inn, a man who says his greatest joy comes when someone visits the kitchen to compliment him on one of his creations.

A graduate of one of Austria's top culinary academies, Wolfgang thrives on pleasing people. And the pleasure comes in many forms. The Cold Roast Pork Sandwich is a popular lunch item, featuring slow-roasted pork loin piled high on dark rye bread and served alongside traditional, homemade potato salad. The Rindsroulade (Beef Rolls) are tender strips of beef stuffed with bacon, carrots, onions, and pickles and braised in a delicious brown sauce.

The Black Forest features a variety of side dishes, but none yummier (for this guy, anyway) than the spaetzle, an egg-dough noodle that straddles the line between pasta, dumpling, and gnocchi all at once. First boiled and then fried in butter, the spaetzle are firm yet soft, bouncy little nuggets of deliciousness that taste even better when covered in one of Wolfgang's famous sauces.

All this warmth, love, and comfort make me want to yodel, but I'll spare you the performance. Like everything at the Black Forest Inn, the traditional Bavarian undertakings are best left to Wolfgang.

Hungarian Goulash

Makes: 4 to 6 servings

A signature dish at the Black Forest Inn, Hungarian Goulash is a hearty stew chock full of beef chunks in a yummy gravy.

½ cup lard or corn oil

3 onions, finely chopped

4 tablespoons sweet Hungarian paprika

¼ cup white vinegar

6 garlic cloves, finely chopped

2 tablespoons dried marjoram

1 tablespoon caraway seeds, ground

A pinch of salt and pepper

2 pounds stewing beef, cut into 1-inch cubes

4 tablespoons all-purpose flour

In a large casserole dish over medium heat, melt the lard or heat the corn oil. Add the onions and fry gently until soft and golden. Remove from heat and stir in the paprika, vinegar, garlic, marjoram, caraway, salt, and pepper. Add 5 cups of water and the beef and stir well. Turn heat to medium-high and bring to a boil. Reduce heat and simmer for about 45 minutes or until the meat is tender and cooked through.

In a small bowl, whisk together the flour and 1 cup water. While stirring, slowly add the flour mixture to the casserole dish. Simmer for another 10 minutes, until the goulash has thickened.

Serve goulash with boiled potatoes or spaetzle.

Black Skirt

EST. 2012
974 COLLEGE STREET
TORONTO, ON · M6G 1H4
416-532-7424
WWW.BLACKSKIRTRESTAURANT.COM

Ask me where to eat in Toronto, and I'll tell you Black Skirt. Ask me for a list of great Italian restaurants in Canada, and one of the first names out of my mouth will be Black Skirt. Ask me my favourite article of clothing to wear when nobody's watching, and I'll tell you . . . Well, better to skip that last part, I think.

Clothing obsessions notwithstanding, Black Skirt is an Italian food fantasy, a place where inspired cooking meets old-world dedication. Ask owners and life partners Aggie Decina and Rosa Galle what drives them, and they'll tell you one thing: they know nothing about fancy. Their food comes from family. So, sit down, eat, share, and feel the love all around.

Nothing says *amore* to a guy like me better than Black Skirt's Osso Buco, a meal so good it almost brings me to tears. The dish is served with Black Skirt's signature Purè di Patate, a baked, multi-tiered extravaganza that sandwiches Parmesan and mozzarella cheeses between layers of mashed potatoes and is topped with the crunch of seasoned bread crumbs. Baked to a crispy golden brown, the potatoes soak up the rich sauce and are a perfect complement to the delicate hunks of veal. I think I'm going to cry.

Aggie is as loving as they come. She's also a perfectionist when it comes to her culinary creations. Take, for example, her arancini. Sure, she humoured me by letting me mould a few of the baseball-size delights in my greedy little hands, but I knew they couldn't meet her exacting standards. No wonder! Making the arancini is an involved undertaking, one that starts with mixing cooked rice with butter, shredded mozzarella, grated Parmesan, and eggs, then forming it into a tight little ball. Aggie then created a pocket in the centre of the ball, into which she stuffs a mixture of ground veal, peas, homemade tomato sauce, and mozzarella cheese. After the ball is closed up again, it's coated in egg whites and seasoned bread crumbs before hitting the deep-fryer en route to becoming a light, crispy, gooey ball of finger-snappin' *mama mia*.

Rosa is equally exacting in the kitchen, and her Domenica (Sunday) sauce is a throwback to a simpler time, one that reminds me of Sunday afternoons at home with my dad. The Domenica starts with Black Skirt's homemade tomato sauce, to which the ladies add slow-cooked hunks of pork shoulder, Italian sausage, and homemade meatballs. It's the kind of sauce that's so substantial, you can just eat it with a piece of bread, though Rosa and Aggie like to serve it with al dente

Rosa (middle) and Aggie (right) serve up authentic Italian fare, and their rich homemade cooking was a trip to the dinnertime tables of my youth.

spaghetti to make sure you're good and stuffed. *Mangia!*

Black Skirt's menu is a testimony to family recipes and runs the gamut from antipasti (appetizers) like marinated octopus to an Italian mackerel panini. The Pistachio Pasta is a legendary dish with spaghetti tossed in Aggie's top-secret pistachio sauce, fresh crushed tomatoes, and grated Parmesan. And if you've got a hankering for something sweet, *do not* leave without sampling the Chocolate Cake, a warm, oozy hunk of dreamy goodness.

And yeah, the ladies just might offer you some more, but don't be surprised if they ask you to wash the dishes, too. That's what you get when you're home.

You can look . . . and taste . . . but don't ask! Aggie's Pistachio Pasta has been imitated countless times, but nobody can match her secret recipe and heavenly taste.

Osso Buco

Makes: 8 servings

Co-owner Aggie Decina starts off her Osso Buco with a tomato-based sauce spiked with red wine and mushroom and beef stock, to which she adds a massive hunk of veal shank that's been dredged in flour and seared for texture. Baked for 4 or 5 hours, it's one of the most tender, fall-off-the-bone dishes my lips have ever touched.

Sauce

4 tablespoons olive oil
1 cup finely chopped onion
2 cups finely chopped carrots
1 cup finely chopped celery
1 bottle (25 fluid ounces/750 mL) red wine
1 cup tomato paste
3 cups mushroom stock
3 cups beef stock

Osso Buco

8 veal shanks (1 inch to 1¼ inches thick)
Salt and pepper
1 cup all-purpose flour
4 tablespoons olive oil

Sauce

In a large stockpot over medium-high heat, heat the oil. Add the onions to the pan and sauté for 1 minute, then add the carrots and celery and cook, stirring often, until the onions are soft and translucent. Add the wine and bring to a boil. Reduce heat to medium and cook until the liquid is reduced by half. Add the tomato paste, mushroom stock, and beef stock and continue to cook for 1 hour, stirring regularly to prevent burning.

Osso Buco

Preheat oven to 300°F.

Pat the veal shanks dry with paper towel. Season both sides with salt and pepper. Place the flour in a shallow bowl, then dredge each veal shank in flour and set aside.

In a large skillet over medium-high heat, heat the oil. Fry each veal shank on both sides until golden brown. Transfer the veal shanks to a deep baking dish. Add the prepared sauce to the baking dish. Cover the dish with aluminum foil and cook on the middle rack of the preheated oven for 4 hours. Serve with cheesy mashed potatoes.

The Bungalow

EST. 2009
910 WATERLOO STREET
LONDON, ON · N6A 3W9
519-434-8797
WWW.BUNGALOWHUB.CA

love classic burger joints. You know, those tiny side-of-the-road places that visitors overlook but locals crave? Well, The Bungalow takes burger joints to the next level, filling out the menu with dozens of other offerings in a warm, homey setting that feels like you're eating in your neighbour's living room . . . only the food's WAY better!

Smack in the middle of London's Old North neighbourhood, The Bungalow looks much like, well, a bungalow from the outside, and carries that feeling to its inviting interior, where local business people eat side by side with couples, friends, and families. They know that no matter what they choose from The Bungalow's varied menu, it's going to be fresh, delicious, and made from scratch.

Burgers! The Bungalow does them up many and varied. Pick from the menu or build your own, they're all freakin' outrageous. Chef Nick Patterson tempted me with The Black & Blue Burger, a Cajun-coated delight (covered in "secret Cajun stuff," Nick says) topped with blue cheese and a crispy, buttermilk-marinated onion ring. More refined tastes might talk about the myste-rious conflict between the spicy seasoning and the blue cheese; I say any time you can top a burger with an onion ring, you've got a winner.

While there's no sushi on The Bungalow's menu, the Tuna Burger comes close. I had mine served alongside sweet potato fries, though you can choose from a dozen of The Bungalow's side dishes, including their Homemade Mac & Cheese (which features a trio of Cheddar, moz-zarella, and smoked Gouda) and Deep-Fried Pickles (which look like pickle potato chips).

If you're the creative type (or one of those people who hates being told what to do), go off the charts and create your own burger. Start

Chef Nick Patterson is young and energetic, and the man responsible for the made-from-scratch delights that have made The Bungalow a dining mecca in London.

by choosing your patty (beef, lamb, turkey, wild boar, buffalo, tuna, salmon, portobello mushroom) and your bun, then one of 12 cheeses (hey, nobody said it would be easy). Things get even more involved with the toppings, where you've got 46 to choose from, including such unique offerings as smoked chorizo, grilled pineapple, and horseradish.

But burgers are just the beginning at The Bungalow. The menu features selections from escargot to sirloin steak, and most everything in between. Don't miss the Bungalow Hot Dog, an all-beef dog smothered in deep-fried pickles, baked beans, bacon, Cheddar cheese, and jalapeños. Southwest Chicken Spring Rolls are among the more popular appetizers, and are stuffed with black beans, corn, cheese, and cilantro, then served with a chipotle mayo dip. Thin-crust flatbreads are hugely popular, and range from the Greek (feta, pesto, kalamata olives, roasted red peppers, marinated chicken breast) to the Indian (curried chicken, jalapeños, mango, cilantro, green onions, and yogurt sauce). And OK, so there's no *Italian* flatbread on the menu, but the Spaghetti Puttanesca brings me right back home.

With so much going for it, it's no surprise that The Bungalow has quickly carved out its niche—not only in this quiet little neighbourhood but throughout London, too. And if you happen to walk into someone's living room by mistake, just ask them for The Bungalow. They'll know what you're talking about.

Like your burgers with a bite? The "secret Cajun stuff" that coats the Black & Blue Burger makes this a deliciously spicy hand-held marvel.

Bungalow Tuna Burger

Makes: 4 servings

At The Bungalow, chef Nick Patterson serves up a thick slab of seared ahi tuna, topped with Asian slaw and wasabi aïoli, on a toasted ciabatta bun. Almost crispy on the outside but soft and succulent on the inside, the burger is a delicious exercise in competing textures.

Asian Slaw

4 cups shredded cabbage (1 to 2 heads)
1 cup roasted red peppers, julienned
1 cup grated carrots
1 cup chopped fresh cilantro
½ cup soy sauce
½ cup chili paste
¼ cup sesame oil

Wasabi Aïoli

½ teaspoon wasabi powder
3 tablespoons mayonnaise

Tuna Burger

1 teaspoon vegetable oil
2 pounds skinless boneless sushi-grade ahi tuna, cut into four 8-ounce steaks

Assembly

4 ciabatta or hamburger buns, toasted
Salt and pepper

Asian Slaw

In a large bowl, combine all of the ingredients. Set aside.

Wasabi Aïoli

In a small bowl, combine wasabi powder with 1 teaspoon of water to form a paste. Let stand, then add mayonnaise and stir well.

Tuna Burger

In a skillet over medium-high heat, heat the oil. Reduce heat to medium and sear the tuna steaks for about 1 minute each side (the tuna will be brown on the outside but still pink on the inside). Remove from heat.

Assembly

Place the tuna on the bottom halves of the toasted ciabatta buns. Top with Asian slaw and wasabi aïoli, and season with salt and pepper to taste. Sandwich with the bun tops and serve.

Burger Barn

EST. 2011
3000 FOURTH LINE
OHSWEKEN, SIX NATIONS OF THE GRAND RIVER RESERVE, ON · N0A 1M0
519-445-0088
WWW.BURGERBARN.CA

When you think of Canada's First Nations fare, "delicious burgers" might not be the first words to pop into your mind. Well, pay one visit to the Six Nations of the Grand River Reserve, my friends, and you'll start to associate the two. This is the place of the Burger Barn, a joint whose energy and vitality have built a reputation far beyond the borders of the reserve it calls home. Here you'll find just as many people who have journeyed from nearby Brantford just to get a taste of chef Brad Fennema's and Brian Skye's stupidly delicious creations.

The Barn is the brainchild of the Hill family, who call the reserve home. Husband and wife Jason and Celeste partnered with Jason's sister, Joanie; Steve and Sandra—Jason's mom and dad—pitch in as well. The Hills lamented the fact that even though they lived on Canada's largest reserve, there were very few dining options. They wanted to bring the best of old-school diner food home, and the Burger Barn was born. Now Brad runs a kitchen with a smile on his face all day long, a smile matched by everyone who gets their hands on his food.

Huh? Chef Brad Fennema knows a good burger when he sees one, but sometimes even he's surprised by the sheer mass of his own creations.

Brad knows that the foundation of a good burger is the beef, which is why he insists on prime rib that's ground fresh in-house every day. You won't find a stitch of filler in these burgers, just 100% beef, plus a bit of salt and pepper. And you can taste the love in every bite of The Blaz'n Burger, a 7-ounce charbroiled patty with deep-fried jalapeños, gooey Monterey Jack cheese, spicy barbeque sauce, roasted garlic mayonnaise, and a pile of traditional fixings. It's spicy and flavourful, smoky and sweet, all at the same time. *Ka-pow!*

Big appetites know their best choice is The Barnyard, a massive meal that manages to provide both quantity and flavour. This sky-high sandwich is built around two 7-ounce beef patties topped with Swiss and Cheddar cheeses. Between the two is a Cajun-seasoned chicken breast, while two strips of bacon and a heaping dose of garlic mayonnaise complete the menagerie. Served with a pile of fries, it's a piece of carnivore heaven.

Sure, there are a million different burger options at The Barn, but that's not all. One of their most well-loved dishes is the storied Indian Taco, which is built on a delicate and fluffy foundation of freshly made bannock, or frybread as it's known here. If hot dogs are more your thing, try The Footlong, a wiener so big it's served on a submarine bun. As if 8 ounces weren't enough, The Footlong is topped with onions, tomatoes, and shredded pickles. Smokehouse Poutine is buried under pulled pork that's been smoked for 50 hours (*not* a typo) and a dollop of sour cream. Barn Wings are gargantuan, tossed in Cajun flour and served with one of nine sauces.

Yes, people, it's road trip time. If you're looking for a fun, bright, and lively place to get your fix of hand-held heaven, the Burger Barn is a must-visit. There may not be an empty table in the joint, but there's something special happening at the Six Nations of the Grand River Reserve, and it's worth the wait.

If Old MacDonald had a burger, this would be it! The Barnyard Burger has all the animals on the farm running for cover . . . and eager customers drooling.

Indian Taco

Makes: 4 servings

In this dish, frybread is topped with ground prime rib that's been cooked in a savoury stew with tomatoes, red kidney beans, and Brad's not-so-secret taco seasoning. The top of the tower is shredded Cheddar and mozzarella, followed by lettuce, diced tomatoes, and red onion. This is comfort food like you've never tasted before, and your tongue will thank you for it.

Taco Seasoning

3 tablespoons cornstarch
2 tablespoons chili powder
1 tablespoon salt
1 tablespoon sweet paprika
1 tablespoon sugar
2¼ teaspoons chicken soup base
1½ teaspoons onion powder
1 teaspoon ground cumin
¾ teaspoon garlic powder
¾ teaspoon cayenne pepper

Taco Meat

2 pounds ground prime rib beef
2 tablespoons unsalted butter
1 can (14 ounces) red kidney beans,
   drained and rinsed
1 can (19 ounces) stewed tomatoes, with
   juice

Frybread

2 cups all-purpose flour
1 tablespoon baking powder
1 teaspoon salt
1 cup buttermilk
Canola oil

Taco Seasoning

In a bowl, combine all of the ingredients. Set aside.

Note: This recipe makes more seasoning than you'll need for the tacos. Store extra in an airtight container.

Taco Meat

In a large skillet over medium-high heat, brown the ground beef with the butter. Drain any excess liquid. Add the kidney beans, stewed tomatoes, and 3 tablespoons of the prepared taco seasoning and stir to combine. Bring to a boil, reduce heat, and simmer for 45 minutes to allow flavours to meld.

Frybread

While the meat is cooking, in a medium bowl, combine the flour, baking powder, and salt. Stir in the buttermilk until the dough just comes together, adding more flour if dough is too sticky to handle.

Turn the dough out onto a lightly floured work surface and knead until smooth (do not over-knead—less is more).

In a large, deep, heavy skillet over medium-high heat, heat ¾ inch of oil.

Using your hands, tear dough into 8 to 10 equal-sized pieces, each about ¾ cup (the size of a base-ball). Shape into round discs about ¼ inch thick, making a thinner depressed area in the centre of each.

Fry the breads in the hot oil until golden on both sides, turning only once. Drain on paper towel.

Assembly

Scoop taco meat onto frybread and top with desired taco toppings (shredded cheese, lettuce, tomatoes, red onion, sour cream, etc.).

The Burger's Priest

EST. 2010
3397 YONGE STREET
TORONTO, ON · M4N 2M7
416-488-3510
WWW.THEBURGERSPRIEST.COM

All foods need to secure a spot in the afterlife. Whether you call it heaven or nirvana, there's a place for every meal on the other side. But some items—as popular as they may be—need a lift to make it to the promised land. Enter The Burger's Priest, whose self-proclaimed mission is to redeem the lowly hamburger and help it claim its rightful place in the next world.

Confused? Me too. But what can you expect from a joint with a Secret Menu (an underground menu whose items are never displayed at the restaurant) and where religious puns flow as freely as the french fries? Top it off with owner Shant Mardirosian, a seminary dropout and true believer whose new calling is to redeem a part of food culture he says has been lost in the blur of the fast-food generation. From the ridiculous to the sublime, Shant's burgers have earned a reputation of biblical proportions in Toronto, and he's converting people by the thousands every week.

With a few exceptions, devotees of The Priest worship the god of beef, and Shant approaches this, the foundation of his business, with requisite reverence. Different cuts of meat are freshly ground every day by a secret technique witnessed by a select few. The beef is then hand-formed into loose hockey pucks, placed on a tray, and wrapped in plastic until they're summoned to the flattop for judgment.

You get a double dose of meat with the Red Sea, a Secret Menu item that starts with a single cheeseburger. Things get messy when Shant pours on a heap of his signature chili—a slow-cooked blend of burger chunks, kidney beans, tomato sauce, and seasonings. If your heart's up to the task, throw in an order of Chili Cheese Fries, a basket of fries blanketed in fresh chili and Cheddar cheese.

Is that a halo? Owner and chef Shant Mardirosian spent eight months working in New York City kitchens and meat processing plants to learn the soul of the true burger.

Piety meets hypocrisy in The Religious Hypocrite, a pseudo-vegetarian burger that features two sizzling slices of bacon. But what makes The Hypocrite extraordinary is its main feature: two giant portobello mushroom caps that have been grilled, stuffed with a secret mixture of three cheeses, then coated in flour, eggs, and panko before being baptized in the deep-fryer. Sure, you can add bacon to flesh it out a bit (get it . . . *flesh* it out?), but once the hot cheese blend begins to ooze out of the tender mushroom, you'll know you've found the holy grail. Remove the bacon and you've got The Priest's true vegetarian option, called . . . well . . . The Option.

Burgers come in all shapes and sizes at The Priest, and each name is punnier than the last. Holy Smokes is a classic double cheeseburger topped with "smoke": panko-breaded jalapeño rings deep-fried to order. The Armageddon burger heralds the end of your appetite for days to come with its two cheeseburger patties and two portobello "Options." Or go straight to Hades with The Tower of Babel, which squishes The Option between two cheeseburger patties, themselves jammed in an envelope of grilled cheese sandwiches.

More adventurous pilgrims who visit The Priest can order their burgers Jarge (*Jarz-sh*) Style, which means the meat will be fried in ballpark mustard. It may sound blasphemous, but your tongue will be singing a different tune: delicious! Hell (sorry), even the desserts are burger shaped. Shant's chocolate chip cookies are a sermon of peace in your piehole.

Bow down your head and worship, burger lover. The service is about to start, and The Priest is in the house.

Divine inspiration is easy to find at The Burger's Priest, where the meals are so tasty, they'll drop you to your knees.

Vatican City

Makes: 4 burgers

If you're looking for something to worship, The Priest's Vatican City is a Secret Menu item (and *Toronto Life*'s 2011 Burger of the Year) sporting two quarter-pound patties smashed flat on the flattop, where they sizzle in their own juices before being covered in a blanket of cheese.

Grilled Cheese Buns

8 hamburger buns (white or whole wheat)
Butter
16 slices processed cheese

Burgers

2 pounds quality ground beef
Salt
8 slices processed cheese

Toppings (optional)

Lettuce
Tomato
Pickle
Onion
Ketchup
Mustard
Mayonnaise

Grilled Cheese Buns

Split the buns and liberally butter the insides. Place 1 slice of cheese on the outer part of each half while it is toasting on the grill. As the cheese starts to melt, sandwich the cheesy sides of each bun together and press until flat.

Burgers

Preheat a cast-iron grill over high heat.

Form the beef into 8 even patties, being careful not to overwork the meat. Generously season both sides of the patties with salt.

Cook the patties until a nice crust forms on the bottom, about 3 minutes, then flip. As soon as you flip the patty over, top with a slice of cheese and cook for another 3 minutes. Do not squeeze the patties or flip more than once. Once the cheese is melted, the burger should be done.

Assembly

Top the bottom of a grilled cheese bun with two patties. Garnish with your desired toppings and sandwich with another grilled cheese bun.

Chino Locos

EST. 2008
4 GREENWOOD AVENUE
TORONTO, ON · M4L 2P4
647-345-5626
WWW.CHINOLOCOS.COM

love burritos. And I love Chinese food. Luckily for me, there's Chino Locos, so I can get the best of both worlds. Now I don't have to eat out twice to get my fixes! And with unbelievably massive portions, I can order one of chef Minh La's creations and enjoy it twice in the same day: half for lunch, and the rest for dinner. Sound loco? That's Chino Locos to you, amigo.

But these two cuisines did not meet by accident. Owners and compadres Minh La and Victor Su opened Chino Locos after watching their parents—Asian immigrants to Canada—work their butts off to make a living for their families. The restaurant is the product of their intense collective drive and the desire to give Torontonians delicious, inventive, and hip-hop cool food for a reasonable price. Nailed it!

Minh is the driving force in the kitchen, a funky, fun, and talented dude who demands the best in everything he serves. Born in Saigon, Minh immigrated to Canada when just five years old, and cooked his way into Toronto's George Brown College Culinary program. Though he cut his teeth in the world of fine dining, his current mission is to feed what he calls "ordinary people." Well, nobody's more ordinary than I am, so bring it on!

And bring it he does. The Slow Roast Pork Burrito is built on a white or whole-wheat tortilla slathered with guacamole and stuffed to overflowing with cheese, sour cream, hot sauce, homemade chipotle sauce, ginger relish, black bean mix, and delicious slow-roasted pork. What makes the burrito extraspecial, though (pay attention, this is where the Chino part comes in), is that Minh uses chow mein

This is the good stuff, baby! Minh La stuffs his burritos with the best ingredients, plus the one that puts the "Chino" in Chino Locos: chow mein noodles.

noodles instead of rice. Once you get over the sheer size of the thing, you'll be delighted by the texture of the noodles and the party of flavours.

Minh also gets busy with Da Finest Fish Burrito, a simple-yet-complex (confusing, eh?) delight that starts with Vietnamese basa pan-fried in Chino Loco's signature chipotle sauce. The fish keeps company in the tortilla (hey man, they've got gluten-free options, too) with a fiesta of guacamole, tomatoes, edamame, red onions, black beans, green peppers, cilantro, cheese, and sour cream. Don't forget those chow mein noodles, which blend perfectly with the tender fish.

Minh is a master of variety, and it shows on the menu. The Pollo Loco is built around shredded white chicken meat and chipotle, while the Biggie Bean Burrito is a black bean lover's dream come true. And the Juicy Vegan—featuring pressed tofu, eggplant, shitake mushrooms, and glass noodles—is so damn good, you'll wonder why you ever eat meat.

It's these kinds of paradoxes that define the vibe at Chino Locos. The joint is bright but chilled, nonsensical but hip. Sure, there's red-and-white checkered floors, but you're more likely to hear Jay-Z than Fats Domino pumping through the speakers.

Assuming you can hear anything over the sound of food being stuffed into your mouth, that is.

Minh and Victor are cosmopolitan dudes who know that there's more to food than just meat. That's why you won't find a stitch of it in their Juicy Vegan Burrito, which doesn't sacrifice taste—or heft!—in the bargain.

"Off Da Hook" Rib-Eye Steak Burrito

Makes: 4 servings

Surprisingly perfect blends are always on hand at Chino Locos. Asian fusion meets protein over-dose with the gargantuan Off Da Hook burrito. I don't know what's more amazing: how tasty and tender this thing is, or how chef Minh La manages to wrap it so tightly that nothing falls out.

Noodles

16 ounces chow mein noodles

2 tablespoons oil

4 pinches of chopped green onions

2 teaspoons salt

4 tablespoons black bean sauce

Burrito

12 ounces rib-eye steak, cut into
   bite-size pieces

2 tablespoons salt

2 tablespoons cornstarch

2 tablespoons oil

1½ cups chipotle sauce, divided

¼ cup black bean sauce

Assemby

4 12-inch tortillas

4 tablespoons sour cream

4 tablespoons guacamole

1 cup shredded cheese (of your choice)

1½ cups pico de gallo

4 pinches of chopped fresh cilantro

1 cup cooked black beans

1 lime, cut into wedges

Noodles

In a large saucepan of boiling water, blanch the chow mein noodles for 1 minute. Drain and set aside to cool.

In a skillet over medium-high heat, heat the oil. Add the onions, season with salt, and sauté for 30 seconds. Add the chow mein noodles and stir-fry for 2 minutes, then flip all of the noodles over and stir-fry for another 2 minutes. Stir in the black bean sauce and cook until heated through. Remove from heat and set aside.

Burrito

Season both sides of the steak with salt and cornstarch.

In a skillet over medium-high heat, heat the oil. Sear the steak on both sides until medium rare, about 1¼ minutes per side. Add 1 cup of the chipotle sauce and the black bean sauce and stir-fry until evenly coated. Remove from heat and set aside.

Assembly

To each tortilla, add 1 tablespoon each of sour cream and guacamole and one-quarter of the cheese. Top with 1 teaspoon of pico de gallo and a pinch of cilantro. Divide chow mein noodles and remaining ½ cup chipotle sauce among tortillas. Top each with 4 tablespoons cooked black beans. Divide the steak into 4 even portions and add to tortillas. Squeeze 1 lime wedge over each burrito. Wrap up each burrito and toast in a hot dry pan or on a panini press to seal the edge.

The Crepe House

EST. 2011
2012 PARK STREET
PORT DOVER, ON · N0A 1N0
519-583-9018
WWW.CREPEHOUSE.CA

As far as life-changing experiences go, trips to Europe are right up there. The Crepe House is the product of one such excursion. Back in 2002, Penny Nunn and her children travelled through the Netherlands and Germany, stumbling upon a crêpe vendor. One chocolate-and-banana crêpe later, Penny's life would never be the same. She knew that she had to bring the simple, versatile, and delicious treats back home to Port Dover.

And bring them back she did. Penny started out small, selling crêpes from a propane-powered street cart she set up at strategic locations around town. As her customer base grew, so did Penny's confidence. She and partner Jim Loshaw converted a house in the downtown core, painted it bright yellow and blue, and have been serving up sweet and savoury creations there ever since.

Perhaps the most difficult thing about eating at The Crepe House is making a decision. That struggle starts with the crêpe itself, where you can opt for either traditional white flour or buckwheat batter. Things only get more difficult once you've crossed the batter bridge, because the next step is deciding which of your taste buds need satisfying. Will you go for a sweet temptation or something more savoury?

Savoury is well represented at The Crepe House, and nothing is more comforting than Penny's Turkey Dinner Crêpe, which takes everything you love about Thanksgiving and rolls it up in a nifty little package, all topped

Penny Nunn is the picture of contented concentration as she works with the versatile little pancake that makes The Crepe House a destination for everyone.

with even more gravy. For a guy like me—who thinks turkey shouldn't be just for holidays—it was a cozy reminder that, well, I'm right.

Yet as open as I was to the idea of an entire Thanksgiving meal being handed to me in a warm little pouch, I wasn't sold on the idea of morphing cannelloni—a traditional Italian stuffed-pasta dish—into crêpe form. Skeptic or not, I was won over by Penny's Cannelloni Crêpe (sorry, I'll hand in my Italian National card now), which got slightly crispy when baked, adding a nice texture to hold the cheesy filling together, even under the tomato sauce. I give it two Italian thumbs up!

Not one to ignore tradition, Penny happily serves The Pirate, the chocolate-and-banana crêpe that stole her heart. Penny uses European dark chocolate, which she drizzles generously over the sliced bananas. The folded crêpe is topped with more bananas, homemade whipped cream, and even more melted chocolate. Sweet teeth also find their fix with the Summer Garden, Penny's most popular offering. This tangy delight starts with homemade lemon curd (a recipe Penny learned from her grandmother), followed by heaps of fresh fruit topped with maple syrup, icing sugar, and more fruit, and served with a dollop of whipped cream on the side. It was, in a word, heavenly: bright, tart, and . . . fruity!

And if you think Penny is the only person whose life can be changed by crêpes, you're sorely mistaken. Just show up here on Friday the 13th, when leather-clad bikers line up outside her doors. That's right, people, it takes a real man to eat a crêpe.

Who needs pasta? Well, I do. But that didn't stop me from loving Penny's Cannelloni Crêpe, which transforms an Italian classic into an indulgent crêpe. The dish can be ordered with a range of fillings that change with the seasons.

The Crepe House's best seller, the Summer Garden Crêpe, is built around zesty lemon curd and fresh fruit, but the whipped cream, maple syrup, and icing sugar render it utterly divine.

Lemon Curd

6 eggs

2 egg yolks

2 cups white sugar

¼ cup lemon zest

¾ cup lemon juice

1 cup butter

Batter

2 cups all-purpose flour

¼ teaspoon salt

2½ cups milk

2 eggs, beaten

1 tablespoon canola oil

Assembly

Seasonal fresh fruit (peaches, strawberries, raspberries, blueberries)

Maple syrup

Icing sugar

Lemon Curd

Bring water to a boil in the bottom of a double boiler (or a saucepan), then reduce heat to a simmer. In the top of the double boiler (or in a heatproof bowl), whisk together the whole eggs, yolks, and sugar. Whisk in the lemon zest, lemon juice, and butter, stirring frequently until the butter has melted and the mixture is smooth and thick. Remove from heat and set aside to cool before using.

Note: This recipe makes 8 cups of lemon curd. Store unused portion in airtight containers and refrigerate for up to 3 weeks or freeze for up to a year.

Batter

In a blender, combine all of the ingredients and blend until smooth. Let batter rest at least 1 hour before preparing the crêpes.

Assembly

Preheat a greased crêpe pan. Pour a scant amount of batter in the centre of the pan. Swirl the pan or use a crêpe spreader to spread batter as thinly as possible. When the edges begin to lift, using your fingertips or your crêpe paddle, carefully turn the crêpe over to brown the other side. Transfer cooked crêpe to a plate, keeping warm. Repeat with remaining batter.

To serve, fill the crêpes with 1 tablespoon lemon curd and fresh seasonal fruit. Fold the crêpe into a triangular pouch and top with a drizzle of maple syrup and a dusting of icing sugar. Serve with a dollop of whipped cream on the side. Make it really pop with a fresh fruit garnish.

Summer Garden Crêpe

Makes: 4 to 6 crepes

Dr. Laffa

EST. 2011

401 MAGNETIC DRIVE

NORTH YORK, ON · M3J 3H9

416-739-7134

WWW.DRLAFFA.COM

love my job. Not only do I get to *eat* for a living, but along the way I learn new and exciting things and meet some of the coolest people anywhere. Well, at Dr. Laffa I hit the jackpot.

Food? Laffa sandwiches are massive and tasty, and just one part of a huge and varied menu. Learning? Who knew that laffa bread is made by sticking dough to the inside of something called a "taboon"? And people? Lovable co-owners Yoram Gabay and Sasi Haba are yin and yang. Yoram is Dr. Laffa's jokester and front man, while Sasi is the behind-the-scenes guy who keeps the place running.

Yet as well as Yoram and Sasi work together, their relationship is a relatively young one. Sasi moved his family from Israel to Montreal back in 2006, bringing the stainless-steel interior of his beloved taboon with him. It sat in his backyard for years, but when Sasi moved to Toronto, the taboon came along. Good thing it did: here he met Yoram—a fellow Israeli expat and baker—who rented some commercial space to Sasi.

The pair hit it off, and they were soon making culinary music together: Dr. Laffa had found its niche. The restaurant was so popular that it had to be relocated to a bigger space. And while Dr. Laffa might not be right in the heart of downtown Toronto, it is SO worth the trip for me.

Especially if you're hungry. Like, starving. Because that's exactly how you have to be if you expect to finish one of Yoram's laffa

Sasi Haba may not be Dr. Laffa's front man, but he's a star when it comes to the warm, crusty pitas he bakes by the hundreds every day.

sandwiches. The Falafel Laffa starts with a 7-ounce ball of dough (think medium pizza) lovingly stretched before being slapped inside the taboon, where it bakes to crusty goodness. Then the laffa is filled with *six* (yep, six!) crispy and creamy falafel balls, along with hot sauce, tahini sauce, amba (sour mango sauce), a cucumber-tomato-onion salad, and french fries (the real Israeli way!). From there you're on your own, and free to add any of the dozen or so other garnishes on the menu. Just beware: this monster weighs in at two to three times the size of a "normal" falafel sandwich, so bring your friends along for the ride.

Shawarma also gets a boost at Dr. Laffa, where Yoram is quick to point out that only shawarma made from the thigh of a female turkey qualifies as the real deal. The broad slabs of meat are seasoned with a blend of 17 spices imported from a Jerusalem market, then assembled on a giant skewer, where they marinate for at least 24 hours. Then the skewer is hoisted onto a rotating grill, roasting in its own juices and fat. For the Shawarma Platter, the tender, flavourful meat is carved off and served alongside ample portions of classic sides. The sandwich is much the same, only stuffed inside a laffa with your choice of fillings. How was it? Easy: best shawarma ever.

Traditional Iraqi Kubba (beet soup) is as beautiful as it is filling: handmade meat dumplings swim in a bright red beet bath.

Who says a visit to the doctor can't be fun? At Dr. Laffa, the prescription is for a daily dose of delicious.

Quick-witted jokester Yoram Gabay makes everyone feel like family, with both his good-natured teasing and the delicious food he creates in Dr. Laffa's kitchen.

Dr. Laffa Hummus

Makes: 4 to 6 servings

Co-owner Yoram Gabay's hummus plate is more than just an appetizer. The creamy hummus—a perfect balance between garlic and lemon—is spooned into a bowl, then hollowed in the middle for a scoop of pan-fried ground beef. It's a warm and creamy Israeli hug.

Timing note: chickpeas must soak in water for 12 hours.

Hummus

4 cups dried chickpeas
1 teaspoon baking soda
A pinch of salt
3 garlic cloves
4¼ cups mineral water
1½ cups raw tahini
3 tablespoons olive oil
3 tablespoons lemon juice
3 tablespoons ground cumin

Beef Topping

½ onion, finely diced
1 tablespoon olive oil
1 garlic clove, crushed
7 ounces beef chuck, coarsely ground
Pinch of sweet paprika
Pinch of spicy paprika
Salt and pepper
1 tablespoon toasted pine nuts
Chopped fresh parsley

Hummus

Place the chickpeas in a large bowl and cover with about 12 cups of water. Set aside to soak at room temperature for a minimum of 12 hours. Drain the chickpeas well.

In a large pot, combine about 12 cups of fresh water, the soaked chickpeas, and the baking soda. Bring to a boil over medium heat and cook for 3 to 4 hours, stirring occasionally, until chickpeas are tender. (To test for doneness, crush a single chickpea between your thumb and index finger. If the chickpea doesn't crush easily, continue cooking.) Drain the chickpeas and rinse with lukewarm water.

Transfer the chickpeas to a food processor fitted with the metal blade. Add the salt, garlic, mineral water, tahini, olive oil, lemon juice, and cumin and process until creamy, about 10 minutes. If any lumps remain, continue processing. Set aside.

Beef Topping

In a large skillet over medium heat, fry the onion in the oil until golden. Add the garlic and ground beef, stirring and breaking up the meat with the back of a spoon as it cooks. Season with the paprikas and salt and pepper to taste and stir to combine well. When the beef is well browned and cooked through, stir in the toasted pine nuts.

Assembly

Place a large scoop of hummus in a shallow serving bowl. Using the back of a spoon, spread the hummus around the rim of the bowl, creating a well in the centre. Fill the well with a scoop of beef topping. Sprinkle with chopped fresh parsley. Repeat for remaining servings.

The Early Bird

EST. 2012
355 TALBOT STREET
LONDON, ON · N6A 2R5
519-439-6483
WWW.THEEARLYBIRD.CA

I realize the purists out there are going to have a field day with me, but sometimes you've gotta put yourself out there. So here goes: The Early Bird's perogy poutine may be the best I've ever eaten. Yes, fries plus cheese curds plus gravy is one of the most delicious creations known to humankind. But substitute handmade perogies—which stand near the top of the comfort-food chain—for fries, then top them with *duck* gravy, and you can see why this one stands out in my mind.

Delicious food is not the only thing that makes The Early Bird memorable. The place is as long on personality as it is on cuisine, thanks to rockin' brothers Justin and Gregg Wolfe, whose mission is to serve up wacky twists on diner food . . . when they're not playing in their heavy metal band, that is. This all comes in a funky retro package featuring everything from pop art to groovy posters. Oh, and *massive* portions, too.

Massive comes in many forms at The Early Bird, perhaps none more ridiculous than the 6 inches of triple-decker heaven known as the Turducken-Style Club, which features turkey, chicken, and duck, each prepared in a unique way and assembled on thick slabs of homemade bread. Slathered in maple aïoli and topped with a variety of fixings, it's a sandwich that customers swear is one of the greatest on the planet. I say that's one tasty 'gweech (that's how we tough guys say "sandgweech" back in the 'hood)! Go from ridiculous to sublime by siding the Turducken with bacon-wrapped pickles, which are deep-fried and paired with smoked garlic aïoli.

Yo! Early Bird co-owner Justin Wolfe not only rocks a sweet beard, he rocks delicious twists on diner classics *and* rocks the tunes with his metal band, Beards of Prey.

The Turducken-Style Club features meat, three ways: smoked turkey; cured, bacon-like duck breast; and panko-coated, deep-fried chicken come together in fowl harmony.

If you're getting the picture that Justin is a freakin' magician in the kitchen, you're right. Awesome dude and amazing chef, he dazzles his clientele with dishes like Ginger Beer Battered Tofu (served on focaccia and topped with spinach, peppers, deep-fried lotus root chips, and shredded leeks), The Popper (a grilled-cheese sandwich with melted mozzarella, cream cheese, sliced pickled jalapeños, tortilla chips, and homemade jalapeño pepper jelly), and Egg McJustin (English-style toast topped with a ground pork patty, smoked bacon, fried egg, aged Cheddar, baby spinach, and chipotle aïoli).

It's dishes like these that catapult The Early Bird into the annals of the *You Gotta Eat Here!* Hall of Fame. Funny, brilliant, generous, happy, and rockin' it inside and outside the kitchen, Justin and Gregg know a good time and serve it up hundreds of times every day.

The Pancake Stacker

Makes: 4 servings

Breakfast gets supersized at The Early Bird with the Pancake Stacker, a sky-high arrangement that starts with four of the fluffiest pancakes I've ever put in my piehole. But co-owner Justin Wolfe's not the kind of guy to serve you cakes alone. That would be just too . . . ordinary. Sandwiched between the cake layers are hash browns, homemade peameal bacon, and house-smoked bacon, all topped with a sunny-side-up egg. Drizzle with a bit of maple syrup or let the yolk be your sauce—either way, it's a sweet, savoury, and smoky mound of love that you'll need months to train for and days to recover from.

Special equipment: smoker

Peameal Bacon

2 cups brown sugar

½ cup kosher salt

½ cup **Prague salt (pink curing salt)**

¼ cup blackstrap molasses

2 teaspoons fennel seed, ground

2 teaspoons mustard seed, ground

2 teaspoons black pepper, ground

2 bay leaves

1 pork loin (2 to 3 pounds)

Cornmeal

Smoked Bacon

1 cup brown sugar

½ cup kosher salt

1 teaspoon black pepper

¼ cup fennel seeds

Pinch of hot pepper flakes

1 pork belly (3 to 4 pounds)

½ cup maple syrup

Potato Hash

4 to 6 large russet potatoes, diced

2 tablespoons butter

1 onion, diced

Salt and pepper

Pancakes

2 cups 2% milk

1 teaspoon white wine vinegar

2 cups all-purpose flour

½ cup sugar

2 teaspoons baking powder

½ teaspoon baking soda

2 eggs

½ teaspoon vanilla extract

Assembly (per stacker)

4 pancakes

3 to 4 slices peameal

4 to 6 slices smoked bacon

1 egg, cooked sunny-side up

Maple syrup

Peameal Bacon

Prepare the brine: Combine all of the ingredients—except the pork loin and cornmeal—with 4 cups of water in a medium stockpot and bring to a boil. Remove from heat and set aside to cool slightly, then transfer to an airtight container, cover, and refrigerate until cooled completely.

Place the pork loin in the container with the cooled brine. Cover and refrigerate for 3 to 5 days to cure the meat.

After 3 to 5 days, the pork loin will start to darken and firm up—it's now peameal bacon. Drain the peameal and rinse under cool running water. Pat dry with paper towel and roll peameal in cornmeal.

Using a sharp knife, cut the peameal crosswise into thick coins.

In a greased skillet over medium-high heat, fry the peameal until browned on both sides, about 4 minutes per side. Set aside and keep warm.

Smoked Bacon

Prepare the dry rub: Combine all of the ingredients—except the pork belly and maple syrup—in a small bowl.

Place the pork belly in an airtight container. Smother and rub the belly with the dry rub, pour the maple syrup over top, cover and refrigerate for 2 to 3 days to cure.

Once cured, rinse the rub off the bacon under cool running water. Pat dry with paper towel. The bacon is ready to be smoked, if desired, or simply sliced and panfried.

If smoking, cook in a smoker at 225°F for about 2 hours (the outside will start to darken). Allow the smoked bacon to cool.

Using a sharp knife, slice lengthwise in thin strips. (For best results, slice the bacon using a meat slicer.)

In a greased skillet over medium-high heat, fry the bacon until crisp. Transfer to a plate lined in paper towel to drain. Set aside.

Potato Hash

In a medium saucepan of boiling water, blanch the potatoes until just tender.

Heat a cast-iron skillet over high heat. Add the butter and onion and cook, stirring often, until the onion is translucent. Add the potatoes and cook, stirring occasionally, until potatoes are browned and crisp. Set aside, keeping warm.

Pancakes

In a small bowl, combine the milk and vinegar and set aside to "sour."

In a large bowl, combine the flour, sugar, baking powder, and baking soda. Make a large well
in the centre of the dry ingredients. Crack the eggs into the well and stir, slowly pulling dry
ingredients into the centre of the mixture. Add the soured milk and vanilla, and stir just
until combined (the mixture should be thick and lumpy).

Scoop a ladleful of the mixture into a hot greased skillet or onto a hot flattop to form pancakes.
Cook for 2 to 3 minutes per side, until browned (when air bubbles form throughout the top of
the pancake, it's ready to be flipped). Repeat with remaining batter, to make 16 pancakes in
total. Keep warm in a low oven.

Assembly (per stacker)

Place one pancake on a serving plate. Cover evenly with potato hash and top with a second
pancake. Follow by a layer of the peameal bacon and a third pancake. Top with smoked
bacon, then the fourth and final pancake. Top the stacker with a sunny-side-up egg. Smother
in maple syrup and stab with a knife!

Earth to Table Bread Bar

EST. 2010
258 LOCKE STREET SOUTH
HAMILTON, ON · L8P 4B9
905-522-2999
WWW.BREADBAR.CA

You can taste Earth to Table's philosophy—Good Ingredients Matter—in every bite of food you eat at the Bread Bar, whether you're feasting on sweet bakery treats, sandwiches, or pizzas. In this restaurant, fresh and local ingredients add up to delicious food!

Long-time partners in the kitchen, Bettina Schormann and Jeff Crump came together at an upscale restaurant in Ancaster, Ontario, where they co-authored a cookbook called *Earth to Table*. When Bettina felt the urge to strike out on her own, Jeff was quick to join her. Given the response from nearby Hamiltonians, it's a partnership that's built to last.

On the bakery side of the ledger, Bettina is as knowledgeable as she is passionate. A graduate of Toronto's George Brown College's culinary school, she's won numerous awards for her pastry making, and it shows in every heavenly creation she serves.

The divine comes in many forms at the Bread Bar, and you'll think you've met your maker when you eat Bettina's croissants and pain au chocolat, which are made melt-in-your-mouth fresh every day. Her Really, Really Fudgy Brownie is a decadent chocolate treat spiked with salted caramel and toffee bits and served warm with vanilla ice cream. The Butterscotch Budino features a creamy butterscotch pudding topped with vanilla crème fraîche and candied pumpkin seeds.

Jeff steps into the picture with lunch and dinner, and his pizzas are so popular that Bread Bar makes some 200 pounds of dough every day. I opted for the Eggplant Parmesan Pizza, a simply spectacular 'za smothered in tomato sauce and mozzarella, then topped with fresh basil, lemon zest, hot pepper flakes, sliced eggplant, Parmesan cheese, bread crumbs, and a homemade buttermilk dressing. *Yuh-me!*

The Wise Guy Pizza is a made man's dream and features homemade pork sausage seasoned with toasted fennel (which I didn't like as a kid . . . but love now) piled alongside roasted onions and red peppers. Topped with fresh basil after it comes out of the oven, the pizza is an explosion of flavour, an experience only enhanced by the crust, which is like none I've ever tasted before.

Accomplished chef that he is, Jeff doesn't limit his culinary chicanery to pizza. The menu is chock-a-block with soups and salads (try the Kale Caesar), as well as sandwiches, burgers, and entrées. The Chop Chick Pea Tartine is an open-faced sandwich of marinated chickpeas, roasted red peppers, and lemon confit. If it's potatoes you crave, the Loaded Fries Special is Jeff's take on poutine, a creation that changes with his whim. Über-popular is the Green Goddess, which sees the fries loaded up with cheese curds, wild mushrooms, green onions, and homemade green goddess dressing.

If all this variety has got you confused, fear not. Whether you come in the morning, afternoon, or evening, there's always something delicious waiting at the Bread Bar. Or you could go for the Full Catucci and just stay all day.

Good ingredients matter at Earth to Table Bread Bar.

The secret to all of Jeff's pizzas is that he lets the dough rise for a day and a half in the fridge, a process that lets it build up a stupid amount of flavour.

Monkey Bread
Makes: 1 dozen

One of my favourites at Earth to Table is Bettina Schormann's Monkey Bread, a cross between a cinnamon bun and a doughnut. Bettina starts with brioche pastry dough, which is hand-rolled into balls and tossed in a blend of cinnamon and sugar. Bake four lumps in each cup of a muffin pan and top with a drizzle of sweet glaze, and you've got little pillows of brioche heaven.

Timing note: dough must chill ovenight

Brioche Dough

2⅓ cups all-purpose flour

3 tablespoons white sugar

1 tablespoon instant dry yeast

2 large eggs

1 large egg yolk

⅓ cup warm (not hot) water

2 teaspoons salt

1 cup unsalted butter, cubed and softened

Monkey Bread

1 cup white sugar

1 tablespoon ground cinnamon

1 cup icing sugar

1 tablespoon milk

Brioche Dough

In the bowl of a stand mixer fitted with the paddle attachment, combine the flour, sugar, and yeast.

In a separate bowl, whisk together the whole eggs and yolk with the water.

With the mixer on a low speed, add the egg mixture to the flour mixture and mix until well combined. Add the butter, one cube at a time, and mix until a smooth dough forms (it will seem more batter-like at this point).

Transfer the dough to a lightly oiled bowl, cover in plastic wrap, and refrigerate overnight. The dough should be cool and firm before use.

Monkey Bread

Line a 12-cup muffin pan with paper liners.

In a shallow bowl, whisk together the white sugar and cinnamon.

Once the prepared brioche dough is cool and firm, use a spoon to scoop up 1-inch dough balls and toss them in the cinnamon sugar until evenly covered (you should end up with 48 balls; any remaining dough can be wrapped and refrigerated for up to 3 days). Place 4 balls into each paper-lined muffin cup. Loosely cover the pan with plastic wrap and set aside in a warm spot (e.g., on top of the fridge) for about 40 minutes to allow dough to proof slightly. Once proofed, bake in a preheated 350°F oven for 10 to 15 minutes, or until golden brown and firm to the touch.

Meanwhile, in a small bowl, combine the icing sugar and milk to form a smooth glaze.

Drizzle each monkey bread with icing sugar glaze. Best served slightly warm.

Edgar

EST. 2010
60 RUE BÉGIN
GATINEAU, QC · J9A 1C8
819-205-1110
WWW.CHEZEDGAR.CA

One word: lovely.

That is the only way to describe Marysol Foucault and the magical delights she whips up every day at Edgar, the restaurant that bears her father's name. Small but mighty, Marysol is one of those rare personalities who lives for what she does. Cooking is Marysol, and Marysol is cooking.

Yet it wasn't easy for this tiny woman with the infectious giggle to break into the restaurant biz. Although she landed her first cooking gig as a teenager, Marysol wasn't a fan of hard-edged commercial kitchens, so she got a job at a local cooking school. But serendipity had more in store for Marysol: she was detoured down an unfamiliar road one day, where she noticed a For Rent sign on a local business. A few days later, Marysol had quit her job, and Edgar was on its way.

The world needs more restaurants like Edgar, where people feel like they are part of a kinder, simpler time. The place is tiny and intimate, and a throwback to the '50s and '60s, the decades Marysol most connects with. That's why you'll often find her riding to work on a powder-blue scooter or wearing a vintage-style dress in her kitchen.

While Marysol and her restaurant are old school, her recipes are 100% cutting-edge, spinning old favourites into modern-day works of art. Take, for example, La Bûcheronne ("Lady Lumberjack"), which she says is just another way of serving bacon and eggs. Uh . . . no! La Bûcheronne is a multifaceted breakfast feast that has so much going on, you won't know where to stick your fork first.

Small-but-mighty Marysol Foucault runs her kitchen and her restaurant with heaps of love, and you can taste it in every dish she serves at Edgar.

Should it be the cheesy potato gratin, a 2-inch tower of heart-pounding goodness? Or maybe the home-baked beans peppered with smoked ham and topped with maple syrup? Of course, you could always opt for the maple syrup–soaked candied bacon, the poached eggs, or the herbed popover. Regardless of where you start, you'll love how all the different elements blend together into one gooey, sweet, salty mess.

The delicious variety of La Bûcheronne is matched flavour-for-flavour by the Pork Belly Dutch Baby, which features some of the best "bacon" I've ever had. The Baby starts with rich pork belly, which is lovingly rubbed with a sugar-and-spice mix, then baked in apple juice for 5 hours. It's served in a giant baked "bowl" (a cross between a pancake and Yorkshire pudding) that's been sprinkled with sugar and cinnamon, and filled with homemade apple sauce, chunks of aged Cheddar, and an unfathomable amount of the pork.

Guaranteed you've never seen eggs done like Marysol's sinfully delicious Huevos Rancheros, where the eggs are cooked in homemade salsa and served with a bevy of Mexican fixings.

Smothered in tons of maple syrup, this is a table-slapper (as in table-slappin' good!). Marysol also delighted me with her Huevos Rancheros, where the eggs are cooked in salsa and served in a tortilla basket filled with homemade refried beans.

Breakfast dishes may play a huge part in life at Edgar, but Marysol is no one-meal gal. Her Vegetable Sandwich is served hot on black olive bread slathered with spicy mayo and topped with avocados, roasted Roma tomatoes, red onions, goat cheese, and red peppers. The Fig Sandwich is an in-season delight served with provolone, Brie, prosciutto, and a balsamic reduction sauce on a rosemary and roasted garlic panino.

Marysol is also a gifted pastry chef, so don't miss her desserts. Whether it's the Bread Pudding, Blueberry and Lemon Curd Dutch Baby, or famous Lemon Beignets, you'll likely set up a tent in Edgar's kitchen once you get a taste of these delights. Because when you've found a restaurant as lovely as this, you won't want to leave.

Blueberry and Lemon Curd Dutch Baby

Makes: 4 Dutch Baby pancakes

Edgar's Blueberry and Lemon Curd Dutch Baby is a bowlful of baked love, only this time bursting with a gorgeous sweet filling featuring homemade lemon curd, yogurt, and fresh blueberries.

Special equipment: double boiler (optional), oven-safe cast-iron pan

Lemon Curd
3 eggs
1 egg yolk
¾ cup sugar
Zest and juice of 2 lemons
⅓ cup butter

Dutch Baby
1 cup all-purpose flour
1 cup milk
⅓ cup sugar
Zest of 1 lemon
½ teaspoon grated nutmeg
6 eggs
½ cup butter, softened

Assembly
Icing sugar
Ground cinnamon
Greek yogurt
Fresh wild blueberries

Lemon Curd
Bring water in the bottom of a double boiler (or a saucepan) to a boil, then reduce heat to a simmer. In the top of the double boiler (or in a heatproof bowl), whisk together the whole eggs and yolk. Whisk in the sugar and lemon zest and juice. Continue whisking, continuously, until the mixture thickens, about 6 minutes (it should heavily coat the back of a spoon). Remove from heat and whisk in the butter until fully incorporated and mixture is smooth. Cover with plastic wrap and refrigerate to cool.

Dutch Baby
Place a cast-iron pan in the oven and preheat oven to 425°F.

In a jug or tall container, using an immersion blender, blend the flour, milk, sugar, lemon zest, nutmeg, and eggs until smooth.

Remove the hot cast-iron pan from the oven. Add 1 heaping tablespoon butter to the pan and swirl to coat the pan well. Pour one big ladleful of the batter into the pan and return pan to the oven. Cook for about 8 minutes or until golden brown and Dutch Baby starts to climb the sides of the pan, and remove from pan. Repeat with remaining batter.

Assembly
Place a Dutch Baby onto a serving plate. Sprinkle with sugar and cinnamon and top with a dollop of lemon curd, a dollop of yogurt, and a large handful of blueberries.

Fanny Chadwick's

EST. 2010
268 HOWLAND AVENUE
TORONTO, ON · M5R 3B6
416-944-1606
WWW.FANNYCHADWICKS.CA

There's nothing quite like Mom's cooking. Now Fanny Chadwick might not be your mother, but the neighbourhood restaurant that bears her name is a haven for the rich, old-fashioned, and delicious meals that most of us hold near and dear to our hearts when we think of home cooking. Named after a local woman whose open-door policy made her home a focal point of daily life on Howland Avenue, the restaurant has continued the tradition, serving as a hub for the hordes of regulars who consider Fanny's their second home.

The actual owner of Fanny's is Sarah Baxter, a local resident who became fed up with corporate life and sought out something simpler, homier, and more meaningful. Fanny Chadwick's is the fruit of that labour, and it's frequented by friends and families, as well as visitors looking for a touch of home away from home. The place is teeming with activity all the time, but weekend brunches are absolutely bonkers, and most tables are full by 11:00 a.m. You gotta get up early to catch this worm!

While Sarah may be the inspiration behind Fanny's, its on-the-ground mojo comes from chef Vega Janic, who studied math and physics in university, only to realize that her true calling was in the kitchen. And it shows! Her Shepherd's Pie, for example, is a classic rendition that warms both heart and soul. It starts with a lamb shoulder that's been braised overnight, until the meat is fall-off-the-bone tender. Chopped and mixed in a succulent gravy, the meat is layered into a baking dish, then topped with a layer of butter-sautéed leeks, followed by piped dollops of creamy mashed potatoes. Served with seasonal vegetables, it's warm and delicious, and the potatoes are the fluffiest little balls of love you'll ever eat.

Fanny's classics come in many flavours, and the Tourtière Turnover is an ode to the Québécois kitchen, but with a twist. Rather than the family-size pie most people are used to, Fanny Chadwick's version is a single-serving turnover that stuffs savoury, clove- and cinnamon-spiked ground chuck and potato filling into a flaky, golden-brown pastry. The turnover is served with a fresh green salad, a perfectly light complement to the wintry warmth of the tourtière.

Home cookin' keeps on coming at Fanny's, and the Buttermilk Fried Chicken is like a visit to a southern-fried country kitchen. The dish is served with creamy mashed potatoes, homemade

If the line-ups at Fanny Chadwick's are around the corner, you can thank Vega Janic. Her dishes have become the stuff of legend in this Toronto neighbourhood.

chicken gravy, and butter-sautéed vegetables. Pan-Seared Fish and Chips features fish fillets that are cornmeal-crusted and pan-fried, a refreshing twist on a deep-fried classic. The House-Made Sausage changes with Vega's mood, which likely explains why it's so popular. Flattop-fried until crispy but juicy, the sausages are served with freshly braised cabbage and fluffy mashed potatoes. Classic Mac and Cheese includes a dollop of mustard for a special kick.

So if you find yourself lamenting the fact that Mom's cooking isn't being served in your kitchen every night, take heart. Fanny Chadwick is happy to play substitute. Of course, you might never visit Mom again, but that's something you're going to have to work out on your own.

No ground meat here! Fanny Chadwick's Shepherd's Pie one-ups the standard ground beef-and-peas number with savoury hunks of chopped lamb and a surprising layer of butter-sautéed leeks with mashed potatoes.

Three-Bean Ragout with Stilton Polenta

Makes: 8 to 10 servings

This comfort masterpiece begins with chickpeas, navy beans, and black-eyed peas, all of which are sautéed in a rich tomatoey stew spiked with white wine, veggies, and spices.

Timing note: polenta must chill for several hours, and beans must soak overnight

Veggie Ragout

½ cup dried chickpeas

½ cup dried navy beans

½ cup dried black-eyed peas

1 tablespoon butter

1 cup finely diced onion

2 garlic cloves, minced

¼ cup finely diced celery

½ cup white wine

4 cups canned whole tomatoes, with juice

¼ cup capers, drained

3 tablespoons tomato paste

2 tablespoons yellow mustard seeds

Salt, pepper, and sugar

Polenta

½ cup cornmeal

¼ cup crumbled Stilton cheese

¼ teaspoon salt

2 to 3 tablespoons butter, for frying

Assembly

Olive oil

Pea shoots

Veggie Ragout

Place the chickpeas, navy beans, and black-eyed peas in three separate bowls, cover with water, and set aside to soak overnight.

Drain the beans. Bring three separate saucepans of water to a boil, place one type of bean in each pan, and simmer for 45 minutes to 1½ hours, until the beans are soft enough to crush between your fingers (each type will have a different cooking time; chickpeas usually take the longest). Drain and set aside.

In a large pot over medium heat, melt the butter. Add the onions, garlic, and celery and cook until the onions start to turn translucent, 7 to 10 minutes. Add the white wine, bring to a boil, and allow wine to reduce completely. Add the tomatoes, cooked beans, capers, tomato paste, and mustard seeds and cook for 30 minutes. Season with salt, pepper, and sugar to taste.

Polenta

In a large pot, bring 2 cups of water to a boil over high heat. Reduce heat to medium and add the cornmeal. Cook, stirring constantly, for 4 minutes. Remove from heat and stir in the cheese until melted. Season with salt and stir to combine. Pour the polenta into a plastic wrap–lined loaf pan and cover with additional plastic wrap. Set the polenta aside to cool, then refrigerate for several hours or overnight to allow it to set. Once the polenta is completely set, use a sharp knife to cut it into fingers about 1 inch wide. In a nonstick skillet over medium heat, melt the butter. Cook the polenta fingers, flipping to ensure all sides are brown and crispy.

Assembly

Place a polenta finger in the middle of a serving plate. Ladle ragout over top, leaving the polenta partly uncovered. Garnish with a pinch of pea shoots and a drizzle of olive oil.

The Flying Spatula Diner

EST. 2010
125 COLLINGWOOD STREET
FLESHERTON, ON · NOC 1EO
519-924-2424

We all have different ways of dealing with things we don't like. Some of us shy away from conflict, others get angry. Shawn Adler, the owner and chef at The Flying Spatula Diner, has his own unique approach. When Shawn was dissatisfied with a breakfast at a local diner one morning, he vowed he would take over the place if it ever went up for sale. The next day Shawn saw an ad in the local paper proclaiming the building for rent, and leapt to action.

It wasn't as if Shawn was sitting around on his hands waiting for fate to present itself to him. He was, at the time, in the throes of opening *another* restaurant in the area, The Flying Chestnut. And while The Chestnut may be a fine dining experience, The Flying Spatula is a quintessential country diner, where meaty, mouth-watering classics are the rule of the day, and locals come often and stay long.

Shawn pays tribute to The Spatula's hometown with his Putting the "Flesh" in Flesherton Meat Platter, which is enough food to choke a starving trucker. The components of this meat-and-potatoes classic might change from time to time, but you can bet yer arteries it's going to be good. Mine started with a marinated strip loin steak (enough for a meal in itself), but then went high-octane with buttermilk-fried chicken, farmer's sausage, a dry-rubbed pork loin chop, and some bacon for good measure. Served with seasonal veggies and french fries or mashed potatoes, it's a waist-builder that a family can share . . . even if Shawn insists it's for one person.

Chef Shawn Adler's motto is simple: Make the food better than anywhere else! It's a mantra that has won over legions of devoted fans.

If you're looking for something a little more manageable but no less satisfying, go for The Spatula's Roast Prime Rib Dinner, a Friday-night special that tastes like cozy winter evenings at your grandma's house. The centre of this meal is a massive slice of juicy roast prime rib, but Shawn's Yorkshire Pudding—huge, fluffy, golden pillows of flaky, bready goodness—will steal your heart, too. The meal comes with country smashed potatoes and Shawn's legendary creamed corn, which may be the most decadent side of veggies I've ever eaten.

Now, as much as I love Shawn's mains, the one dish that really sent me into a spin of nostalgia was his Hot Turkey Sandwich, hands-down one of my all-time favourite comfort foods. There's just something so soothing about white bread soaked in gravy, and Shawn's is rich and thick. To make it even better, the sandwich is served with Shawn's creamed corn and ridiculously delicious smashed potatoes.

The Flying Spatula looks like a classic diner/truckstop, and Shawn stays true to appearances with many of his menu items. Meat Loaf comes as two thick slices spiked with bacon bits. The Rack of Ribs is humungous and saucy; the 2-pound Burger piles four patties on a homemade bun with all the fixings. Need more? Add some Cheddar cheese, a fried egg, peameal bacon, mushrooms, caramelized onions, or pickles to max out your burger. Polish off the plate (including the fries!) in under an hour and you get a free T-shirt! Speaking of massive, The Breakfast Club sandwich is a simply ludicrous breakfast, a triple-decker using French toast and pancakes instead of bread, and filled with eggs, ham, bacon, and Cheddar cheese.

Wait, I know what you're thinking: John, it wouldn't be a classic diner without classic home-made pies! Enter Chris Carvahlo, resident baker at The Flying Spatula, and a magician of the crust. Of all Chris's pies, customers go wild for his Coconut Cream Pie, a soft and textured dream that ends much too quickly after one piece—so order a second!

Hell, you only live once, right? So load up on The Flying Spatula's classics-on-steroids approach to diner food and get 'er done. Shawn likes that kind of attitude.

The Flying Spatula is a classic truckstop diner.

Meat Loaf

Makes: 4 to 6 servings

Owner and chef Shawn Adler's Meat Loaf starts with premium ground beef mixed with chopped onion, bread crumbs, ketchup, eggs, dried thyme, salt, pepper, and chili powder. But what makes this dish full-on stupid good is the bacon that lines the loaf pan before being filled with the beef mixture. Your mama never made meat loaf this way . . . though you'll wish she had!

20 strips bacon
2 pounds ground beef (preferably local and organic)
2 cups finely diced onion
1¼ cups toasted bread crumbs
⅝ cups ketchup
4 eggs, lightly beaten
2½ tablespoons chili powder
1¼ tablespoons kosher salt
¾ teaspoon dried thyme
¼ tablespoon freshly ground black pepper

Preheat oven to 350°F. Line a standard loaf pan with the bacon.

In a large bowl, combine all of the remaining ingredients. Using your hands, pat the mixture into a loaf shape and place in the prepared loaf pan. Bake in preheated oven for about 1 hour, or until the meat loaf reaches an internal temperature of 160°F.

Serve with smashed potatoes, creamed corn, and broccoli, or in a sandwich.

Meat-Free Morsels to Make Your Mouth Sing

Don't be a neanderthal, bud. There's more to life than eating meat. OK, so I love meat as much as the next guy, but sometimes it's just . . . well . . . unnecessary. And never has that been more true than with these dishes, which show that less is often more.

LOROCO PUPUSAS
EE Burritos,
Saskatoon, SK

Salvadorian cornmeal pancakes that walk the line between soft and crispy are filled with cheese and the mysterious Central American herb loroco.

POTATO CRUST MUSHROOM AND SWISS QUICHE
Tess, Halifax, NS

The potato crust is just the beginning—or rather, the ending—of this ridiculously rich, fluffy, and cheesy treat. Line up with your appetites, folks!

JALAPEÑO BUTTER BEANS
Slickity Jim's Chat 'N' Chew, Vancouver, BC

Another side dish? You got it. Like no beans I've ever had, and main-dish-worthy in every sense of the word.

PHILLY CHEESESTEAK
The Hogtown Vegan,
Toronto, ON

Yeah, it's imitation steak doused in imitation cheese sauce, but you'd never know. Tastes like the real thing.

MARGHERITA PIZZA
Via Tevere Pizzeria,
Vancouver, BC

Perfect crust. Perfect cheese. Perfect sauce. And a touch of fresh basil. Perfection in simplicity.

FALAFEL LAFFA
Dr. Laffa,
North York, ON

Yeah, it's massive. Yeah, it's meatless. And yeah, it's friggin' righteous.

BEET ROOT CHIPS
Holy Grill, Calgary, AB

It's not often that I'm wowed by a side dish, but this is no ordinary side. Better yet, they're served with Holy Grill's delicious panini and burgers.

The Hogtown Vegan

EST. 2011
1056 BLOOR STREET WEST
TORONTO, ON · M6H 1M3
416-901-9779
WWW.HOGTOWNVEGAN.COM

When you think vegan food, you can't help but think "healthy," right? You know: toned, fit people running in slow motion through fields of flax and barley? Well, I'm happy to say that there's a vegan joint out there that embraces its deep-fried side as much as any truckstop does. This is The Hogtown Vegan, where southern soul food is reinvented, meatless-style. And what this joint lacks in meat it makes up for in flavour and inventiveness, thanks to the magical culinary tricks of co-owners Madeleine Foote and Scott McCannell.

OK, so Madeleine and Scott are not meat eaters. But they love indulgent food, and The Hogtown is a perfect blend of these philosophies. With a surprising amount of experience under their belts for 20-some-things, the two have built a restaurant that appeals to everyone from neighbourhood elders to punky teens and everything in between. And don't be surprised if you cross paths with a few carnivores along the way, too. Many are brought here by their vegan friends and find themselves coming back for more!

And why wouldn't they?

The Hogtown's Pulled Unpork Sandwich is a saucy marvel with enough smoky zing to satisfy the direst barbeque craving. The secret to this sandwich is Scott's homemade barbeque sauce, a sticky mess full of good-ies like molasses, garlic, paprika, ballpark mustard, ketchup, and puréed chipotle peppers. Bathed in the sauce is the unpork, textured vegetable protein with a healthy dose of liquid smoke. Assembled on a bun with homemade coleslaw, the sandwich is tangy and filling, a delicious mess you'll be glad you ordered.

Hey, I can cook vegan, too! (As long as Hogtown co-owner and chef Madeleine Foote is there to tell me exactly what to do, that is.)

Of the dishes Madeleine stuffed into me, nothing matched the Philly "Cheesesteak" for mind-blowing similarity to its meaty counterpart. Taking the place of meat in this sub is seitan (no, not the prince of the underworld), a meat substitute that starts out as a nutritional yeast-and-flour dough that is baked and cooled overnight before being sliced like deli meat and fried on the flat-top. The cheesesteak's assembly is a straightforward affair, burying the seitan under caramelized onions and red peppers, then blanketing it all in vegan cheese sauce. Now, let me be the first to admit that I have NO idea what goes into vegan cheese sauce, but it tasted exactly like what I was used to. In other words . . . delicious! This is vegan indulgence at its finest.

Scott and Madeleine's inventiveness seems to have no limit when it comes to morphing unmeat into meat. The Mushroom Po' Boy uses meaty, deep-fried shiitakes instead of traditional oysters, then stuffs them into a toasted sub bun slathered in tartar sauce and overflowing with traditional fixings. The Unchicken Burger is a fluffy white bun coated in homemade vegan mayonnaise and weighed down with a crispy battered "chicken" cutlet and piles of fixings. The Big Hog is Hogtown's answer to a double cheeseburger, while Chili "Cheese" Fries is a junk-food dream, where shoestring fries buckle under the weight of black bean chili, cheese sauce, guacamole, sunflower seed "sour cream," and fresh green onions.

Meat or not, there's one surefire reality when it comes to The Hogtown Vegan: the food is stupidly delicious, no matter how you slice it. Embrace your unmeat side! You'll be glad you did.

Whether you call yourself a meatosaurus or a flesh-eater, you'll never know that the Hogtown's Philly Cheesesteak is 100% vegan.

Unchicken and Waffles

Makes: 4 servings

This dish tastes like a carnivore's delight . . . but it ain't. Instead, co-owner Madeleine Foote coats vegan "chicken" breasts and deep-fries them until perfectly crispy and golden. Then she lays them atop her fluffy corn-flour waffles and drizzles the entire concoction with maple syrup. Served with sweet potato mash and collard greens, it's southern-fried cooking at its finest.

Special equipment: waffle iron

Waffles

1 cup all-purpose flour

⅔ cup corn flour

1 tablespoon sugar

2 teaspoons baking powder

¼ teaspoon salt

1⅓ cups soy milk

1 tablespoon canola oil

Vegan Buttermilk

2 cups soy milk

1 tablespoon white vinegar

Unchicken

4 cups canola oil

4 frozen vegan "chicken" breasts

Dredge

1 cup all-purpose flour

⅔ cup corn flour

⅓ cup cornstarch

1 tablespoon onion powder

1 tablespoon garlic powder

1 tablespoon sweet paprika

1 tablespoon dried oregano

2 teaspoons dried thyme

Waffles

Preheat a waffle iron. In a large bowl, whisk together the flour, corn flour, sugar, baking powder, and salt until well combined.

In a measuring cup, combine the soy milk and oil. Slowly stir the wet ingredients into the dry ingredients until no lumps remain. Pour the batter onto the waffle iron and cook until golden brown. Set the waffles aside, keeping warm.

Dredge

Combine all of the ingredients in a shallow bowl and whisk until no lumps remain. Set aside.

Vegan Buttermilk

Whisk together the soy milk and vinegar in a shallow bowl and set aside for 5 minutes to sour.

Unchicken

Heat the oil in a large saucepan over medium heat (oil should reach 375°F before you start frying; you can also use a deep-fryer).

Coat both sides of the frozen "chicken" breasts in the vegan buttermilk. Using your fingers or tongs, dredge the coated "chicken" in the prepared dredge mixture until well coated on both sides. Transfer to a plate and repeat with remaining "chicken."

Once the oil has reached 375°F, carefully drop 1 piece of "chicken" into the oil and fry until golden and the tip of the "chicken" starts to float (about 4 minutes). Transfer to a plate lined in paper towel and repeat with remaining "chicken." (It's important to fry each piece of "chicken" separately so as not to crowd the pan and cool down the oil.)

Assembly

Place one waffle on each serving plate and top with your desired amount of fried chicken. Drizzle with maple syrup and top with vegan butter, if desired.

Icehouse

EST. 2011
51 RUE ROY EST
MONTREAL, QC · H2W 2S3
514-439-6691

There's a tendency in some parts of the restaurant world for people to take themselves too seriously. That's definitely *not* the case at Montreal's Icehouse, a *You Gotta Eat Here!* Fan Favourite, where food often comes in a bucket and gets dumped on your table, and the music *du jour* is all rock 'n roll, baby. In other words, if Icehouse was a kid you went to high school with, it'd be the one in the black leather jacket giving the teacher the finger from the back of the class.

Icehouse owes much of its devil-may-care personality to owner and chef Nick Hodge, a native Texan who tells it like it is and leaves his pretense at the door. After graduating from university, Nick funded his travels by cooking in kitchens around the world. Eventually he settled in Montreal, where he co-founded a café chain called Java U. Now Nick's cooking the kind of food he grew up loving, and Montrealers are lined up outside to get some.

Born and raised outside Austin, Nick grew up in a family of food junkies. And with a beard like that, you *know* he means business.

Icehouse offers a huge range of stick-to-yer-gut appetizers and entrées, but if there's a single dish that defines this place and its attitude, it's the Bucket Service of Fried Chicken. What? No plates or cutlery on your table? That's by design, people. The modus operandi at Icehouse is roll up your sleeves and dig in, so when the half or whole fried chicken arrives and is dumped on your paper-lined picnic table, dig in!

But don't go thinking that there's something wrong with your bird just because they're tossing it in front of you. In fact, Nick's fried chicken is some of the best I've ever eaten, in part because of Nick's signature sauce, which he has unceremoniously dubbed "Chicken Shit" sauce. Names aside, this sauce—which combines red wine vinegar, honey, and hot pepper sauce—adds a flavour to

If it's fine dining you're after, you've come to the wrong place. The Icehouse is all rock 'n' roll, where having a bucket o' chicken dumped on your table is all part of the show.

Icehouse's fried chicken that you can't find anywhere else. To top it off, the bucket is served along with homemade buttermilk biscuits, southern coleslaw, and what has become one of my all-time favourite side dishes: smoked potato salad. Oh, and if fried chicken's not your thing, fear not. Bucket service is also available for Dr. Pepper Pork Ribs, peel-and-eat shrimp, and authentic southern crawfish.

But that's just the tip of what Icehouse has to offer on a menu where each item seems to pack more *whamo!* than its predecessor. I feasted on a Lobster Burrito, a dish that proves that blue collar and upper crust can happily co-exist. The dish fills a 12-inch flour tortilla with lobster meat sautéed with onions, roasted poblano pepper, pico de gallo, and black beans, and tickled by homemade tarragon aïoli. Not enough flavour bomb? Toss in some corn, grilled onions, and shredded Monterey Jack cheese and you've got a dish most of us dream about: hefty and yummy!

Nick also offers an ever-morphing variety of tacos, of which the Teriyaki Short Rib Tacos are his all-time faves. Fried Chicken Tacos are as tasty and crunchy as they are filling, and Fried Shrimp Tacos add a seafaring flair to a traditional assembly. True to Nick's roots, fried food is also a part of Icehouse's dessert menu: Nick serves Chicken Fried Peach Pie battered and deep-fried, and with a scoop of his homemade vanilla ice cream.

If all of this seems, well, terribly un-Quebec, don't worry. Montrealers from all over the city are willing to wait in line for a chance to have one of Nick's employees dump a bucket of food in front of them. As our Super Fans like to say, it's a bit trashy . . . in a sexy way.

In keeping with owner and chef Nick Hodge's southern roots, the Oyster Po' Boy features six succulent deep-fried oysters piled high on a hamburger bun, followed by homemade coleslaw, shredded lettuce, pimento cheese, ranch sauce, and a generous spritz of Chicken Shit sauce (it tastes *way* better than it sounds!). If happiness were measured in the number of napkins you use, this bad boy is one small step from paradise.

Special equipment: deep fryer (optional)

Coleslaw

1 carrot, peeled and shredded
½ green cabbage, cored and shredded
½ Vidalia onion, julienned
½ cup mayonnaise
½ cup rice vinegar
Salt and pepper

Pimento Cheese

2 cups shredded Cheddar cheese
1 roasted red pepper, finely diced
1 shallot, finely diced
1 cup mayonnaise
Salt and pepper

Chicken Shit

1 cup red wine vinegar
1 cup honey
½ cup hot sauce (Tabasco-style)

Chipotle Mayo

2 to 4 marinated chipotle peppers
2 cups mayonnaise

Ranch Dressing

1 bunch fresh chives, finely chopped
1 garlic clove, finely chopped
1 shallot, finely chopped
1 cup buttermilk
1 cup mayonnaise
Salt and pepper

Chicken-Fried Oysters

Canola oil
20 oysters, shucked
2 cups buttermilk
3 cups all-purpose flour
½ tablespoon garlic powder
½ tablespoon onion powder
½ tablespoon chili powder
1 teaspoon cayenne pepper
Salt and pepper

Assembly

Lettuce, shredded
Tomato, sliced
Hamburger buns (soft white buns)
Dill pickles (optional)

Oyster Po' Boy

Makes: 4 servings

Coleslaw

In a large bowl, combine all of the ingredients and mix well. Cover and refrigerate until ready to use.

Pimento Cheese

In a bowl, combine all of the ingredients. Cover and refrigerate until ready to use.

Chicken Shit

In a glass or plastic bowl, whisk together all of the ingredients. Cover and refrigerate until ready to use.

Chipotle Mayo

In a food processor, blend together all of the ingredients until smooth. Cover and refrigerate until ready to use.

Ranch Dressing

In a glass or plastic bowl, whisk together all of the ingredients. Cover and refrigerate until ready to use.

Chicken-Fried Oysters

In a deep iron skillet, preheat 1 inch of oil to 350°F. (You can use a deep-fryer instead if you have one.)

Prepare your breading stations: In a large bowl, combine the oysters and buttermilk (this is your "wet" station). In a shallow bowl, combine the flour, garlic powder, onion powder, chili powder, cayenne, and salt and pepper to taste (this is your "dry" station).

Working with one hand, place the oysters in the dry station and coat well. Using your other, dry hand, transfer the battered oysters back to the buttermilk. Repeat the process once more, then transfer the double-battered oysters to a clean tray.

Carefully deep-fry the oysters until golden and crispy, about 3 minutes. Transfer to a large bowl and coat with Chicken Shit.

Assembly

Spread pimento cheese on the bottom half of the bun. Place 5 oysters on the cheese, drizzle ranch dressing on top, and add a mound of coleslaw. Spread chipotle mayo on the top half of the bun and close the sandwich. If desired, serve with a skewered dill pickle.

L'Avenue

EST. 1994
922 AVENUE DU MONT-ROYAL EST
MONTREAL, QC · H2J 1X1
514-523-8780

Montreal may be known for its night life, but you've gotta get up pretty early in the morning if you want to nail down a table at the city's legendary brunch spot, L'Avenue. Here the lines start soon after the restaurant opens its doors, as people happily hunker down for a chance to sample some of the most decadent brunch combinations around. What is it they say in French? Oh yeah: good things are worth the wait!

How else can you explain the success of a restaurant that's been going strong since the mid-1990s? L'Avenue is the creation of its spirited owner Johnny Ditomasso, a born-and-raised Montrealer who started the restaurant on a whim when he was just 22 years old. Over that time, L'Avenue has aged beautifully and now shares its funky-and-fun atmosphere with students, hipsters, and families alike.

L'Avenue is all about inventive combinations, and nothing speaks to these daring blends like the Sucré-Salé-Croustillant (Sweet-Salty-Crispy), which marries French toast with eggs Benedict. The dish—which was made for me by the über-fun Andrea Matwiy—starts with a pool of maple syrup on a long plate filled with thick, fluffy slabs of panko-crusted brioche French toast. The sweet and crunchy mixture gets its salt from the slices of Jarlsberg-covered ham that come next. This ridiculous exercise in decadence is finished off with two poached eggs and a river of delicious hollandaise sauce, which is

L'Avenue manager Andrea Matwiy loves food almost as much as she loves watching people enjoy her restaurant's insanely complex—and equally delicious—meals.

made in-house by the bucketful every day. I loved the mixture of the warm yolk and the maple syrup, and that panko-crusted French toast was out of this world. The Sucré-Salé-Croustillant is served with a side of L'Avenue's signature triple-threat hash browns, which are boiled, then baked, then pan-fried.

I know what you're thinking: *Stop, John. We don't need to read any more.* You're probably right. But as insanely delicious as the Sucré-Salé-Croustillant may be, it's not the only delectable offering on Johnny's menu. The Benedict Confit Canard (duck confit eggs Benedict) is as rich as it sounds, piling hunks of fat-cooked duck on an English muffin and burying it under poached eggs and hollandaise sauce. The flavour of the duck is deep and rich, a perfect juxtaposition to the lemony bite of the creamy hollandaise.

The party goes on and on at L'Avenue, where you can choose from as many as a dozen different eggs Benedict dishes, including the Mon Agneau Bénédictine (lamb and squash Benedict) and Benedict Berceau (chicken and potato Benedict). The L'Idaho Omelette is a tribute to America's potato state, and combines eggs with mashed potatoes, bacon, and Cheddar cheese. Think omelette meets perogy, and you won't wonder why it's served with sour cream. The Gaucho Loco Brunch Burger is an 8-ounce beef patty topped with a fried egg, aged Manchego cheese, and two different sauces served on a soft bun, a spicy way to start your day.

It's this kind of variety and inventiveness that has sealed L'Avenue's reputation as the go-to brunch spot in Montreal. Just make sure you set your alarm clock—or be prepared to wait a while.

The Sucré-Salé-Croustillant may be a tongue twister for anglophones, but this French toast/eggs Benedict hybrid speaks for itself once it hits your taste buds.

For a trip to Over-the-Topville, try these pancakes with caramelized apples and Cheddar, a L'Avenue marriage of sweet and savoury on a parade of classic buttermilk pancakes. Yet it's no maple syrup that these pancakes get. Instead, they're covered in a pile of crumbled bacon and handfuls of shredded Cheddar cheese. A few seconds in the oven later, the melted cheese is covered with a blanket of caramelized apples in thick caramel sauce. Fluffy pancakes . . . meet crispy bacon. Sweet apples . . . meet sharp Cheddar. English pancakes . . . meet Montreal ingenuity. John Catucci . . . meet your maker, because you must be in heaven!

Caramelized Apples

2 cups brown sugar

1 cup butter

½ cup whipping (35%) cream

8 small apples, cored and sliced (leave peel)

Bacon

1 teaspoon butter (or substitute
   1 teaspoon oil)

1 pound bacon (about 16 slices)

Pancakes

4½ cups all-purpose flour

5 tablespoons sugar

1 teaspoon salt

3 eggs

4½ cups buttermilk

¼ cup butter, melted

1 tablespoon vanilla extract

1 teaspoon oil

Assembly

2 cups shredded Cheddar cheese

Caramelized Apples

In a saucepan over high heat, bring the sugar, butter, whipping cream, and ½ cup water to a boil; cook, stirring constantly, until thickened. Add the apples and cook for 2 to 4 minutes, until softened. Reduce heat to lowest setting and simmer until you are ready for assembly.

Bacon

In a skillet over medium heat, melt the butter. Once the butter is sizzling, add the bacon and cook to desired crispness (turn bacon over periodically to prevent burning). Remove from heat and transfer the bacon to a plate lined in paper towel. Set aside.

Pancakes

In a large bowl, sift together the dry ingredients. Add the wet ingredients and stir well to form a batter.

In a large skillet or griddle over medium heat, heat the oil. Using a ladle, pour the batter into the pan (each scoop makes 1 pancake). Cook the pancakes for 2 to 3 minutes, until batter begins to form bubbles on top and the bottom is golden brown, then flip and cook until the other side is golden brown. Repeat with remaining batter. Divide servings of 4 to 5 pancakes each on oven-safe plates or a cooking tray.

Assembly

Preheat oven to low broil.

Sprinkle each serving of 4 to 5 pancakes with ½ cup cheese. Warm in oven for 2 to 4 minutes, until cheese has melted. Remove from oven and add 4 pieces of bacon to each plate. Top with a generous serving of caramelized apples. Serve immediately.

Made in Mexico Restaurant and Cantina

EST. 2011
185 MAIN STREET SOUTH
NEWMARKET, ON · L3Y 3Y9
905-235-7722
WWW.MADEINMEXICORESTAURANT.COM

Don't be fooled by that innocent face. Chef Romina Bravo has years of experience in the kitchen, and is almost grandmotherly in her love for feeding people.

You don't have to be a grandmother to cook like one. But that's the gift of 20-something Romina Bravo, the culinary engine behind the Made in Mexico Restaurant and Cantina. A native of Mexico, Romina started her cooking apprenticeship at her grandmother's apron strings. Now her authentic Mexican creations are creating a stir in Newmarket.

But Made in Mexico is hardly a one-woman show. Romina's father, Fernando, and stepmother, Janet Walker, are its owners. Fernando specializes in homemade tortillas and nachos that will have you begging for more. Janet runs the front of house, and is intensely passionate about Mexican cuisine, despite the fact that she's a born-and-raised Newmarket girl.

Romina's specialties run the gamut of Mexican cuisine, but it's her Carne Asada Quesadilla Mexicana that steals the show, even though it's nothing like that cheesy thing you've been eating for years. True to her calling, Romina makes it authentic, served on homemade corn tortillas baked until warm and gooey. The tortillas are stuffed with delectable *carne asada* (roast beef), marinated and slow-roasted before being pulled apart. Topped with pico de gallo, Monterey Jack cheese, cilantro, and taco sauce, these quesadillas are a Mexican street classic rich on taste and texture.

Fernando matches Romina's verve in the kitchen, only he focuses his cooking skills on nachos, which he has turned into an art form. The basis of Fernando's creations are the tortilla chips themselves, which start as handmade corn tortillas. Fernando cuts the tortillas into wedges, microwaves them for texture and shape, then deep-fries them for a few seconds before adding salt. The resulting chips are the lightest, crispiest, and most delicious this guy's ever had.

Made In Mexico's nachos come in three varieties. I had the Nachos Rancheros, which are topped with heaps of homemade chorizo (stupidly tasty!), refried beans, salsa roja, and Monterey Jack and Cheddar cheeses. The result is something as tasty as it is beautiful. Crispy but somehow soft, with a little heat from the guajillo chili pepper hiding in the chorizo, this is a fist-pumping delight.

Mexicans are as big on dessert as anyone, and Made in Mexico's menu is Exhibit A. Churros are tempting sticks of fried dough sprinkled with cinnamon and sugar and served with caramel dipping sauce. There's also Mexican Flan (baked caramel custard) and ChocoFlan, a homemade chocolate cake topped with a layer of flan.

So if you're bummed that your grandmother hasn't boned up on her Mexican-cooking skills, fear not. Romina may be just starting out on her life's journey, but she's a wise old woman in the kitchen. Your taste buds will understand.

If you think a quesadilla is that thing you order down at the pub, think again. Romina's carne asada version is the real deal, from the homemade corn tortillas to the tender beef.

Flautas Verdes

Makes: 4 servings

Scoring high on the how-freakin'-delicious-is-this-food scale are chef Romina Bravo's Flautas Verdes, chicken flautas topped with her signature salsa verde. The dish sees five corn tortillas stuffed with perfectly seasoned chicken, then deep-fried until golden brown. The flautas are topped with salsa verde, which adds a delightfully tangy bite to the meal, followed by lettuce, queso fresco, and a drizzle of sour cream. Add fresh guacamole on the side for dipping (no utensils allowed!), and you'll see why they've become a favourite among locals.

Salsa Verde

6 to 8 boiled green tomatillos

2 garlic cloves

½ Spanish onion, chopped

1 small jalapeño pepper, chopped (seeds removed if you don't want too much heat)

½ cup chopped fresh cilantro

2 tablespoons vegetable powder

1 teaspoon salt

Canola oil

Flautas

Canola or corn oil

5 cooked boneless, skinless chicken breasts, shredded

1 teaspoon garlic powder

1 teaspoon salt

1 teaspoon black pepper

20 corn tortillas (5- to 6-inch)

Assembly

½ Spanish onion, shredded

1 cup shredded lettuce

1 cup queso fresco (fresh cheese)

1 cup sour cream

Salsa

In a blender, combine the tomatillos, garlic, half of the onion, jalapeño, cilantro, vegetable powder, 2 cups of water, and salt, and blend until smooth.

Cover the bottom of a saucepan with a thin layer of oil and heat over medium heat. Once the oil is hot, add the tomatillo mixture and cook, stirring occasionally, for 15 to 20 minutes, or until it starts to thicken and get lighter in colour. Set aside.

Flautas

Shred the remaining half onion. In a skillet over medium heat, heat 1 teaspoon of oil and sauté the shredded onion until soft. Add the chicken and season with the garlic powder and salt and pepper to taste. Cook until the chicken is golden. Remove from heat and set aside to cool slightly.

Soften the tortillas in the microwave for 1 minute to make them more pliable.

Lay a single tortilla flat on a clean work surface. Spoon some of the chicken mixture down the centre of the tortilla. Roll the tortilla tightly around the filling into a flute shape to make the flautas and secure with a toothpick. Repeat with the remaining tortillas.

Fill a deep skillet halfway with oil and heat over medium heat until a thermometer inserted into the oil reads 375°F. Using tongs, place the flautas in the oil and cook, turning occasionally, until crispy (you can also cook these in a small deep-fryer if you have one). Transfer the cooked flautas to a plate lined in paper towel and set aside to cool slightly. Remove the toothpicks.

Assembly

Place 5 flautas on each serving plate. Cover with salsa verde and garnish with lettuce, queso fresco, and sour cream.

Memphis Fire Barbeque Company

EST. 2010
1091 HIGHWAY 8
WINONA, ON · L8E 5H8
905-930-7675
WWW.MEMPHISFIREBBQ.COM

They say breakfast is the most important meal of the day. Well, if it's fuel you need, the Memphis Fire Barbeque Company is going to turbo-charge you with some of the biggest, baddest (in a good way!), barbequed-est morning fare imaginable. And if you're one of those folks whose day starts after noon, fear not: these guys serve it up all day long, and the smoker never seems to stop.

Now, if you're thinking that Winona, Ontario, isn't big enough to host a world-class barbeque joint, think again. MFBC's owners Steve and Lori Popp—after years of cooking in other restaurants—realized their true foodie love lay in the cuisine they sought out every time they had a day off: barbeque. Enter a 60-square-foot smoker imported from Kansas, and the stage was set for Memphis Fire Barbeque Company to carve its own unique path in the world.

And so it has. Steve and Lori have succeeded in making the transition from high-end training to southern pig-out food, and nothing speaks to that metamorphosis more than the Bar-beque & Breakfast, an all-star team of the best they have to offer. No bacon here, you've got a choice of anchoring the plate with tender beef brisket or pulled pork, both of which spend a full day in the smoker before being mixed with root-beer-spiked smokehouse barbeque sauce. Add some slow-cooked Pit Beans (simmered for 2 hours and smoked for another 12 in a brew of molasses, mustard, and smokehouse sauce), and you're halfway there. The platter is filled out with two freshly baked biscuits and two eggs, enough to feed a four-man bobsled team. Wait, they don't bobsled in Memphis?

I know this guy! Co-owner and chef Steve Popp may be a classically trained chef, but he knows no greater culinary joy than stuffing a double patty with bacon and Sneaky Cheese.

As if things couldn't get any bigger at MFBC, there's The Big Kahuna, a smoky and tropical breakfast built around a stack of three malty pancakes spiked with coconut emulsion and shredded coconut, then topped with roasted pineapple sauce and whipped cream. That alone is enough to feed any surfer, but Steve ups the ante with three eggs and three meats: black forest ham, double-bacon, and house-smoked garlic sausage.

To-die-for dishes pepper the lunch and dinner menus at Memphis Fire. The Sneaky Cheese Burger is arguably one of the best double cheeseburgers ever created, and features two patties with Steve's signature Sneaky Cheese—a smoked blend of cream cheese, Imperial Cheddar, and whipping cream—smeared between. Pair it up with a heart-thumpin' serving of Coney Island Fries, which are twice-fried and topped with Coney Beef Chili, Sneaky Cheese, onions, melted Cheddar, and green onions. They've also got smoky and stupidly tasty ribs, and fried chicken that's so crispy and tender, I'm sure it bathed in buttermilk every day of its life.

So drop your cereal and bag your bagels, people. If it's *real* morning inspiration you're after, set your sights on Winona. Everybody else around here has, so why should you be any different?

Feeling tropical? The Big Kahuna—an outrageous combination of salty, sweet, and rich— is enough food to feed everybody at the luau.

Big and bold are served up daily at Memphis Fire, and The Lobotomizer is as bold as it is big—the product of co-owner Steve Popp's active imagination. Hungry for something different one day, Steve threw some diced bacon on the griddle, then covered it with pancake batter and some shredded Cheddar. Once he managed to flip it (note to self: practice two-spatula pancake flipping in spare time), Steve topped it with three over-easy eggs, more Cheddar, and Texas Pete hot sauce. Crack those yolks and this is a breakfast dish that will blow your mind. Literally . . . you won't have a mind afterwards. But you'll die happy!

1 box (32 ounces) just-add-water instant pancake mix
½ cup malt powder
1 pound diced and cooked side bacon
5 cups shredded aged Cheddar cheese
12 eggs
4 tablespoons hot sauce
1 bunch of green onions, thinly sliced
Maple-flavoured table syrup (pure maple syrup just isn't the same in this dish)

In a large bowl, prepare the pancake mix following package instructions and adding enough water to make a thick muffin batter. Add the malt powder and stir well, being careful not to over-mix or the pancake will not rise properly. Set aside for 10 minutes to rise, and then knock it down by whisking it lightly.

Preheat a griddle to medium-hot and the oven to 300°F. Line a baking sheet with parchment paper and place in the oven.

Divide half of the diced bacon into two portions and place each onto the griddle, leaving at least 8 inches of space between each portion to allow the pancakes to spread. When the bacon begins to sizzle, pour 2 ladlefuls of the prepared pancake batter over top of the bacon. Cook for 1 minute, then generously sprinkle each pancake with cheese. Cook for another minute, or until the edges start to curl. Using two large spatulas, flip the pancakes (if the pancakes crack or break, don't worry: the still-moist pancake batter will fuse them as long as you push the pieces back together). Generously sprinkle the pancakes with additional cheese (but reserving some for the final topping). Once the pancakes are cooked through, transfer them to the prepared baking sheet in the oven to keep warm. Repeat with the remaining bacon and batter.

In a skillet over medium heat, working in batches, fry the eggs over easy and set aside, keeping warm. (For larger groups, you can also poach the eggs—just make sure the yolks are runny.)

To serve, place one pancake on each serving plate. Top each pancake with 3 eggs and drizzle with hot sauce. Sprinkle with the remaining cheese and green onions. Serve with syrup and extra hot sauce at the table.

Mickey's Dragon Pizza

EST. 2010
1900 LAKESHORE ROAD WEST
MISSISSAUGA, ON · L5J 1J7
905-822-1411
WWW.FEEDYOURDRAGON.COM

At most restaurants, you place your order and wait until the magic appears on your table. What happens in the kitchen is a mystery. Dining at Mickey's Dragon Pizza is also a spectator sport, thanks to Canada's one and only revolving pizza oven, which is surrounded by glass and provides a bird's-eye view of dough, sauce, cheese, and a gorgeous variety of toppings coming together in freshly baked harmony.

Mickey's is the product of husband-and-wife team Mick and Sandi Stoyan, who have made pizza an integral part of their lives. Long before opening the Dragon, Mick dragged Sandi to every pizza joint they could find across the globe and spent hours in their kitchens trying to make the perfect pie. When they finally took the plunge and opened their very own place in 2010, they sunk every dime they had into the undertaking. But the gamble paid off: Mickey's is now one of the most popular pizza joints in the Greater Toronto Area, despite its unassuming home in a local strip mall. As for the dragon, you'll find him or her—I haven't checked—perched atop the roof of Mickey's, a fire-breathing beacon for some damn good 'za.

Like all good pizza joints, Mick and Sandi know the foundation of great pizza is the dough and the sauce, and they work hard to get them perfect every time. Sandi's sauce features a hand-selected tomato variety from California, which she combines with garlic, olive oil, salt, and pepper. As for dough, Sandi is a master, mixing perfect proportions of ingredients and forming them into loving mounds for proofing. Deep-dish dough is pressed in the pan and left to rest in the refrigerator; classic-crust dough is formed into balls and refrigerated until needed.

The dough doesn't wait very long, given the droves of diehard Mickey's fans across the GTA. They love the massively ridiculous Meat King, a 3-pound deep-dish monster that hates vegetables. The King starts with sauce and cheese, then goes hog-wild with a mound of barbequed Italian sausage, about 100 slices (no joke) of pepperoni, crumbled homemade meatballs, and bacon. Finished with more sauce and cheese, and livestock everywhere is afraid.

As much as the Meat King screams caveman, the Mediterranean is a far more artistic pursuit, as beautiful as it is delicious. It starts with a classic crust brushed with olive oil on both sides (for extra moistness), then tomato sauce and a layer of mozzarella. Then the Mediterranean hits, with red onions, roasted red peppers, sundried tomatoes, spinach, kalamata olives, and crumbled feta cheese. Then it's on to the 5-foot spinner for 20 to 25 glorious minutes of top-and-bottom baking.

You can build your own pizza at Mickey's, but you can't go wrong with Sandi's signature creations. The deep-dish Steak & Mushroom Pie is a delicious marriage of meat pies and pizza, while the Texas Hold'em is a hefty deep-dish blend of pepperoni, bacon, meatballs, green peppers, red peppers, and barbeque sauce. There are lots of vegetarian options, too, including the Green Dragon, a colourful mountain of mushrooms, red onions, green and red peppers, green olives, sautéed spinach, and crumbled feta.

So forget about going to the movies tonight. A meal at Mickey's is a two-for-one undertaking: you get to eat out, and the entertainment is free.

Fiery, inviting, and effervescent, Sandi Stoyan found true pizza passion when she married husband Mick, a self-avowed pizza freak.

Got meat? Barnyard animals everywhere fear the Meat King, which combines stupid amounts of sausage, pepperoni, house-made meatballs, and bacon into a tidy package.

Mango Tango Chicken Pizza

Makes: Makes two 10- to 12-inch pizzas

The Mango Tango is a yummy creation that tickled every one of this guy's taste buds. Sauce and cheese are topped with carmelized onions, tender pieces of chicken breast, hot peppers, mango, and an exotic sprinkle of garam masala spice for a hint of India.

Dough

2¾ cups all-purpose flour

¼ cup cornmeal

1½ teaspoons sugar

1½ teaspoons sea or kosher salt

1½ teaspoons instant dry yeast or 1 pkg
   (¼ ounce)

1 tablespoon olive oil

1 tablespoon sunflower oil

Sauce

1 can (28 ounces) whole tomatoes, with juice

2 teaspoons finely chopped roasted garlic

1 teaspoon olive oil

1 teaspoon salt

Assembly

12 ounces mozzarella cheese, shredded

1 cup yellow onions, chopped

Balsamic vinegar

Sugar

2 skinless, boneless chicken breasts,
   cooked and diced

1 cup mango (fresh or frozen), diced

Hot peppers, sliced

Garam masala

Dough

In a food processor fitted with a dough hook, combine the flour, cornmeal, sugar, salt, and yeast.
   On low speed, mix in the oils, then slowly add ½ cup warm water. Blend no more than 5 minutes, until mixture forms a smooth dough ball.

Place the dough ball in a generously oiled mixing bowl and turn to coat. Cover with plastic wrap
   and set aside in a warm place for about 1 hour to rise.

Sauce

In a clean food processor fitted with the metal blade, purée the tomatoes until smooth.

Transfer the purée to a large saucepan over low heat. Stir in the roasted garlic, oil, and salt.
   (Optional: Add 1 tablespoon of sugar and season with spices to taste.) Simmer until thickened.

Assembly

Set the oven rack in the middle position and preheat oven to 550°F or highest temperature.
   Lightly grease 2 pizza pans. Sauté yellow onions in a little balsamic vinegar and sugar.

Divide the dough into two even portions and roll the dough out on pans to edges. Using your
   fingers, press until even.

Divide the sauce between pizzas and spread evenly over dough, leaving ½ cm around the edges.
   Sprinkle each with the cheese and then caramelized onions. Top with the chicken (for even
   better results, cook the chicken in a light curry sauce beforehand). Add the mango and hot
   peppers. Season with garam masala.

Bake in preheated oven for 7 to 10 minutes, until crust and toppings are golden brown.

Motor Burger

EST. 2009
888 ERIE STREET EAST
WINDSOR, ON · N9A 3Y9
519-252-8004
WWW.MOTORBURGER.CA

When the recession hit in 2009, it didn't stop restaurateurs and partners Jay Souilliere and Gino Gesuale. They recognized that the market for fine dining was coming to an abrupt halt, and their high-end Italian restaurant NOI would have a hard time surviving. But rather than close down, Jay and Gino simply switched gears, recognizing that their changing community still wanted to eat out, just in a different way. Motor Burger—a gourmet burger joint whose name pays homage to Windsor's rich automotive history—was born, and judging by its success, Jay and Gino were right on the money.

Casual and warm, Motor Burger is as unpretentious as it is inventive. The restaurant is a blend of Jay and Gino's personalities, two wild and crazy guys who are passionate about what they serve. Gino is the front-of-house guy, taking care of customers and serving as the face of Motor Burger. Jay is the culinary heart of the place, meticulously constructing each burger as if it were someone's last meal.

Motor Burger is casual, warm, and inviting, and judging by its wild success, just what the good people of Windsor were looking for in a casual eatery.

Jay prides himself on offering his customers a variety of patties, and his Fire Bird burger is a high-performance creation featuring chicken spiked with Thai chilies. Then the chicken is ground, breaded in crunchy Japanese panko, deep-fried for a crisp coating, and baked to finish. From there the patty is topped with a spicy four-pepper medley and Muenster cheese, followed by spicy, shaved, crispy onions and Jay's signature Motor Sauce, a smoky-yet-tangy blend that's attained legendary status 'round these parts.

The Autostrada burger was born of Jay's desire to have a sausage and a burger at the same time. The burger features a pork sausage patty drizzled with chili oil, which is topped with Gorgonzola cheese and homemade apple-fennel coleslaw. I've had a lot of burgers in my day, but this was a treat I won't soon forget, thanks to the complex taste of that slaw.

Motor Burger's Jay Souilliere has turbo-charged Windsor's food scene by offering up fast and furious burger options named after the cars we love.

As you've likely surmised by now, Motor Burger's is a menu you should work your way through one by one. My favourite was the Lamb-orghini, a tasty lamb patty covered in sundried tomato tapenade and goat cheese, all served on a bed of mixed greens. Deux Chevaux is Jay's fave, a beef patty complemented with Gruyère cheese, baby spinach, caramelized onions, and smoked bacon. The Pinto is a delicately seasoned ground turkey patty topped with spicy slaw. Fishtailing tops ground ahi tuna with sesame oil, garlic, shredded cabbage, and Motor Sauce.

Jay is equally demanding with his side dishes and starters. Dip Sticks are corn dogs made from in-house sausages and served with roasted garlic Dijon mustard for dipping. Chili Spring Rolls are stuffed with smoked cheese and chorizo-and-black-bean chili, then topped with sour cream. Finally, Fried Pickles are coated with plain and ranch-flavoured taco chips and served with a homemade horseradish dipping sauce.

Rest assured, if the world economy goes sideways, Jay and Gino will be reinventing themselves once again. Until then, I'm filling my tank every time I get to Windsor.

Built for speed . . . and comfort! The Lamb-orghini is a Motor Burger original, a high-performance meal that combines style with power. Yeah, and it's pretty dang tasty, too.

The Shrimp Fuel Burger

Makes: 4 burgers

The Shrimp Fuel Burger is an ingenious combination of puréed and chopped shrimp that holds its shape (the puréed shrimp acts as a binder in place of eggs or bread crumbs) but still offers chunky bits of sweetness. The patty is fried at medium-high temperature, giving it a perfect crust. The Fuel is a delight on its own, but restaurateur Jay Souilliere goes high-octane with sweet and tangy avocado and mango salsa.

Lime-Chipotle Crème Fraîche

1 to 2 chipotle peppers (depending on how spicy you like it)

8 ounces crème fraîche or sour cream

Zest and juice of 1 lime

2 garlic cloves, finely chopped

Salt and pepper

Avocado and Mango Salsa

2 ripe avocados, peeled, pitted, and quartered

2 Roma tomatoes, quartered

1 ripe mango, peeled, pitted, and quartered

½ red onion, finely chopped

2 tablespoons canola oil

1 teaspoon minced garlic

1 teaspoon finely chopped Thai chilies

Juice of 1 lime

Shrimp Burger

2 pounds black tiger shrimp, peeled and deveined

½ cup chopped fresh cilantro

1 teaspoon grated fresh ginger

¼ teaspoon ground cumin

¼ teaspoon smoked paprika

2 garlic cloves, finely minced

1 to 2 bird's-eye chilies, finely chopped

Salt and pepper

1 tablespoon canola oil

Assembly

4 brioche hamburger buns

Baby spinach leaves or lettuce

Lime-Chipotle Crème Fraîche

In a small bowl, combine all of the ingredients. Chill until ready to use.

Avocado and Mango Salsa

In a small bowl, combine the avocados, tomatoes, and mango. Add the onion, oil, garlic, chilies, and lime juice, and stir to combine. Set aside for 10 to 15 minutes to marinate.

Shrimp Burger

Divide the shrimp into 2 even portions. Using a sharp knife, roughly chop 1 portion. Using a food processor fitted with the metal blade, purée the second portion. Transfer both to a large bowl and stir to combine. Add the cilantro, ginger, cumin, paprika, garlic, and chilies. Mix well.

On a piece of parchment or waxed paper, using a wet spoon, divide the mixture into 4 even portions and shape into patties. Season with salt and pepper to taste.

In a skillet over medium-high heat, heat the oil. Fry each patty for 2 minutes per side, until nicely caramelized, firm, and cooked through.

Assembly

Split the buns. Spread the bottom halves with lime-chipotle crème fraîche. Top with baby spinach or lettuce and a shrimp patty. Garnish with avocado and mango salsa. Add the top buns.

Murray Street Kitchen

EST. 2008
110 MURRAY STREET
OTTAWA, ON · K1N 5M6
613-562-7244
WWW.MURRAYSTREET.CA

Creative genius comes in many forms. From painting to dancing to TV show hosting (!), there are many ways to express our inner Michelangelo. Well, there's some genius goin' down at Ottawa's Murray Street, and it's coming at the hands of co-owner and master chef Steve Mitton.

Steve is not one of those guys who stumbled onto his profession by accident. He grew up in Germany, where he was so enamoured with local cuisine that he started a three-year stint as a butcher's apprentice at the age of 17. From there, Steve started plying his trade at local restaurants before coming to Canada to earn a degree at St. Mary's University in Halifax. But cooking never left Steve's blood, and after graduation he went straight to the Culinary Institute of Canada.

Are we happy? Steve Mitton is the man behind Murray Street and proudly proclaims that he has never entertained ideas about changing his livelihood since he opened the restaurant.

Steve soon found himself working in Ottawa and began to make his mark in restaurants around town. When Steve's first employers at Bistro 115 decided to sell, he leapt, teaming up with buddy Paddy Whelan. Now Murray Street is a mainstay of the Ottawa dining scene.

Taste one of Murray Street's offerings and you'll see why. Each dish is an exercise in brilliance, beginning with Murray Street's Spaetzle Poutine, which combines a Quebec classic with Steve's German roots. This dish is built upon handmade spaetzle, a noodle/dumpling thingy that's boiled and butter-fried, then topped with chunks of duck confit and fresh cheese curds. Served in a cast-iron mini-cauldron, the poutine goes from ridiculous to sublime with a bath of Murray Street's signature "Beast" Gravy, a rich concoction made fresh from the meat and bones of that day's specials.

Steve is not so high-brow to think that his meat is too good for a stick, and his Candy Apple Pogos are the reason why. The dish begins with a giant log of sausage/bologna made by Steve's right-hand man, Paul Dubeau. Cut into wedges and pierced on a stick, the meat is dipped in a cornmeal batter, then deep-fried. The finishing touch is homemade apple jelly, which adds a sweet and tangy touch.

There's no stick in Steve's Potaco, but it's still freakin' yummy. The most popular item on Murray Street's brunch and lunch menus, the Potaco is a hybrid between a taco, pulled pork sandwich, and potato pancake. It starts with a thick and crispy potato pancake that's filled with tender pulled pork, aged Cheddar cheese, and a generous helping of smoky baked beans (home-made, of course . . . Steve's mother's recipe!). Folded over on itself, the bulging Potaco is topped with salsa, shredded lettuce, and sour cream. The crispy pancake is a perfect accompaniment to the melt-in-your-mouth pork and savoury beans. I call it the Mo'Taco!

You guessed right if you figured that the genius doesn't end after three dishes at Murray Street, though you never really know what you're going to get since the menu seems to change daily. The Ain't No Thang duck wings are a local staple, featuring massive duck wings oven-poached in their own delicious fat before hitting the deep-fryer and being tossed in homemade barbeque sauce. Über-popular on the brunch menu is a combo of braised corned beef, poached egg, bone marrow hollandaise, and Steve's quirky take on hash browns, his "cheezy potato hasherole."

In the end, Murray Street is a place where the ordinary becomes extraordinary, and the unexpected is a daily occurrence. And I don't know if Steve's IQ actually places him in Einsteinian territory, but with food this good, I'm thinking he's a genius!

Junk food meets culinary wonderment with Steve's Candy Apple Pogos, which prove the age-old theory that meat on a stick can be a thing of beauty after all.

Baked Beans

Makes: 4 to 6 servings

Steve's mom created this recipe, and you can taste the love in every savoury bite. The white navy beans are soaked overnight, boiled, then oven-baked with salt pork in a rich barbeque sauce, and they make for the perfect accompaniment to any meal.

1 pound dried white navy beans, soaked overnight
¼ pound salt pork (homemade if possible), cut into chunks
2 cups molasses
1 cup brown sugar
½ cup apple cider vinegar (preferably Hall's)
¼ cup tomato paste
2 tablespoons Worcestershire sauce
1 tablespoon salt
2 onions, finely chopped
6 garlic cloves, finely chopped
1 smoked ham hock
Stock

In a saucepan of unsalted boiling water, cook the beans until tender.

Drain the cooked beans and transfer to a large casserole dish (large enough to hold the beans and twice the volume of liquid). Set aside.

Preheat oven to 350°F.

In a frying pan over medium heat, lightly brown the salt pork to render a little fat. Reserve both the meat and rendered fat.

In a bowl, combine the molasses, brown sugar, vinegar, tomato paste, Worcestershire sauce, and salt. Add the mixture to the beans and stir to combine. Add the onions, garlic, ham hock, and reserved salt pork (with its fat). Add just enough stock to cover the mixture and stir to combine.

Cover the casserole dish with aluminum foil and place on the centre rack of preheated oven. Bake for at least 2 hours, until the ham hock pulls apart easily and the sauce has thickened.

When ready to serve, pull the meat from the hock (discard the bone) and stir into the beans.

Pie

EST. 2010
31 COMMERCE PARK DRIVE
BARRIE, ON · L4N 1XB
705-725-9663
WWW.EATMYPIE.CA

For most people, pizza is not a gourmet undertaking. They want their slice and they want to get on with it. Well, to those people I say "boo hoo!" Why? Pie.

Yes, Pie is a pizza joint, but it's like few pizza joints you'll ever visit in your life. This is the place where everyday pizza meets gourmet attitude, seemingly insane combinations of toppings, and the highest-quality ingredients on the planet. Want *real* pizza? Pie is your place.

Like most good restaurants, Pie does not come by its genius accidentally. Indeed, when co-owner Craig Russell found a location that tickled his pizza fancy, he knew there was only one man he wanted to go into business with: enter Randy Feltis, who has a lengthy career in fine dining under his belt. But you'd never know it by talking to him now: Randy radiates a passion for pizza that few people can match . . . and it shows with every dish he makes. It doesn't hurt that Randy and Craig had the foresight to import a traditional Italian wood-burning pizza oven, which gives their food a taste of the old country.

The Cow Pie is a creation whose flavour belies its name. This pie passes on tomato sauce, opting for a stupidly creamy béchamel sauce jacked up on goat cheese, fresh mozzarella, white Cheddar, and Parmesan cheese. Then come the roasted potatoes, sautéed spinach and mushrooms, red onions, more Parmesan, and the featured performer:

If it's an appetizing name you're looking for, the Cow Pie might not fit the bill. If you're looking for a rare pizza treat, this is it.

pulled, slow-cooked beef shank. It's the creamiest pizza I've ever eaten, and all its flavours blend perfectly with the rich piles of beef.

If you're feeling brave, then tackle Pie's Furious Cannucker, a giant that few people have ever managed to finish. This beast is a three-pizza tower, each of which is topped with tomato sauce, mozzarella, triple-smoked bacon, pepperoni, and a sunny-side-up egg. Wait! You don't get named after Furious Pete (a Canadian competitive eating champion) with just three measly pies. To make this truly daunting, the Cannucker is buried under a pound of poutine. Eat it in 35 minutes and it's free. Me, I'm happy with just a piece . . . and even that's a meal in itself.

Randy's got more surprises under his belt, and enough varieties to keep you coming back for months. The Captain Pie Liner is a so-called Crazy Pie, topped with tomato sauce, poached shrimp and scallops, and creamy hunks of horseradish-smoked ricotta cheese. The Slow and Low Pie is covered in homemade barbeque sauce, pulled pork, and caramelized onions, with a heap of homemade fennel and carrot coleslaw in the centre and a swirl of garlic aïoli for good measure. The Nutty Pie is a dessert-lover's dream: a thin crust blanketed in chocolate-hazelnut spread, sliced bananas, caramel, and a scoop of vanilla ice cream.

Hey, there's even un-pizza at Pie, everything from starters to pasta to sandwiches to soup . . . and more. Me, I'm sticking with the pizzas. Call it an obsession, I guess, but a guy like me knows that when someone does something *this* good, you take advantage of it.

Champion competitive eater Furious Pete is not just a big man with a big appetite, he's also the inspiration for Pie's massive Furious Cannucker triple-decker.

Whether they have a traditional oven or not, there aren't many people in Italy feasting upon a Green Egg and Ham pizza. But it's a huge hit at Pie, and now I know why. The pizza substitutes homemade pesto for tomato sauce on the thinly stretched dough, then follows with slices of fresh mozzarella, roasted chunks of Yukon Gold potatoes, double-smoked bacon, spinach, and an egg cracked right in the middle of the party. Pizza for breakfast!

Special equipment: pizza stone

Dough

3½ to 4 cups bread flour

1 pkg (¼ ounce) instant dry yeast

2 teaspoons kosher salt

2 tablespoons + 2 teaspoons olive oil

Toppings

2 Yukon Gold potatoes, halved then sliced
  into 10 wedges

Olive oil

1 teaspoon fresh rosemary leaves

1 teaspoon each salt and pepper

2 teaspoons minced garlic

6 cups spinach

Assembly

2 cups basil pesto

2 eggs

Sliced fresh mozzarella cheese, to taste

2 cups thinly sliced double-smoked bacon

1 cup grated Parmesan cheese

Dough

In the bowl of a stand mixer, combine 3½ cups flour (using bread flour will give you a very crispy crust), yeast, and kosher salt. With the mixer running, add 1½ cups warm water (110°F) and 2 tablespoons of the oil and beat until the dough forms a ball. If the dough is sticky, add additional flour, 1 tablespoon at a time, until the dough comes together. If the dough is too dry, add additional water, 1 tablespoon at a time. Scrape the dough onto a lightly floured work surface and gently knead into a smooth, firm ball.

Grease a large bowl with the remaining 2 teaspoons olive oil. Place the dough in the bowl and cover the bowl with plastic wrap. Set it aside in a warm area for about 45 minutes, until doubled in size. Turn the dough out onto a lightly floured surface. Divide it into 2 even portions. Cover each with a clean kitchen towel or plastic wrap and set aside for 15 minutes to rest.

Toppings

Preheat oven to 375°F.

On a baking sheet, toss the potatoes with the oil and rosemary, and season with salt and pepper. Roast in preheated oven for 25 to 30 minutes, until tender. Set aside. Meanwhile, in a skillet over medium heat, heat some oil. Sauté the garlic for about 1 minute, until softened. Add the spinach and cook, stirring often, just until wilted. Remove from heat and set aside.

Assembly

Preheat the oven to 550°F or highest temperature. Punch down each of the dough balls. Turn out onto a lightly floured pizza stone and roll each out to a 12- to 14-inch circle. Spread the pesto over the surface of each and cover evenly with roasted potato. Crack 1 egg into the centre of each pizza. Top with mozzarella, spinach mixture, and bacon and drizzle with oil. Bake in preheated oven for 23 minutes, or until crusts are golden brown. Garnish with grated Parmesan.

Pressed

EST. 2011
750 GLADSTONE AVENUE
OTTAWA, ON · K1R 6X5
613-680-9294
WWW.PRESSED-OTTAWA.COM

Leave your laundry at home, Mother. The only thing being ironed at Pressed is the food, where Jeff Stewart knows that squishing bread and batter between two hot griddles not only heightens flavours, it gives fillings of all kinds a chance to come together in foodie harmony.

A disenchanted civil servant, Jeff left a job on Parliament Hill to pursue his passions in the kitchen, not the cubicle. A survey of the local dining landscape convinced Jeff that what Ottawa needed was something between fast food and fine dining. Pressed—where patrons can leisurely enjoy delicious, well-made, and creative dishes—was born.

Jeff's the kind of guy who likes a challenge, so while other places might be highlighting pulled pork on their menu, Pressed opts for something a little wilder: the Southern-Style BBQ Wild Boar. The meat—which hints of pork but with a wilder disposition—is rubbed, then smoked for more than half a day, after which it's so tender it falls apart with a stern look. Mixed with Pressed's signature homemade barbeque sauce, braised in the oven, and squashed between two pieces of gorgeous ciabatta with some freshly crafted apple coleslaw, the result is decidedly upscale. The sandwich is served with Jeff's sweet potato chips, a salty, crunchy complement to the deep, savoury flavours of the boar.

But boar is just the tip of the iceberg when it comes to things Jeff will mash between two pieces of hot metal.

It didn't matter a stitch to quick-witted entrepreneur Jeff Stewart that he had little restaurant experience; he knew his passion for food would carry the day. And it has!

Pressed's House-Made Falafel pairs crunchy falafel patties with pickled turnip on a ciabatta bun smothered in baba ghanoush spread. The Eggplant Tempura Sandwich is not just for vegetarians, as the combination of deep-fried eggplant and homemade miso aïoli has a surprisingly meaty feel. And for my people, the Tuscan! is an Italian dream . . . on a ciabatta bun, that is. Garlicky black olive tapenade forms the base for fresh mozzarella, basil, smoked grape tomatoes, and layers of prosciutto.

Like your pressed products to come with nooks and crannies? Look no further than Pressed's waffles, which are not just for breakfast anymore. Jeff's New South Waffle is an ingenious variation on the ever-popular chicken and waffles. Yet unlike the fried chicken pieces that adorn the traditional presentation of this dish, Jeff uses homemade smoked chicken croquettes, then tops them with lemon zest, icing sugar, and cherry compote and serves it up with maple syrup and hot sauce. *Hot dawg!* . . . sweet and spicy.

Waffle creations permeate every corner of Pressed's menu. For breakfast, the Benedict Waffle is a marriage of double-smoked bacon, poached eggs, and decadent hollandaise sauce on a waffle base. Need sweet? Check out The Big Apple Waffle, where Jeff layers caramelized apples atop a fresh waffle, followed by homemade lemon mascarpone, a blizzard of icing sugar, and a wash of pure maple syrup. Uh . . . yeah, I'll have just a little more, please.

If your head is spinning from all the options that Pressed throws at you, join the club. The good news is that no matter which of Jeff's fillings and toppings you introduce to bread, batter, and hot iron, the result is lick-your-plate-clean yummy.

Eggs benny . . . Pressed style! The Benedict Waffle is for those who can't decide if they want eggs or waffles for breakfast, bringing both together in sinful harmony.

The Pressed Hangover Waffle

Makes: 4 to 6 servings

Entrepreneur Jeff Stewart's Hangover Waffle is a treacherous creation that starts with a crispy-yet-chewy waffle base, piled high with slices of smoked beef brisket, St. Albert cheese curds from Quebec, and light brown gravy made from in-house chicken stock.

Special equipment: smoker (optional), waffle iron
Timing note: brisket requires 8 to 10 hours in smoker or 4 hours in oven

Brisket

½ cup sweet paprika

¼ cup kosher salt

¼ cup brown sugar

1 tablespoon black pepper

1 tablespoon chili powder

1 tablespoon chipotle powder

1 tablespoon mustard powder

1 tablespoon onion powder

1 tablespoon garlic powder

1 tablespoon cumin seeds

1 tablespoon anise seed

1 pound beef brisket

Waffles

3 cups all-purpose flour

2 tablespoons sugar

½ tablespoon baking powder

1 teaspoon salt

6 eggs

3 cups milk

1 cup butter, melted

Gravy

3 cups chicken stock

1 cup all-purpose flour, sifted

Salt and pepper

Assembly (per serving)

½ cup cheese curds

4 tablespoons finely chopped green onions

Brisket

Preheat smoker to 225°F or oven to 325°F.

In a small bowl, combine all of the ingredients—except the brisket—to make a dry rub.

Rub the brisket all over with a generous amount of prepared rub.

Place the brisket in the smoker for 8 to 10 hours or place the brisket in a medium baking dish and bake for 4 hours, or until internal temperature registers 160°F on a meat thermometer.

Waffles

Preheat waffle iron. In a bowl, sift together the flour, sugar, baking powder, and salt.

In another bowl, combine the eggs, milk, and butter. Add the wet ingredients to the dry ingredients and mix until just combined.

Pour the batter onto the waffle iron and cook until golden brown. Set aside, keeping warm.

Gravy

In a saucepan over medium heat, bring the stock to a simmer. Slowly whisk in the flour and cook, stirring often, until the gravy thickens to the consistency of maple syrup. Season to taste with salt and pepper.

Assembly (per serving)

In a skillet over medium-high heat, combine ½ cup of brisket, shredded, and a ladleful of gravy and cook until warmed through. Stir in ½ cup of cheese curds. Remove from heat. Arrange 2 waffles on a serving plate. Top with brisket mixture. Garnish with green onions. Repeat with remaining waffles.

Smoke & Spice Southern Barbeque

EST. 2008

7470 TECUMSEH ROAD EAST

WINDSOR, ON · N8T 1E9

519-252-4999

WWW.SMOKENSPICE.COM

Anyone who's ever been in love knows that passion is a powerful thing. Well, passion is the driving force behind Smoke & Spice Southern Barbeque, and it shows. Owners Ryan and Tina Odette love barbeque so much that once they decided to open their own joint, they sent emails to dozens of pit bosses across the southern US, looking for a place to train . . . for free. Pat Martin at Martin's BBQ Joint in Nolensville, Tennessee, answered the call, and Ryan and Tina were well on their way to bringing authentic southern barbeque to the good people of Windsor, Ontario.

Despite his eagerness to learn the way of the smoke, cooking is nothing new to Ryan. A graduate of Niagara College's culinary arts program, he cooked at many high-end restaurants before

Pit Boss Ryan Odette has a passion for food and a love of all things barbeque, two things that come together beautifully at Smoke & Spice.

he and Tina opened Mamo Bistro in 2004. Yet the couple felt that what Windsor really needed was an everyday joint that the typical family could mosey on down to as often as they wanted. Smoke & Spice was born.

And what a birth it was! From the outside, Smoke & Spice looks like an Alberta ranch house with its giant flaming sign, impressive stone features, and welcoming timbers. The inside is as laid-back and homey as it is huge, and everyone feels like family. Come as you are, people. There's no dress code other than make-sure-it's-something-you-don't-mind-getting-dirty!

Messiness comes in various shapes and sizes at Smoke & Spice, from traditional classics to lesser-known barbequed delicacies. Checking in on the more obscure (but insanely tasty) side of the scale is Ryan's Smoked Bologna Sandwich. No Alice, this is definitely *not* the bologna of your youth, even if it does taste a bit like childhood. To make it extra-special, Ryan smokes an entire bologna for 2 hours, giving it a deep, rich flavour. When it's time to make your sandwich, he cuts off a slab, deep-fries it, and serves it up on a hamburger bun along with his Original Barbeque Sauce (one of five served at Smoke & Spice), mayonnaise, and white cabbage coleslaw.

Smoking is an art form at Smoke & Spice, and the Smoked Chicken Wings are Exhibit A. After coating with a dry rub, the wings are smoked for 2 hours, then deep fried for an added level of crispiness while still being plump and juicy. The wings hit the table plain, so you'll have to choose yer sauce: Original (tangy Kansas City–style), Chipotle (smoky!), Carolina Mustard (mustard and spice), Memphis Sweet, and the one that nearly sent me to the hospital, Triple X Hot.

Smoke & Spice's food parade continues with St. Louis Cut Spare Ribs, which are smoked for almost 5 hours before emerging tasty and tender. The pork for the Pulled Pork Sandwich spends 12 hours in the smoker before being served on Wonder Bread (true to its southern US roots) with Original Barbeque Sauce and coleslaw. The El Ray sandwich is a Ryan original, overflowing with smoked beef brisket tossed in barbeque sauce, then topped with Monterey Jack cheese, homemade coleslaw, and an onion ring. Mac & Cheese isn't high-brow enough to avoid processed cheese, while the Redneck Nachos are loaded with heaps of melted cheese, homemade chili (with brisket ends!), pulled pork, sour cream, and jalapeños.

So, if you're wandering the streets of Windsor and wondering what that smoky smell is, follow your noses to the end of the rainbow, my friends. You won't find a pot of gold there, but the offerings at Smoke & Spice are culinary treasures nonetheless. And you'll taste the passion in every bite.

If you remember bologna as that painfully lifeless thing your mom threw on white bread, you haven't tasted it here, where the meat is sinfully redefined.

Pulled Pork Sundae

Makes: 4 to 6 servings

Dessert is not an option at Smoke & Spice, at least not the sweet variety. Rather than ice cream, this treat is built upon a foundation of co-owner Ryan Odette's beans, which are buried under a heavy layer of pulled pork. Who needs pie?

Special equipment: smoker (optional)

Timing note: pork butt requires 10 to 12 hours in smoker or 6 to 8 hours in oven

Pulled Pork

1 cup white sugar

½ cup sweet paprika

2 tablespoons black pepper

4 tablespoons granulated garlic

4 tablespoons onion powder

3 tablespoons chili powder

3 tablespoons ground cumin

1 teaspoon salt

1 teaspoon dry mustard

7 pounds pork butt

BBQ Baked Beans

1 can (14 ounces) beans with pork in tomato sauce

½ cup brown sugar

⅓ cup barbeque sauce

1 teaspoon barbeque rub

1 teaspoon black pepper

Coleslaw

⅓ cup apple cider vinegar

6 tablespoons white sugar

½ tablespoon salt

2 cups mayonnaise

2 pounds cabbage, shredded

Pulled Pork

Preheat smoker to 225°F or oven to 250°F.

In a bowl, combine all of the ingredients—except the pork butt—to make a dry rub.

Rub the pork butt all over with a generous amount of prepared rub, reserving a few tablespoons for beans and garnish.

If cooking in smoker: Place the pork butt in the smoker for 10 to 12 hours, or until internal temperature registers 195°F on a meat thermometer. If cooking in oven: Place pork butt in a medium baking dish, cover, and bake for 6 to 8 hours, until the internal temperature registers 195°F on a meat thermometer. Remove from heat and set aside to cool, then pull apart.

BBQ Baked Beans

In a saucepan over medium heat, combine all of the ingredients and 1 teaspoon of reserved barbeque rub and cook, stirring often, for 30 minutes.

Coleslaw

In a saucepan over medium heat, combine the salt, sugar, and vinegar and cook, stirring often, until the salt and sugar are dissolved. Remove from heat and set aside to cool completely. Once cooled, whisk in mayonnaise.

In a bowl, toss the cabbage with the prepared dressing. Cover and refrigerate until ready to use.

Assembly

Divide the baked beans among serving bowls. Top with the pulled pork and then the coleslaw. Drizzle with your favourite barbeque sauce and sprinkle with barbeque rub to taste.

The Smokin' Buddha

EST. 2007
OLD TRAIN STATION
265 KING STREET
PORT COLBORNE, ON · L3K 4G8
905-834-6000
WWW.THESMOKINBUDDHA.COM

Port Colborne is perched on the southern end of the Welland Canal, which connects Lake Ontario to Lake Erie. The ships that run through here are many and massive, and hint more at beers and burgers than international cuisine. At least that's what Kevin Echlin was worried about when he opened The Smokin' Buddha, which brings the flair of the Far East to the St. Lawrence Seaway. But as time has proven, Kevin had nothing to worry about: his restaurant and its eclectic offerings have been met with rave reviews from locals and visitors alike.

Raised in small-town Ontario, Kevin cultivated his love of Asian food while living in Japan and travelling through Asia in the late 1990s. When he got home, he decided to give his cus-tomers the opportunity to travel without ever leaving home . . . through their taste buds. In 2005, The Buddha debuted at the Port Colborne Farmers' Market; two years later Kevin made good on his dream, opening The Buddha's doors in an old train station.

Over the past few years, The Smokin' Buddha (a *You Gotta Eat Here!* Fan Favourite) has developed a dedicated following among those wishing to tempt their tongues with decidedly less-than-ordinary fare. Though the menu boasts time-tested faves like Pad Thai and Chicken Samosas, it's Kevin's specialties that made my mouth sing. Take the Pea-nut Chicken, a red curry Thai dish that perfectly balances spicy with sweet and

Chef Kevin Echlin plays world tour guide with The Smokin' Buddha's bevy of international dishes, but he should know not to get between a man and his cutlery.

Now that's *my* kind of diety! He may have been the sage upon whose teachings Buddhism was found, but Buddha also signifies good eats to the people of Port Colborne.

made this Italian beg for more! Kevin makes his own curry paste, which allows him to customize the heat of the dish to the diner's liking. I had mine mild—call me a wimp and I'll beat you with an udon noodle.

India is well represented at The Smokin' Buddha, as Kevin's menu boasts a flurry of curries (yep, did that on purpose) like Vindaloo, Butter Chicken, Saag Paneer, and Chana Masala. But the dish that sent me straight to nirvana (yep, I did that, too) was the Lamb Popsicle Rogan Josh, an exotic dish that features grilled lamb chops pressed against a mound of rice and bathed in rogan josh sauce, a mysterious combination of more spices than most of us have in our entire spice drawers! The lamb is grilled to tender perfection, and the sauce adds a creamy heat.

Old world and new world combine in the Buddha's Naan Pizza, a fusion dish that tops an Indian flatbread with Japanese curry, a blend of mozzarella and Cheddar cheeses from the local farmers' market, a smattering of red onion, and red and green peppers. Thai Chili Fish is a hefty, pan-fried piece of local whitefish that's doused with a spicy-sweet Thai chili sauce and served alongside rice and salad in a signature lime-mint dressing.

In the end, The Smokin' Buddha is a trip to the tastes of Asia, and Kevin is your guide. The best part? No lost luggage, no jet lag, and no annoying tourists!

Pizza comes in many forms, and the Naan Pizza is one of Kevin's fusion specialties, where Indian naan bread meets Japanese sauces.

Korean Beef Noodles

Makes: 2 servings

The Buddha's Korean Beef Noodles features a heaping mound of noodles tossed with slices of marinated sirloin, portobello mushrooms, and homemade bulgogi sauce.

½ **cup soy sauce**
¼ **cup sesame oil**
1 teaspoon brown sugar
2 garlic cloves, chopped
One 1-inch piece fresh ginger, chopped
1 tablespoon oil
½ **pound sirloin beef, sliced**
1 large portobello mushroom, sliced
1 pkg (14 ounces) udon noodles
½ **carrot, grated**
2 tablespoons green onion, chopped

In a small bowl, whisk together the soy sauce, sesame oil, brown sugar, garlic, and ginger. Set aside. In a wok over medium heat, heat the oil. Stir-fry the beef and mushrooms until browned. Add the noodles and prepared sauce and cook, stirring constantly, until the noodles are softened. Add the carrots and simmer for about 1 minute.

Divide the noodles among serving bowls and garnish with the green onions.

Thai Chicken Salad

Makes: 4 servings

Part salad, part noodle dish, The Smokin' Buddha's Thai Chicken Salad consists of a bed of egg noodles and greens, topped with roasted cashews and a signature spicy dressing.

Marinade and Dressing

1 cup soy sauce
1 cup rice vinegar
2 tablespoons sesame oil
1 tablespoon Thai chili sauce

Salad

4 skinless, boneless chicken breasts (4 to 6 ounces each)
4 cups cooked egg noodles
4 cups mixed greens
1⅓ cups bean sprouts
1⅓ cups roasted unsalted cashews
Leaves from 1 bunch of fresh cilantro, chopped

Marinade and Dressing

In a bowl, whisk together all of the ingredients. Reserve 1 cup for the dressing and use the rest for the marinade.

Salad

Combine the chicken and prepared marinade in a resealable bag. Turn the chicken to coat, seal the bag, and refrigerate for at least 30 minutes or up to 4 hours.

Preheat a grill or barbeque to medium-high. Remove chicken from bag, discarding marinade. Cook the chicken for 4 to 5 minutes per side, or until cooked through. Cut into long strips.

In a small saucepan, bring the reserved dressing to a boil. Remove from heat.

Divide the egg noodles, mixed greens, chicken strips, bean sprouts, cashews, and cilantro equally among 4 serving bowls. Serve with dressing on the side.

The SmoQue Shack

EST. 2011

129 YORK STREET

OTTAWA, ON · K1N 5T4

613-789-4245

WWW.SMOQUESHACK.COM

No one loves barbeque as much as this guy. So when the words "Jamaican barbeque" were used to describe Ottawa's SmoQue Shack (a *You Gotta Eat Here!* Fan Favourite), I suspected we were in for a treat. And The Shack did not disappoint. In fact, its Jamaican Jerk Pork is one of the most delicious pork dishes I've ever eaten. Earthy, tantalizingly flavourful, and spicy without being too hot, this dish is a testament to chef Warren Sutherland's heritage and talent, and the poster dish for The SmoQue Shack's parade of slow-cooked Jamaican delights.

A native of Kingston, Jamaica, Warren studied electrical engineering at Michigan State University but realized one afternoon that his calling likely lay elsewhere when he found himself contentedly writing out a recipe in the middle of class. Warren stuck with engineering, though, and it was by no coincidence that he took a job in Barre, Vermont, just a few miles from the New England Culinary Institute, which is exactly where Warren ended up.

The twists and turns of a chef's life eventually led Warren to Ottawa, where he started the Sweetgrass Aboriginal Bistro. After eight years of fine dining, though, Warren was ready for something different, and decided to return to his roots. With help from childhood friend Marlon Franklin and former sous chef Adam Kelly, The SmoQue Shack was born.

Warren Sutherland is passionate about food and a master of the smoker. He loves that The SmoQue Shack is homey and approachable, and offers people a taste of his home.

The Shack offers a wide variety of delicious barbequed dishes, but for this guy, nothing touches the Jamaican Jerk Pork, Warren's self-proclaimed pride and joy. Pork shoulders are rubbed, then left to sit overnight in an exotic marinade. They spend much of the next day in the smoker, after which they're sliced into quarter-pound steaks, charbroiled, chopped, and tossed

The Jamaican Jerk Pork is a masterful blend of exotic spices and chef Warren's point of pride, a dish that comes as close to home as any you'll taste here.

in the jerk sauce. Serve with red beans and rice and a chunk of cornbread, and you've got a dish so spicy and flavourful it makes you crave a Red Stripe and a beach.

Warren understands if you can't decide which meat to stuff in your face, so he'll make it easy on you. I'm talking about the Sample Platter, which allows customers to choose any three barbequed meats on the menu. Mine was jerk chicken, baby back ribs, and smoked beef brisket, each of which was better than the last. The chicken—which can be hard to smoke because it has a tendency to dry out—was beautifully crispy on the outside but juicy on the inside. Warren's Memphis-style pork baby back ribs are rubbed, smoked, and finished on the charbroiler with a honey chipotle sauce that brings home the heat and sweet. Finally, smoked beef brisket is coated in a house rub before being smoked for about half a day. Sliced thin and served with coffee barbeque sauce, it's a damn thing of beauty.

Want veggies? Warren's got 'em, but be prepared for something *way* better than the stuff your mama forced you to eat when you were a kid. The Shack's creamed corn is made with heaps of butter and cream. Southern-style greens (kale and Swiss chard) are cooked in bacon fat, pork stock, and spices, then topped with hunks of house-smoked bacon. My kinda veggies!

There's more on the menu here than you can shake a jerk at (is that legal?), so allow yourself a few hours to make up your mind. The DBK Sandwich is a behemoth with pulled pork, shaved brisket, grilled Polish sausage, coleslaw, and shredded pickles. One word: massive! Another word: yummy! Mac and Cheese is creamy and decadent, The Shack's most popular side dish. Jumbo BBQ Shrimp, Piri Piri Rib Tips (*seriously* hot!), Brisket Poutine, and The Lerner Sandwich (smoked tofu!) are just a few of Warren's other creations, all of which will keep you coming back for more.

Like Warren himself, they're all smoky, saucy, and Caribbean-y. (And yes . . . that *is* a word. I think.)

Jerk Chicken

Makes: 4 to 6 servings

The SmoQue Shack's Jerk Chicken is an epic meat-eating experience, and just one of a litany of menu items that pay homage to Warren's roots. The dish proved so popular that it helped inspire "Jerk Tuesdays," a themed night featuring a Jerk Platter and bottle of Jamaican beer.

Special equipment: smoker
Timing note: chicken must marinate 8 to 12 hours

Jerk Sauce

4 whole Scotch bonnet peppers, puréed
1 cup chopped yellow onion
2 green onions, chopped
2 garlic cloves
2 tablespoons vegetable oil
1 tablespoon salt
1 tablespoon allspice, toasted and ground
2 tablespoons black pepper
2 teaspoons dried thyme
1 teaspoon ground ginger
½ teaspoon ground nutmeg
½ teaspoon ground cinnamon
1 bottle (12 ounces) beer (preferably Red Stripe)

Chicken

2 whole chickens (3 pounds each), butterflied
Juice of 3 limes
Salt and pepper
1 cup Jerk Sauce
Applewood chips (for smoker)

Jerk Sauce

In a food processor fitted with the metal blade, combine all of the ingredients and purée until smooth. Set aside.

Chicken

Rub the chickens with the lime juice and set aside for 5 minutes. Rinse under cool running water and pat dry with paper towel. Season with salt and pepper and set aside for 20 minutes. Coat the chickens in 1 cup of jerk sauce (refrigerate any unused portion for another day), cover with plastic wrap, and refrigerate for 8 to 12 hours (or overnight). Place applewood chips in the smoking tray of the smoker. Preheat smoker to 250°F. Cook the chickens for 2½ hours. Allow the chickens to rest for 10 minutes before cutting into pieces.

Turn Up the Heat!

OK, so I'm not the biggest fan of the hot 'n' spicy. But I'm a sensitive new-age kinda guy, and I appreciate that a little heat (or sometimes, *a lotta* heat) adds that extra something for a whole raft of foodies. And these dishes bring the zip in all its glorious machinations, from the gentle belly warmer to the five-alarm blaze.

SPICY CARIBBEAN PORK

Antoinette's Food Cache,
Whitehorse, YT

*The pork is true to its
name in this combo
platter that features the
best of Antoinette
. . . and the Caribbean.*

BLACKENED BLUES CATFISH

Louisiana Purchase,
Edmonton, AB

*Hell, if it's good enough for
Buddy Guy, it's good enough
for me. A little HOT, mind
you, but the taste is worth
the burn.*

LOUISIANA GUMBO

Slickity Jim's Chat 'N'
Chew, Vancouver, BC

*Gumbos come in all
shapes, sizes, and
temperatures. This one is
a 5 on the "I-Think-I'm-
Gonna-Die" scale, but a
10 on the "Man-This-Is-
Delicious" scale.*

JAMAICAN JERK PORK

The SmoQue Shack,
Ottawa, ON

*Nothing says heat quite
like Jamaican jerk, but this
dish is a complex blend
of flavours that's so much
more than just fire.*

CURRY CHICKEN ROTI

The Reef Restaurant,
Vancouver, BC

*The curry chicken is a
flavour bomb on its own.
Wrap it in a roti shell and
you're taking things to a
whole new level.*

TRIPLE X HOT CHICKEN WINGS

Smoke & Spice Southern
Barbeque, Windsor, ON

*It's not the wings
themselves that make
this dish singularly the
hottest thing I've ever
put in my mouth, it's the
Triple X Sauce. Only for
the bravest of heart . . .
and tongue.*

SOUTHERN CRAB CAKE BENNY

Chewies Steam & Oyster
Bar, Vancouver, BC

*Grab a taste of N'awlins
in Vancouver with
jalapeño-spiked red rock
crab cakes buried under
poached eggs and Cajun
hollandaise. Hot and
sweet, baby!*

Soulyve

EST. 2009
34 MILL STREET
ORANGEVILLE, ON · L9W 2M3
519-307-5983
WWW.SOULYVE.CA

Who says good deeds go unnoticed? Back in 2006, Philip Dewar and Joshua Blake were asked by Josh's dad to help raise money for school-building initiatives in Jamaica. They decided to pitch in by selling some homemade Jamaican classics at a farmers' market, and the response was overwhelming. Soon Philip and Josh had started a catering business to keep up with off-season demand, but locals still weren't getting enough. The answer was Soulyve, where Caribbean "soul" food meets fresh, "live" ingredients. And judging by the continual crowds that fill this cute little joint, the people of Orangeville just can't get enough.

Neither can I, for that matter. Especially when it comes to Philip's Jerk Chicken, which is singularly one of the tastiest things I've ever put in my mouth (and I've put a *lot* of things in my mouth!). Yeah, it was hot. Damn hot. But the thing I love about jerk chicken is it's not hot just for the sake of it. OK, so Philip blends a stupid number of Scotch bonnet peppers into his jerk marinade, but there's so many other flavours happening that I can overlook the five-alarm fire in my mouth.

For a twist on a traditional Jamaican favourite, you gotta eat the Power Patty, which splits a traditional Jamaican patty, lines it with a generous spread of Cajun mayo, then piles on cheese, tomatoes, lettuce, red onions, and a heap of jerk chicken. The crust is flaky and delicious, and the mayonnaise gives a nice kick of heat . . . as if you needed it after the blast of jerk chicken. That's one powerful patty!

As the Power Patty shows, Philip is not afraid to take risks with his food. Take the Jerk Pineapple Pizza, for example. I'm not sure what part of Italy this recipe comes from, but I want to visit! Philip starts with a cornmeal and whole-wheat flour crust, which he coats in marinara sauce and a blend of mozzarella, Cheddar, and Parmesan cheeses. Then he trows (that's "throws" to you, pal) on onion slices, tomatoes, and jerk chicken, and tops it with a sweet chili sauce and yet more cheese. Tangy and spicy, it's a damn good pizza for a Jamaican guy!

Philip also rocks the traditional, and his Curry Goat and Curry Chicken are old-time Jamaican mainstays. In each dish, hunks of meat are marinated, then stewed with an array of hearty vegetables and potatoes. Samosas are crispy and hearty, and come in beef-and-potato or chickpea-and-potato varieties. Trini Doubles are two fried flatbreads filled with mild curried chickpeas

Who, this guy? Chef Philip Dewar is a cool, hard-working, and playful entrepreneur who is as long on charm as he is on culinary inspiration.

and potatoes, and served with tamarind sauce. Ackee & Saltfish takes Jamaica's national fruit and stews it with cured cod and vegetables. For a real taste of the Caribbean, try the Oxtail, which slow-braises oven-roasted pieces of oxtail beef until they're so tender they fall apart before you can hit them with your fork.

If anything, Soulyve is what small-town success looks like. Its owners are busy, its clientele is always satisfied, and it's bringing something different to the local food scene. As for Philip and Josh, they're happy to keep doing their good deeds, one dish at a time.

What started as a modest booth at Orangeville's summer-only farmers' market has exploded into Soulyve, where people can enjoy Jamaican treats all year long.

Jerk chicken takes centre stage in many of Soulyve's menu items, but none wowed me more than the Reggae Wrap, one of my all-time favourite sandwiches. Filled with shredded jerk chicken, homemade pineapple and mango, chef Philip Dewar's tangy Cajun mayo, and a mound of traditional fixings, it's as delicious as it is massive.

Timing note: chicken must marinate 4 to 6 hours or overnight

Chicken

6 green onions, chopped
2 Scotch bonnet peppers, minced
1 yellow onion, chopped
½ cup soy sauce
½ cup sugarcane vinegar or apple cider vinegar
¼ cup vegetable oil
2 tablespoons chopped fresh thyme
2 tablespoons minced garlic
1 tablespoon brown sugar
1 teaspoon ground pimento (allspice)
½ teaspoon ground cloves
½ teaspoon ground nutmeg

1½ pounds skinless, boneless chicken breasts, halved
1 cup chicken stock, warmed

Assembly

4 paratha roti
Cajun mayonnaise (1 cup mayonnaise, 1½ tablespoons Cajun seasoning, ½ tablespoon paprika)
Romaine lettuce, shredded
Tomatoes, sliced
Red onion, sliced
Pineapple and mango salsa
Cheddar cheese, shredded

In a food processor fitted with the metal blade or a blender, combine all of the ingredients—except the chicken and chicken stock—and blend for about 30 seconds, until smooth.

Place the chicken in a medium bowl and coat with the prepared marinade. Refrigerate for 4 to 6 hours (or overnight).

Preheat a grill to medium-high and lightly oil grate. Remove the chicken from marinade (discard the marinade). Grill the chicken, flipping once, for 6 to 8 minutes, or until the juices run clear.

Preheat oven to 375°F.

Transfer the grilled chicken to a baking dish and add the hot chicken stock. Bake in preheated oven for 6 minutes, until cooked through. Remove from oven and allow the chicken to rest for 5 minutes before serving.

Assembly

Warm the roti on an open grill, allowing both sides to toast lightly. Remove from heat.

Top the roti with the following, in this order: mayonnaise, lettuce, tomatoes, onions, salsa, and cheese. Mound the grilled chicken on top and wrap roti carefully, folding and tucking the bottom flap in, then the sides.

That Italian Place

EST. 2008
470 CHRYSLER DRIVE
BRAMPTON, ON · L6S 0C1
905-451-5552
WWW.THATITALIANPLACE.CA

'm an emotional guy. When I eat at a restaurant that serves food reminiscent of my childhood, I get all choked up. So when Paul and Gino Fuda started serving me memory after memory during my visit to their home of fantastic Italian delights, I actually broke down and cried.

Growing up in a food-centric Italian household, Paul and Gino are probably used to the occasional emotional outburst. Their family's catering business introduced them to the art of serving people, and their recipes have been in the family for generations. So when both of them were ready for a change, they opened That Italian Place. Now they cater to eclectic and loyal customers who love their joint's boisterous and loving personality and can't wait to hear one of the boys shout their name when their meal is ready. Yo, Angee-la!

A signature sandwich at That Italian Place is the impressively large Porchetta and Rapini. The heart of the sandwich is fall-apart-tender pork shoulder, which bakes for hours in a rich broth of herbs and vegetables before being pulled apart. When the porchetta is so tender it melts in your mouth, the boys heap it on a toasted baguette with garlic-sautéed rapini (bittersweet Italian broccoli) and a slice of smoked provolone or mozzarella. The sandwich is oozy, rich, and insanely tasty . . . a tear-jerker, for sure.

The customer base at That Italian Place is many and varied, and includes former Maple Leaf star Bill Derlago, who visits the joint on a weekly basis.

Tradition hits the fork with Spaghetti and Meatballs. The meatballs are a combination of ground veal and pork, grated Parmigiano Reggiano, eggs, a touch of bread crumbs, herbs, and spices. Yet unlike many cooks, the Fudas don't fry or bake their meatballs. Instead,

A meal fit for a village. The Big Mouth stromboli is a challenge for your big mouth, your big stomach, and everything in between.

they go directly into the pot of their basil pomodoro sauce, itself a gorgeously simple concoction of crushed and strained San Marzano plum tomatoes, puréed onions and garlic, olive oil, salt, pepper, and fresh basil.

True to their roots, the Fuda fellas offer up a variety of pasta dishes, though you never really know what will be offered on the day you arrive. Panini are another house delight, highlighted by The Classic Veal, with fried meat delicately dipped in tomato sauce and topped with your choice of cheese and veggies. The Muffaletta is the sandwich that little Italian kids were sent to school with, a log of hollowed-out bread stuffed with aromatic deli meat and antipasti spread. Desserts are also a national treasure, and you can choose from Italian Cream Puffs, Cannoli with Sugar, and Cannoli with Walnuts.

But really, this is a place where you can't go wrong, no matter what you order. Yes, *miei amici*, That Italian Place is *that* good. And if you happen to see a guy who looks like me weeping in the corner, just give me . . . er . . . him a moment before you ask for a bite of his stromboli.

The Italian Job Stromboli

Makes: 4 to 6 servings

Italian delights come in every shape and size at That Italian Place, though most tip the scales at . . . freakin' massive! That's especially true of their gargantuan stromboli, which is available in two sizes: The Italian Job (1½ pounds) or The Big Mouth Challenge (7½ pounds). Either way, it's as tasty as it is intimidating. The stromboli is layered with six types of Italian cold cuts, along with three types of shredded cheese. The beast is served with the Fuda brothers' legendary Basil Pomodoro Sauce.

1½ pounds pizza dough
1 cup all-purpose flour
½ pound sweet Genoa salami
½ pound sweet capicollo
½ pound hot capicollo
½ pound mortadella
½ pound prosciutto cotto
½ pound sweet soppressata
1 cup shredded mozzarella
1 cup shredded smoked mozzarella
1 cup shredded provolone
1 cup olive oil
2 teaspoons dried oregano
Tomato sauce, warmed

Let the dough rest at room temperature for 2 to 3 hours.

Preheat oven to 400°F. Grease a large baking sheet.

Sprinkle a clean work surface and the dough with flour (to prevent the dough from tearing). Roll out the dough to a 16-inch-wide rectangle.

Making sure to leave a clean 2-inch border all around, arrange layers of salami, sweet and hot capicollo, mortadella, prosciutto, and soppressata on the dough. Combine all of the cheeses and sprinkle over the meats, being mindful to keep the borders clear. Carefully roll the exposed dough borders over the meat and cheese like a burrito. Transfer the Stromboli, fold-side down, to prepared baking sheet.

In a small bowl, combine the oil and oregano. Brush evenly over stromboli. Bake for 30 to 40 minutes, until crust is golden brown. Remove from oven and set aside for 10 minutes to cool.

Using a sharp knife, cut the Stromboli crosswise into 1½-inch slices for appetizers or 4-inch slices for sandwiches. Serve with your favourite tomato sauce alongside for dipping.

Globe-Trotting Gourmet

We Canadians are a quietly nationalistic bunch. Yeah, we love all things Canuck, but that doesn't mean we don't appreciate what everyone else has to offer. Luckily, there are joints in every far-flung corner of the country that specialize in taste sensations born elsewhere. So get your passport out, we're going travelling!

HUNGARIAN GOULASH
Black Forest Inn, Hamilton, ON

Love comes in all forms, and the Hungarians know that sometimes the best kind of love is served up warm on a giant plate.

POTATO PANCAKES
Skinnytato, Victoria, BC

If the crispy deliciousness of the pancake is not enough, fold it like an omelette and stuff it with one of a number of delicious fillings.

CARNE GUISADA BOCADILLO
El Camino's, Vancouver, BC

The tenderest beef ever to be jammed inside a bocadillo, surrounded by caramelized onions, chimichurri sauce, arugula, and Manchego cheese. Someone say "yum" in Spanish.

LE BIFTECK
The American Cheesesteak Co., Vancouver, BC

The shaved top-shelf beef in this cheesesteak variation might be Canadian, but surround it with heaps of double-cream Brie, caramelized onions, arugula, and Dijon, and you're ready to parlez en français.

PULLED PORK LASAGNA
Smokin' George's BBQ, Nanaimo, BC

Italy and the southern US come together in blissful harmony that has nonnas the world over pulling out their hair. One taste is all it takes to realize that traditions or not, this dish is a winner.

ADANA KEBAB
Sofra, Edmonton, AB

Elaborately spiced meat cooked on a sword. What else do you need to know?

SHEPTA
Tibetan Kitchen, Victoria, BC

Don't be fooled by its chow-mein-ish appearance. This noodle-beef-veggie stir-fry is spiked with a mysterious curry flavour that won't soon be forgotten.

DA FINEST FISH BURRITO
Chino Locos, Toronto, ON

Vietnamese basa fish fried in chipotle sauce, then stuffed in a tortilla with an international array of fillings, including Asian chow mein noodles that give this burrito an extra-special something few joints can replicate.

The American Cheesesteak Co.

EST. 2011
781 DAVIE STREET
VANCOUVER, BC · V6Z 2S7
604-681-0130
WWW.AMERICANCHEESESTEAK.COM

always say I have the greatest job in the world. Sure, I eat for a living, but that's not all. Along the way, I get to work with some of the nicest people I've ever met. Anthony Sedlak was one of those guys, a fun, giving, larger-than-life kind of guy who not only showed me his skill in the kitchen, but a little part of his heart, too. Anthony—the gifted chef at The American Cheesesteak Co.—died suddenly just a few months after I met him, and he will be missed. But the Cheesesteak Co. is still cranking out some of the most authentically delicious cheesesteaks you'll ever eat, even if Philadelphia is almost 5,000 kilometres away.

The mind behind the Cheesesteak Co. is owner Andy Eng, a good friend of Anthony's who gambled that health-conscious Vancouverites would embrace this American delicacy. Together the two set out to the City of Brotherly Love, where they sampled countless versions of the sandwich, intent on getting it *just right*. And mark my words, friends, they did! Perfectly selected and prepared meat, the freshest buns, and unique West Coast spins make this place a local destination day and night, any time of year.

Anthony Sedlak was funny, charming, and intensely dedicated to creating delicious food that anybody would enjoy.

Nothing pays homage to the original more than The Classic, a sandwich I seek out every time I'm back in Vancouver. The heart of this beauty—like all creations at The Cheesesteak Co.—is the beef: centre-cut, top-shelf prime rib. Interestingly, they shave the beef when it's frozen to make sure it's the perfect thickness without falling apart. Joining the flattop-fried beef on a gorgeous submarine bun are sautéed Vidalia onions, button mushrooms, and your choice of cheese: provolone, American, or that Philly classic, Cheez Whiz. Damn! That's a good sandwich.

When you use some of the best prime rib money can buy as the foundation of your cheesesteaks, you know they're gonna be good. And trust me, they are.

Like it extra large? Tackle The Big Shot, which mixes a massive pile of meat with a blend of sautéed forest mushrooms, extra-creamy fontina cheese, truffle mayonnaise, and fried shallots. Customers clamour for this one because of the way the flavours blend together perfectly. Creamy, meaty, earthy . . . wow! Serve it up with triple-fried french fries, and your mouth will thank you.

Though the magic of the Philly cheesesteak is in its simplicity, that doesn't mean you won't find a whole lotta variety here. The New Yorker starts with sautéed mushrooms and peppers, but throws in shredded lettuce, tomatoes, and roasted garlic mayo for Good Guy measure. Le Bifteck is an exotic continental twist, using double-cream Brie, caramelized onions, arugula, and Dijon mustard. They even do all-day breakfast cheesesteaks here, featuring fried or scrambled eggs.

In the end, there's nothing typical about The American Cheesesteak Co. The food? Extraordinary. The vision? Peerless. And as for Anthony . . . well, he was a one-in-a-million guy, and his legend lives on with every cheesesteak they serve up.

Of course this bad boy is anchored by perfectly fried meat and a delicious bun, but what takes it to the next level is the bourbon barbeque sauce and bacon mayonnaise it comes with. Sprinkle on a handful of fried shallots for crispiness, and you've got a sandwich I'd like to bring home and introduce to my mama. Stupid good. Seriously stupidly good.

Bacon Mayonnaise

1½ cups mayonnaise

8 pieces crispy cooked bacon, finely chopped

1 tablespoon flat-leaf parsley leaves, roughly chopped

Juice of ½ lemon

2 teaspoons Dijon mustard

1 ounce Parmesan cheese, grated

Pinch of kosher salt and freshly cracked black pepper

Spicy Bourbon Barbeque Sauce

1 small yellow onion, finely chopped

1½ cups ketchup

½ cup molasses

2 tablespoons bourbon whisky

2 teaspoons finely chopped chipotle peppers in adobe sauce

1 teaspoon Sriracha sauce

Pinch of kosher salt and freshly cracked black pepper

Cowboy Cheesesteak

4 small potato dough or whole wheat baguettes (8 inches in length each)

1 teaspoon grapeseed oil

24 ounces beef rib eye, shaved very thin (⅛ inch thick)

Pinch of kosher salt and freshly cracked black pepper

16 slices white Cheddar cheese

2 cups crispy fried onions or shallots

1 tablespoon finely chopped parsley leaves

Bacon Mayonnaise

In a glass or plastic bowl, whisk together all of the ingredients until fully incorporated. Check seasoning and, if needed, add more salt and pepper to taste. Refrigerate in an airtight container or squeeze bottle until ready to use.

Spicy Bourbon Barbeque Sauce

Preheat oven to 350°F.

In an oven-safe saucepan, whisk together all of the ingredients until fully incorporated. Cook in preheated oven for 30 minutes. Check seasoning and, if needed, season with more salt and pepper to taste. Set aside to cool, then refrigerate in an airtight container or squeeze bottle until ready to use.

The Cowboy Cheesesteak
Makes: 4 servings

Cowboy Cheesesteak

Preheat oven to 350°F.

Bake the baguette in preheated oven until crisp and lightly browned, 7 to 10 minutes.

Preheat a griddle to 375°F or a large cast-iron skillet over medium-high heat. Heat the grape-seed oil, then add the beef and season with salt and pepper. Cook the beef until medium, 1 to 2 minutes. Divide the beef into 4 even rectangular shapes and top each with 4 overlapping slices of cheese. Cook until the cheese is melted.

Assembly

Cut the warm baguettes lengthwise in half, leaving a hinge. Top each with the cooked beef and cheese, and garnish with bacon mayonnaise, barbeque sauce, crispy fried onions, and a sprinkling of parsley. Serve immediately.

Belgian Fries

EST. 1999
1885 COMMERCIAL DRIVE
VANCOUVER, BC · V5N 4A6
604-253-4220

Whether fries originated in France or Belgium is something I'll let the historians fight over. My reality is younger than that, and revolves more around taste than origins. And when it comes to mixing the delights of the fried potato with a mind-boggling array of delicious, homemade toppings, Ali Faghani at Vancouver's Belgian Fries is rewriting the history books, one order at a time.

Adventurous by nature, Ali emigrated from Iran when he was 21, then followed his mathematical mind to a career at Microsoft. Ali left Microsoft in 2004, leaping into the unknown and buying a struggling poutine business, despite having zero restaurant experience. Well, creativity, an international flair, and Ali's passion for the humble fried potato have turned Belgian Fries into *the* place to eat poutine in the Vancouver area.

Ali's War Fries are a unique hybrid that hints at the historic Dutch colonization of Indonesia. As with all of Ali's poutines, the dish is built around local Kennebec potatoes that are peeled and chipped before being blanched, cooled, and deep-fried, a process that ensures a crispy exterior and soft interior. The War Fries are topped with an Indonesian peanut satay sauce and a generous layer of mayonnaise. Customers here will attest, it's a strange combination . . . but it works!

Take a trip to northern Africa with Ali's Tunisian Kebob Merguez, which is a spicy and exotic twist on poutine like none you've ever had before. The thing that makes this dish truly unique is the merguez sausage, which features house-ground lamb spiked with a blend of herbs and Tunisian

How many fry joints in the world make their own sausage? It's this kind of dedication that separates Belgian Fries and owner Ali Faghani from the rest.

spices. Fried, cut into generous hunks, and heaped atop a mound of fries and cheese curds, it's the perfect accompaniment for Ali's rich, thick gravy.

I continued my whirlwind global tour with Ali's Beef Kotlet Poutine, which features none other than an Iranian hamburger perched atop a glistening mound of poutine. As with all his inventive poutines, Ali makes this one sing with the beef cutlet, a flavourful combination of ground beef, grated potatoes and onions, egg, and spices (curry powder, too!). I loved the cutlet's crispy crust, which falls away to reveal its juicy and tender inside. An Iranian hamburger on Belgian fries with Canadian cheese curds served to an Italian guy. It's the United Nations of poutine!

Of course, there are more poutine options at Belgian Fries than you can shake a passport at, including the Delux, a local favourite that uses chopped bacon and a sautéed mixture of sliced mushrooms, onions, and red peppers as its topping. The Frites Special is another Dutch specialty, drenched in mayonnaise, onion, and curried ketchup imported from the Netherlands. The Veggie Delight is massive, overflowing with a pile of sautéed eggplant, onions, mushrooms, red peppers, kidney beans, and corn. The Chili Fries feature a steaming mound of homemade chili, which Ali crafts from lean ground beef, crushed tomatoes, kidney beans, chickpeas, corn, and loads of herbs and spices. Bring your lumberjack appetite because this bad boy is big enough to feed two.

Ali's more than happy to stuff you with dessert, too, and his Deep-Fried Pecan Ice Cream is as tasty as it is magical. Deep-fried ice cream? Ali's secret is hand-forming the ice cream into balls, then freezing them to -0.4°F. Then they're rolled in cornflakes, whisked egg, and crushed pecans before being deep-fried for 5 seconds, giving each one a crispy coating but leaving the inside intact. It's one you won't want to miss.

Come to think of it, Belgian Fries is a place you won't want to miss. From Europe to Africa, Canada to the Middle East, it's a globe-trotting foodie destination that everyone should visit before they die.

I don't know what kind of black magic Belgian Fries calls upon to keep their Deep-Fried Pecan Ice Cream from melting, but frankly . . . I don't care! As long as I can eat it, that is.

Sure, this dish is anchored by fries, gravy, and curds, but it's the insanely flavourful chicken that makes it special. Owner Ali Faghani soaks pieces of chicken breast in a rich marinade highlighted by lime juice and cayenne. Soon they're charbroiled, flavour-packed nuggets of love that make this a dish you'll come back for again and again.

Special equipment: 8 bamboo skewers, soaked in water for 15 minutes
Timing note: chicken needs to marinate 6 to 8 hours

½ **bulb garlic**
⅓ **cup olive oil**
¼ **cup lime juice**
1 **teaspoon salt**
1 **teaspoon black pepper**
½ **teaspoon cayenne pepper**
1⅓ **pounds skinless, boneless chicken breast, cut into 1½-inch cubes**

1 **red onion, roughly chopped**
4 **cups canola oil**
4 **pounds Kennebec or Yukon Gold potatoes, peeled and chopped into 1½-inch-wide matchsticks**
1 **pound Cheddar cheese curds**
3½ **cups gravy (of your choice)**

In a medium bowl, combine the garlic, olive oil, lime juice, salt, black pepper, and cayenne to make a marinade. Add the chicken to the marinade, cover, and refrigerate for 6 to 8 hours.

Thread the marinated chicken with pieces of red onion onto the soaked bamboo skewers in an alternating pattern. Set aside.

In a deep pot, heat the canola oil to 155°F to 160°F. Carefully add the potatoes to the oil and blanch for 2 to 2½ minutes. Using a slotted spoon, transfer the blanched potatoes to a plate lined in paper towel to drain.

Increase oil temperature to 175°F and deep-fry the blanched potatoes for 4 to 5 minutes, or until golden brown. Transfer to a colander to drain.

Meanwhile, barbeque the chicken skewers, turning occasionally, for 4 to 4½ minutes, until cooked through.

In a saucepan over medium heat, bring the gravy to a simmer.

Divide the fries among shallow serving bowls. Top with the cheese curds, then gravy. Serve each with 2 skewers of chicken.

Bernie & The Boys Bistro

EST. 1999
305 4TH STREET WEST
DRUMHELLER, AB · T0J 0Y3
403-823-3318
WWW.BERNIEANDTHEBOYS.COM

Dinosaurs are the name of the game in Drumheller, one of the premier fossil-hunting destinations on earth. And while you won't find any velociraptors here, you might encounter a Mammoth and a Megasaurus, two beasts as tasty as they are hefty. Confused? Don't be. This is Bernie & The Boys Bistro, as down-home and fun-loving a joint as you'll find anywhere, where the food comes with witty names and in Jurassic proportions.

A true family-run operation, Bernie's starts with Bernie Germain, a former teacher who's as passionate about food as he is about life. Warm, goofy, and energetic, Bernie funded the purchase of the restaurant in part by selling his prized stamp collection. It was a worthwhile gamble: locals and visitors alike flock to the restaurant, where Bernie's wife, Carol, runs the dining room and children Andrew and Lydia are often seen greeting customers, running food, even working the till.

Just don't ask the kids to carry the Megasaurus Pizza, OK? I mean, it's gotta be illegal for someone that small to heft around an *8-pound* pizza. That's not a typo, people. The Megasaurus starts with a mountain of dough stretched in a massive dish, doused with Bernie's tangy homemade pizza sauce, and topped with layer upon layer of pepperoni, salami, back bacon, ham, ground beef, green pepper, pineapple, mushrooms, onions, olives, (you ready for this?) 18 ounces of cheese, and fresh tomato slices! So it should come as no surprise when Bernie

I love this guy! Bernie Germain describes himself as a 17-year-old trapped in a 45-year-old body, and never seems to stop having fun.

says the Megasaurus will feed a table of eight . . . though he's seen much smaller groups try to polish it off.

Though brontosaurus-size meals are a regular occurrence on Bernie's menu (like the 3-pound Family Poutine or the 2-Pound Milkshake—in 70 possible flavours!), the restaurant also dabbles in more eclectic fare. The Blair Wing Project is a plate of chicken wings so damn hot that you have to sign a waiver before you dig in, just in case the trademark Magna Sauce—which features one of the world's hottest peppers—sets your mouth ablaze. By comparison, the triple-decker Clubhouse Sandwich is stuffed with baked turkey that tastes like Thanksgiving . . . only served on Texas toast.

Yet as big as Bernie's is on portions and flavour, the restaurant is equally committed to a fun dining experience for its customers. It's this rare combination that has earned it *You Gotta Eat Here!* Fan Favourite status. In fact, people from as far away as Calgary—almost 150 kilometres to the west—come to Bernie's every chance they get. Maybe it's the '80s tunes (which Bernie's been known to dance to) or the hand-painted tables. Either way, the secret is out: the Yummysaurus still roams the western badlands.

You: Hungry. Megasaurus Pizza: Big. You: Call friends. Megasaurus: Still too big. You: Eat pizza leftovers all week.

Mammoth Burger

Makes: 4 to 6 servings (for one burger)

Checking in on the gargantuan scale is the Mammoth Burger, which is as straightforward as it is colossal: 1½ pounds of homemade bun, 1½ pounds of Alberta beef mixed with seasoning mix, and a mountain of fixings. Though the Mammoth can easily feed a family of four, thousands have tried to tackle it on their own. To this day, less than two dozen have completed the task. The all-time record? Thirteen minutes, 45 seconds. Do it in less and your burger is on the house.

Bun

Cornmeal
2½ cups all-purpose flour
2 teaspoons sugar
2 teaspoons instant dry yeast
1 teaspoon all-purpose seasoning
1 tablespoon canola oil
2 eggs
Sesame seeds

Patty

1½ pounds lean ground beef
2 tablespoons all-purpose seasoning
2 tablespoons dried bread crumbs

Bun

Grease a 10-inch round baking pan with vegetable spray and lightly coat with cornmeal.

In a large bowl, combine the flour, sugar, yeast, and all-purpose seasoning.

In a separate bowl, combine ¾ cup + 1 tablespoon hot water, oil, and 1 egg. Mix the wet ingredients into the dry ingredients, stirring until a soft (not sticky) dough forms. Set aside for 10 minutes to rise.

In a small bowl, beat the remaining egg to make an egg wash.

Press the proofed dough into the greased pan and brush with the egg wash. Sprinkle with the sesame seeds. Set aside for 45 minutes, or until doubled in size.

Preheat oven to 350°F.

Bake the bun in preheated oven for 15 minutes, or until golden brown. Remove from the pan and transfer to a wire rack to cool.

Patty

Preheat a grill to medium. Line an 8-inch round baking pan with parchment paper and lightly spray with cold water. (Wet your hands as well—it will help keep the meat from sticking to your hands.)

In a large bowl, combine all of the ingredients with ¼ cup cold water and form into a ball. Using your hands, press the mixture evenly into the pan to form a large patty. Place a piece of parchment paper on top and, using a small pan, press down firmly to compress the mixture (this will help the patty cook evenly).

Turn out the patty from the pan and grill, flipping once, for 6 minutes per side, until browned and cooked through (an internal temperature of 180°F on a meat thermometer).

Assembly

Cut the bun in half and lightly toast on your grill or barbeque.

Place the grilled burger on the bun bottom and garnish with your favourite toppings: mayonnaise, cheese, lettuce, tomatoes, pickle relish, corn relish, onions, banana peppers, barbeque sauce . . . the list is endless. Add bun top.

Enjoy your Mammoth Burger any way you would like it!

Big Fish

EST. 2004

1112 EDMONTON TRAIL NORTHEAST

CALGARY, AB · T2E 3K4

403-277-3403

WWW.BIG-FISH.CA

When people think of Calgary's culinary offerings, they usually go straight to the beef. And why not? They don't call this place Cowtown for nothin'! Well, Dwayne Ennest will be the first one to tell you that Calgary has so much more to offer, and his Big Fish restaurant stands as Exhibit A, counsellor. Serving it up fresh and delicious, Big Fish is converting beef-loving Calgarians into seafood aficionados, one stupidly good dish at a time.

And while Dwayne might not have seafood in his blood (he grew up in a logging camp in northern British Columbia, where his mom was the camp cook), he's been a food freak for as long as he can remember. So, at the ripe old age of 15, Dwayne hit the road to seek his culinary fortune. Working his way up from dishwasher to chef in kitchens across the US and Europe, Dwayne (along with his wife, Alberta) is now living his dream of restaurant ownership in a fun, unique, and deliciously different environment.

And it doesn't get much different than Big Fish's Crab Club Sandwich, with its whole deep-fried panko-coated soft-shell crab on fresh rosemary ciabatta covered with crispy wild boar bacon, fresh tomato slices, and tangy lemon caper aïoli. The crab is rich and sweet, a taste that's highlighted by the crispiness of the panko coating.

Dwayne knows that meat and seafood often come together in savoury bliss, and he adds his own creation to the annals of surf-and-turfdom with the Lamb and Lobster Burger. This finger-snappin'-good burger stuffs so many taste sensations between the buns that it's hard to keep track. The foundation is a charbroiled patty of pure ground lamb (I *love* that taste!) that's been dusted in a homemade chili rub. The patty is served on a ciabatta bun coated with paprika

Given the overwhelming success of his first restaurant—Calgary's Diner Deluxe—Dwayne Ennest decided to feed his seafood fancy at Big Fish.

mayonnaise and piled thick with fresh arugula. But that's just the beginning. The patty is then topped with Cambozola cheese, butter lettuce, homemade guacamole, salsa cruda, chipotle barbeque sauce, and . . . oh yeah, sweet, thick hunks of fresh lobster meat! It's a monstrously delicious dish, and one served with fresh yam chips, assuming you've got a square millimetre of space left in your stomach after chowing down.

If it's DIY you're after, order Big Fish's Bucket of Peel and Eat Shrimp, a communal, get-yer-hands-dirty dish served with an in-house cocktail sauce. East Coast Lobster Poutine is a neo-classic that surprises with goat feta curds and Jack cheese sauce instead of traditional gravy. The Steelhead Trout Burger is crunchy and sweet, and served with homemade blueberry barbeque sauce, while the Seafood Pot au Feu is a pot of tantalizingly classic seafood mélange served in a rich saffron broth.

So if you've found yourself at the Stampede dreaming of the smell of the ocean, the crash of the waves, and the lonely cry of the gull . . . well, you're outta luck, my friend. But if it's the taste of the sea that you're craving, Big Fish is your place.

The Lamb and Lobster Burger owes its place on the menu to Dwayne's wife, Alberta, who suggested adding a lamb burger—her personal fave—to Big Fish's menu.

Crab & Shrimp Enchilada

Makes: 4 servings

Crab also plays a big part in Big Fish's Crab & Shrimp Enchilada, a mammoth dish inspired by sous chef Trinidad, who brought his mother's Mexican recipes to the restaurant. As for me, I may have grown up in a family that never put cheese on seafood, but this dish won me over (sorry, Nonna). Topped with fresh salsa verde, a pile of jalapeño Jack cheese, and served alongside mango tomato salsa, it's a creamy seafood delight.

Salsa Crude

5 Roma tomatoes, finely chopped
1 jalapeño pepper, seeded and finely
  chopped
½ red onion, finely chopped
½ cup lime juice
2 tablespoons chopped fresh cilantro
2 teaspoons sea salt

Cream Base

1 large sprig fresh thyme
1 small sprig fresh rosemary
1 shallot, sliced
2 garlic cloves, crushed
1 cup apple juice
½ cup white wine
Zest and juice of ½ lemon
3 cups heavy or whipping (35%) cream
Salt and pepper

Stuffing

2 tablespoons butter

1 cup finely chopped onion

1 cup finely chopped carrots

1 cup finely chopped celery

1 bay leaf

1 tablespoon equal parts puréed garlic and shallots

½ cup white wine

1 cup chopped roasted red pepper

2 tablespoons chopped fresh dill

1 teaspoon ground nutmeg

1 tablespoon Mexican chili rub (store-bought is fine)

2 cups cooked shrimp meat

2 cups cooked crabmeat

2 cups shredded Monterey Jack cheese

Salt and pepper

Assembly

8 to 10 flour tortilla shells (8 inch)

1½ cups salsa verde

3 cups shredded jalapeño Jack cheese

Salsa Crude

In a large bowl, combine the tomatoes, jalapeño pepper, onion, and lime juice. Stir in the cilantro and season with salt. Refrigerate for 1 hour before serving to allow flavours to meld.

Cream Base

In a large saucepan over medium-low heat, combine the thyme, rosemary, garlic, shallots, apple juice, and white wine. Bring to a boil and simmer for 8 minutes. Add the lemon zest and juice, cream, and salt and pepper. Bring to a slow boil and then reduce heat to simmer for 30 minutes. Strain the mixture through a fine-mesh sieve (discard solids) and set aside to cool. (Extra cream base can be kept refrigerated for one week.)

Stuffing

In a large saucepan over medium-high heat, melt the butter. Add the onion, carrots, celery, and bay leaf and cook until vegetables are tender. Stir in the garlic and shallot purée. Add two cups of cream base, white wine, and red pepper, and using a wooden spoon, stir, scraping up the brown bits at the bottom of the pan. Bring the mixture to a boil and simmer for 5 minutes. Stir in the dill, chili rub, and nutmeg. Simmer for 5 minutes. Add the shrimp and crab, stir, and remove from heat.

Stir in the cheese until melted. Season with salt and pepper to taste. Set aside to cool.

Assembly

Preheat oven to 375°F.

Spoon about ½ cup of the prepared stuffing along the centre of each tortilla. Roll the tortilla around the stuffing. Place tortilla rolls in a lasagna dish, tightly packed. Top each with more cream base, salsa verde, salsa crude (reserving some for serving), and cheese. Bake in preheated oven until cheese is golden brown. Remove from the oven and top each enchilada with 2 tablespoons salsa crude. Serve immediately.

Big T's BBQ & Smokehouse

EST. 2004
2138 CROWCHILD TRAIL NORTHWEST
CALGARY, AB · T2M 3Y7
403-284-5959
WWW.BIGTSBBQ.COM

Calgarians know their meat, so if you're planning on opening a meatery in this town, you better have a pretty darn good idea what you're doin'. Well, luckily for the good folks of Cowtown, there's Nikki Bond, a tried-and-true student of authentic southern barbeque whose roots in the restaurant business run as deep as her passion for good food. Enter Big T's, the legendary barbeque joint Nikki and her family have carved out of the western foothills.

Rustic, welcoming, and boisterous, Big T's is true to its name in every possible way. From the food to the noise to the fun, this place serves it up large and messy. Take, for example, Big T's signature dish, the ridiculously massive Elvis Platter, which piles six meats on a plate so huge, you need a chuckwagon to haul it into the dining room. The Elvis boasts a mountain of pulled pork, which starts with a dry rub, spends hours in Big T's giant smoker (it holds 650 pounds of meat!), and is finished with a tasty sauce. Also dry-rubbed and smoked are the Elvis's sliced brisket (grade A Alberta beef, baby!), a full chicken (finished on the flattop and basted with Big T's signature barbeque sauce), and a heap of Dusty Rib Ends, bite-size pork riblets that are dangerously easy to eat.

If you think barbeque is a man's world, think again. Big T's owner Nikki Bond is as passionate about it as anyone you'll ever meet, and every dish pays homage to its southern roots.

Not enough meat for ya? Fear not, Elvis hasn't left the building yet, my friends. Throw on some spicy Louisiana-style pork-and-beef Andouille sausage and finish with a saucy mound of St. Louis pork side ribs, and you've got enough to feed five starving oilmen . . . or a small neighbourhood anywhere else. Of course, there's a few (as in, like, *six!*) side dishes thrown in as well, in case you feel the need for a little variety: homemade baked beans, coleslaw, cornbread, dirty rice (that's right . . . I said *dirty*), dinner buns, and fries round out the offering.

Meat comas are a very real risk after a session with the Gut Buster sandwich, a giant hoagie bun stuffed and topped with pulled pork, brisket, and Andouille sausage, then topped off with mounds of shredded mozzarella, jalapeños, and sweet sautéed onions. Wear clothes that, uh, *give* a little: the GB is served with homemade coleslaw, baked beans, and fries smothered in Big T's homemade chunky beef chili.

What else do they serve up at Big T's? Well, there's, um . . . meat! This time, though, it comes in the loaf variety, and it's one damn good loaf. In fact, I'd go so far as to say that Big T's Home-made (smoked) Meat Loaf is what all meat loaf wants to be when it grows up. The secret? I'm not sure (that's why it's a secret, pal), but it probably has something to do with the grade A ground Alberta chuck, homemade maple bourbon sauce, and gravy-drenched mashed potatoes. *Yee-haw!*

The southern-fried party keeps on rollin' at Big T's with unique tastes like Deep-Fried Dill Pickles (a signature "vegetable" dish), Hush Puppies (served Canadian-style, with maple syrup), and Wild Turkey Pie (no birds allowed, just chocolate, pecans, and a couple shots of Wild Turkey Kentucky bourbon).

But when all is said and done, it's the meat—and the smoke they use to cook it—that defines the experience at Big T's. And if your friends can't tell where you've been by the size of your gut, they'll know it by the smell of your clothes, the sauce under your fingernails, and the grin on your face.

You're gonna eat **THAT?** If you're a food lover, the Elvis Platter packs all you could want of the good stuff . . . But you'd better have a few hours to kill.

Wild Turkey Pie

Makes: One 9-inch pie

Big T's Wild Turkey Pie is no pot pie, my friends. Instead, it's a decadent dessert featuring journalist Hunter S. Thompson's favourite bourbon. The buttery chocolate filling is made with eggs, sugar, corn syrup, butter, and (of course!) Wild Turkey. Served warm with heaping scoops of vanilla ice cream and drizzled with rich chocolate syrup, it'll make you forget that you didn't even order dinner.

1 9-inch pie crust
3 eggs
1 cup sugar
1 cup corn syrup
2 tablespoons Wild Turkey bourbon
½ teaspoon vanilla extract
¼ cup melted butter
¾ cup chocolate chips
½ cup pecans

Preheat oven to 375°F. Pull out a 9-inch pie crust.

In a mixing bowl, cream together the eggs and sugar. Add the corn syrup, bourbon, and vanilla and mix until combined. Add the butter and mix until combined.

Sprinkle the chocolate chips and pecans over the bottom of the pie shell. Pour the egg mixture over top. Bake in preheated oven for 35 minutes, or until set. Set aside to cool completely. Reheat in a preheated 350°F oven for 10 to 12 minutes before serving.

Comfort Classics to Warm Your Heart

Eating out is fun enough. I mean, there's nothing better than chowing down on delicious comfort food that someone else has cooked and *not* having to do the dishes afterwards. Here are some good places to start.

BOWDEN FARM CHICKEN

Boxwood Café,
Calgary, AB

There's something incredibly comforting about roasted chicken, and the Boxwood's rotisserie version absolutely nails it.

TURKEY DINNER CRÊPE

The Crepe House,
Port Dover, ON

Thanksgiving in crêpe form. What's not to love?

WEST COAST POUTINE

Wildside Grill,
Tofino, BC

This ain't just any ol' poutine, my friends. Yeah, there are fries and cheese, but add heaps of seafood gumbo, and you're taking it to a whole new level.

ROTISSERIE CHICKEN AND RIBS

Argyle Street Grill,
Caledonia, ON

Who knew that pigs and chickens went so damn well together? It's a match made on a slow-roasted spit.

GARLIC CHERRY SHORT RIBS

The Dish Bistro and the Runaway Spoon, Edmonton, AB

Braised for hours and left for even longer to marinate in their own juices, these ribs are busting with so many complex flavours, you'll never want to leave.

CODFISH CAKES

Chafe's Landing,
St. John's, NL

You don't have to be a Newfoundlander to find comfort in these warm, crispy, buttery, fishy, potatoey treats, now do you, me trout?

SHEPHERD'S PIE

Fanny Chadwick's,
Toronto, ON

Oh yeah, it's tasty. And it's damn pretty to look at, too. But don't let that stop you from tearing it open and shoving it in your piehole.

STEAK AND STOUT PIE

The Churchill Arms,
Charlottetown, PEI

Comfort comes in many forms here, from the rich beef filling to the potato bread crust waiting to soak up any juices that don't make it into your mouth the first time around.

Boogie's Burgers

EST. 1969
A-908 EDMONTON TRAIL NORTHEAST
CALGARY, AB · T2E 3K1
403-230-7070
WWW.BOOGIESBURGERS.COM

One of the greatest joys I know is drinking a good milkshake. Eating one? Well, that takes milkshake pleasure to a whole new level. And that's exactly what you get here at Boogie's Burgers, a classic Calgary burger joint where each menu item tells a story and Fat Elvis is king.

Boogie's Fat Elvis is the milkshake to end all milkshakes, the drink that's also a meal. Got a spoon? You might need it, since the Elvis has vanilla ice cream, peanut butter, banana, and (*ta-da!*) chopped bacon! I'm not sure what kind of nightmare spawned this creation, but it was worth every drop of cold sweat. And in the end, nothing says thirst-quenching quite like bacon does, right?

Food also comes in more traditional forms at Boogie's, which is why the joint has stood in the same spot for more than 40 years. It was founded in 1969 by Gus Pieters (owner of Calgary's famous Peters' Drive-In), his brother, and their friend Boogie. The restaurant was sold a few years later and turned into a family stop, but in 2008 Noel Sweetland and Kipp Teghtmeyer took over, and Boogie's returned to its roots. Now Boogie's is as laid-back as its name suggests, and its classic '80s décor blends perfectly with the food on its menu. From the brightly painted furniture to the retro video games, Boogie's serves it up old school.

And you can't get more traditional than Doug's "Don't Fear the Reaper" Burger, a behemoth that gets its name from a former employee/football player who tipped the scales at 300-plus pounds. Noel and Kipp wanted to keep Doug satisfied, so they brought together four hefty patties, four slices of bacon, Cheddar cheese, a fried egg, and a butterflied hot

Take this job and shove it! Owners Noel (left) and Kipp (right) tried their hands at nine-to-five jobs and *hated* it. For them, the burger life is *the* life.

dog. Accented with Boogie's homemade signature red sauce and a mound of traditional fixings, and held together with a corn dog on a skewer, the burger was such a hit (Doug demolished it without batting an eye) that it's become a mainstay on the menu. As the boys like to say, The Reaper is the perfect marriage of meat and meat.

The one that really set my Italian juices flowing was Keith's Burger, named after the son of a previous owner who woke up one day to divine burger inspiration. Keith's creation has all the flavours of a pizza, but on a burger: two patties, bacon, mushroom sauce, fried mushrooms, fried onions, pizza sauce, mozzarella, Cheddar, and all the fixings! It's sloppy creations like this that have made Boogie's a *You Gotta Eat Here!* Fan Favourite. Like Super Fans say, this thing is so good, someone should write an ode to it.

Come to think of it, these guys should hire their own personal poet, given the endless array of inspiration on the menu. The Blazing Saddles Burger features homemade hot sauce and barbeque sauce. Meaty, spicy, and messy, it's everything a good burger should be. Fay's Burger (with bacon, mushroom sauce, fried onions, and mushrooms) is named after a previous owner and has been on the menu for four decades. The National Lampoon's Hawaiian Vacation is a Boogie's original, topping a fresh chicken breast with grilled pineapple, lettuce, and tomato. Speaking of chicken, June's Jerk Chicken Burger is named after a customer who makes the jerk rub for this tangy, spicy, and ridiculously flavourful creation.

In the end, though, it doesn't really matter what you're ordering at Boogie's, the experience is the same: fun and happy. For when you've got owners who enjoy each other and their business as much as Noel and Kipp do, every customer is The King.

Kipp and Noel originally thought about giving away a T-shirt every time someone finished the Don't Fear the Reaper, but thought better of it when people started polishing them off with alarming regularity!

Deep-Fried Mac 'n' Cheese Burger

Makes: 4 burgers

If you want to stuff all your comfort classics into a burger, look no further than Boogie's Deep-Fried Mac 'n' Cheese Burger, which buries its patty under tasty wedges of deep-fried mac-and-cheese goodness. Um . . . yum!

Mac 'n' Cheese

Macaroni and cheese, cooked from scratch or from a box

Boogie's Signature Red Sauce

½ cup ketchup
¼ cup yellow mustard
¼ cup red hamburger relish

Patties

1 pound 80/20 ground chuck beef
⅛ teaspoon Saskatchewan steak spice (or your favourite steak spice blend)
⅛ teaspoon seasoning salt
⅛ teaspoon onion powder
⅛ teaspoon garlic powder
⅛ teaspoon black pepper
⅛ cup dried bread crumbs

Assembly

4 cups canola oil
12 frozen macaroni and cheese wedges
4 large hamburger buns
½ head iceberg lettuce, finely chopped
1 tomato, sliced
4 slices Cheddar cheese
½ cup chopped onion

Mac 'n' Cheese

Let prepared macaroni and cheese cool and freeze in a resealable container until solid. Cut into 12 wedges.

Boogie's Signature Red Sauce

In a small bowl, combine all of the ingredients. Cover and refrigerate until ready to use.

Patties

In a large bowl, combine all of the ingredients (be careful not to over-mix or the texture of the burger will be too tough). Divide the mixture into 4 equal portions and, using your hands, form into patties. Refrigerate the patties until ready to use.

Assembly

Preheat barbeque to medium-high.

Meanwhile, in a large saucepan over medium heat, heat oil. Deep-fry the wedges of frozen macaroni and cheese until floating and golden.

Grill patties for 5 minutes per side, or until desired doneness.

To assemble the burgers, top each bun bottom with lettuce and tomato. Place a slice of cheese, a dollop of red sauce, onions, and three macaroni wedges on each patty. Place dressed patties on top of each prepared bun bottom. Sandwich with bun top and serve.

Boxwood Café

EST. 2012
340 13TH AVENUE SOUTHWEST
CALGARY, AB · T2R 0W9
403-265-4006
WWW.BOXWOODCAFE.CA

Some restaurants are just that . . . places to eat. Other restaurants manage to combine their love of good food with their desire to give something back to the world. This is the Boxwood Café, where they not only cook up some of the most delicious meals you'll ever get your greedy hands on, they do it while featuring seasonal, sustainable ingredients that make the world—and your stomach—a better place.

The Boxwood comes to us courtesy of its lovely owner Sal Howell, but owes some of its genesis to the City of Calgary, which was looking to revitalize its Central Memorial Park, in part by adding a café to the grounds. Dozens of restaurateurs jumped at the chance to land this unique location, but Sal proved the victor. The City constructed a quaint little cabin based on original 1909 drawings; soon after, the Boxwood moved in.

Rustic yet modern, the Boxwood offers a funky array of vegetarian dishes, but meat is an integral part of the menu, thanks to Sal's rotisserie oven, which she imported from France. The rotisserie is spun by chef Jason Barton-Browne, a business-school dropout who found his true calling in culinary school.

Jason's passion for food is obvious in everything he cooks, and the rotisserie sings the sweet song of his talent. Take, for example, the top-selling Spragg Farm Roasted Porchetta Sandwich. After brining for 24 hours, the pork belly and loin is rubbed with an herb/spice blend and skewered on one of the rotisserie's five spits. Three to five hours later it's sliced onto a house-baked ciabatta bun and covered in salsa verde, slices of roasted BC apples, and salty bits of skin called cracklin'. I was so excited to shove this sandwich in my mouth I did the Happy Dance. Yes, friends, it was stupidly delicious.

Equally local and just as tasty was the Driview Farms Leg of Lamb. After it's de-boned and trimmed, the whole lamb leg is seasoned only with salt and pepper before hitting the rotisserie. It gets sliced to order and served with Jason's homemade merguez sausage (a spicy lamb sausage with a Middle Eastern groove) and mild garlic purée, which imparts all the flavour of garlic without the bite. Tenderness, thy name is rotisserie lamb!

Of all the delights Jason cooked for us, my fave was the chicken. The process starts with whole chickens brined in a brown sugar and water mixture for about an hour before being placed on the rotisserie for another two. While the birds cook, Jason fills the roasting pan underneath with mounds of diced root vegetables, which roast in the fatty drippings from the chickens. Veggies on steroids! When ordered, a breast or leg is removed from the juicy bird and broiled, bringing the skin to a wonderfully crispy finish. The chicken is served on a bed of peppery arugula and topped with the veggies, an amazing combination.

He may have started his career at low-level kitchen jobs, but chef Jason Barton-Browne quickly shot up the culinary ladder and now heads the Boxwood's creative menu.

If fish is your thing, go for the Pan-Seared Lois Lake Steelhead Trout, which is seasoned with a special Boxwood spice mix and lightly browned to flaky perfection. Don't like meat? The Organic Chickpea Fritters sandwich is a homemade pita stuffed with tasty homemade chickpea fritters, cilantro salsa verde, and a heap of greens.

A Boxwood meal wouldn't be complete without dessert, and Jason gives you loads of options. The Panorama Orchard Honeycrisp Apple Tart is sweet but with a bite of tang, while the Fairwinds Farm Chèvre & Pumpkin Cheesecake is as rich as they come. You could go simple with an Oatmeal Cranberry Chocolate Chip Cookie, but the Fiasco Handcrafted Gelato Sandwich is pretty special, too.

Come to think of it, it's *all* special at the Boxwood Café: the owner, the chef, the location, the atmosphere, and the history. And the food. Most definitely the food.

"Low and slow" is the mantra at the Boxwood, and the slow-roasted porchetta sandwich is as tender and delicious as any ever produced by a rotisserie.

Brown Sugar–Brined Roast Chicken
(The Secret to Making a Better Roast Than Mom.!)

Makes: brine for 1 chicken

You can keep a secret, right? Well here's the skinny: you *can* make a better roast chicken than your mom did and you don't even need a commercial rotisserie. The trick lies in the brining, which not only infuses the bird with tons of flavour, it makes for the most tender meat you've ever stuck a fork in.

2 teaspoons fennel seeds
2 teaspoons mustard seeds
2 whole star anise
20 cups water, divided
2 cups packed brown sugar
1½ cups kosher salt
6 bay leaves
4 garlic cloves, crushed
3 cinnamon sticks
1 chicken

In a small dry skillet over medium heat, toast the fennel seeds, mustard seeds and star anise until fragrant. Remove from heat and set aside.

In a large stockpot, bring 8 cups of water to a boil. Add the toasted spices, brown sugar, salt, bay leaves, garlic, and cinnamon. Reduce heat and simmer for 10 minutes. Remove from heat and add the remaining 12 cups of water. Set aside to cool completely.

Place your chicken in a container large enough to submerge it completely in your brine (you may need to weigh the chicken down with a plate to keep it submerged). Set aside at room temperature for 1 hour to brine.

Drain the chicken and pat dry with paper towel.

Roast the chicken according to your mom's recipe and enjoy the compliments (and keeping the secret).

burger 55

EST. 2009
84–52 FRONT STREET
PENTICTON, BC · V2A 1H7
778-476-5529
WWW.BURGER55.COM

Take a couple of best friends, a road trip to Vegas, and an old tire shop and you've got burger 55, a *You Gotta Eat Here!* Fan Favourite burger joint that residents of the Okanagan Valley can't get enough of. Confused? Wait until you see the menu, where owners Chris Boehm and Steve Jones offer enough options to keep your head—and your taste buds—spinning for months.

After becoming friends while working at a chain restaurant in Camrose, Alberta, Chris and Steve hit the road for Las Vegas in 2002, only to be disappointed that every burger they met along the way was cut from the same tired mould: meat, lettuce, tomatoes, onion. Knowing that burgers could be so much more, they decided to open their own joint. Seven years later, they landed in what was once a tire shop in Penticton, and away they went. And while their building may be tiny, their burgers are anything but. Here you get everything you ever dreamt a burger could be . . . and so much more.

The party at burger 55 starts with your choice of a foundation, either beef (grade AAA ground Alberta chuck), turkey, portabella mushroom, pork, or wild BC salmon. From there, you can choose one of the ridiculously delicious menu burgers or (if you're feeling frisky) create your own.

Chris introduced me to the legendary Signature Burger, which Super Fans say tastes like a mystery on a bun. I say the mystery lies in the Buddha Sauce, a concoction that came to life by accident, when Chris and Steve were trying to make a simple barbeque sauce. Accident or not, the Asian tang of the Buddha gives this burger an international flair, one complemented by the cheesy delight of the Signature Spread, a blend of cheeses, lemon juice, herbs, and spices. Pile on some traditional and not-so-traditional fixings, and you've got a burger so massive and messy that it'll find its way up your nose just as easily as it does your mouth.

Some burger 55 fans like to do things their own way, a process that creative whiz kids like Chris and Steve applaud. That's why they let you choose from a raft of traditional fixings, along with not-so-ordinary choices like Montreal smoked meat, grilled peaches, drunk caramelized onions, roasted garlic, pico de gallo, roasted corn, fried eggs, and eight types of cheese. Want more? Got more! Try one of 18 sauces, including 55's Signature Spread, Mole Sauce, Buddha Sauce, Roasted Garlic Sour Cream, Balsamic Reduction, or Curry Sauce. Whoa, daddy!

Sides are as creative as the mains, so don't be surprised if the guy next to you is chowing down on Fries and Curry Sauce or Sweet Whisky Onion Rings. And if he happens to hop up on the roof of the place and starts jamming with a local band, don't ask questions, just join the party. It's just another day at burger 55, where the unexpected is par for the course.

You don't have to be a Super Fan to recognize that the creations at burger 55 are world-class . . . even if you have to enjoy your meal outside in the Okanagan sun!

Hot & Spicy Burger

Makes: 6 burgers

If you've got asbestos lining your gullet, then take a chance on this burger, which tops its patty with enough heat variations to make Beelzebub himself go running for a cold shower. There's the Hot & Spicy Sauce, a blend of sour cream, cream cheese, banana peppers, cayenne pepper, hot sauce, and hot pepper flakes. Then there's the Wasabi Cream, which combines wasabi powder with sour cream, mayo, ginger, and lemon. Not enough? Pile on pico de gallo, banana peppers, and jalapeño Havarti, smashed avocados, and barbeque sauce, and you've got a burger that makes you sweat . . . while still managing to stay darn tasty.

Wasabi Cream

2 cups sour cream

⅓ cup + 2 tablespoons mayonnaise

6 tablespoons dried wasabi powder

2 teaspoons minced fresh ginger

2 tablespoons lemon juice

1 tablespoon salt

Hot & Spicy Sauce

3 cups cream cheese, softened

1 cup sour cream

½ cup hot sauce

1½ tablespoons hot pepper flakes

1 teaspoon cayenne pepper

½ cup banana peppers

½ teaspoon salt

Patties

2¼ pounds ground chuck beef

1 teaspoon salt

1 teaspoon black pepper

Assembly

6 cracked wheat buns

6 tablespoons banana pepper rings, chopped

6 tablespoons pico de gallo

6 tablespoons shredded jalapeño Havarti cheese

½ cup smashed avocados

¾ cup barbeque sauce

Lettuce

Bermuda onions, sliced

Wasabi Cream

In a small bowl, combine the sour cream, mayonnaise, wasabi powder, ginger, lemon juice, and salt. Slowly whisk in 6 ½ tablespoons water, to reach desired consistency. Cover and refrigerate until ready to use.

Hot & Spicy Sauce

In a bowl, combine cream cheese and sour cream and mix until smooth. Stir in hot sauce, hot pepper flakes, cayenne, banana peppers, salt, and 1½ tablespoons water, scraping the edges of the bowl frequently until the mixture is well combined and smooth. Cover and refrigerate until ready to use (will keep in the fridge for up to 2 weeks).

Patties

In a large bowl, combine the beef, salt, and pepper. Divide the mixture into 6 even portions and, using your hands, form into patties. Cover and refrigerate for at least 30 minutes.

Assembly

Preheat barbeque to medium-high.

Grill the patties for 5 minutes per side, or until desired doneness.

Meanwhile, split the buns and toast on grill. Once the buns are toasted, spread the hot & spicy sauce on the bottom halves along with the wasabi cream. Top with banana peppers, pico de gallo, and jalapeño Havarti. Spread the top halves of the buns with the smashed avocados and BBQ sauce and top with the lettuce and sliced onions. Top the bottom halves with cooked patties. Add the top buns and serve immediately.

You Put WHAT on a Burger?

Remember when you were a kid and just putting ketchup and mustard (*gasp!*) on your burger was an adventure? Well, you're all grown up now, and it's time your burgers matured, too. All you need to do to hit the big time is order one of these bad boys, which feature insanely delicious combinations that could only be built by the hand of experience.

LAMB AND LOBSTER BURGER

Big Fish, Calgary, AB

Surf and turf, foothills style. Ground lamb and juicy hunks of lobster meat are just the beginning in this complex taste sensation.

PORK SCHNITZEL BURGER

Cheese Curds, Dartmouth, NS

Is it a burger or is it comfort food? No matter what the definition, the crispy pork schnitzel topped with Cheddar, peameal bacon, and caramelized onion jam will warm your heart and stomach.

HOT & SPICY BURGER

burger 55, Penticton, BC

You'll need some extra taste buds in your mouth to appreciate the sheer variety and depth of heat this baby packs. From chilies to wasabi to banana peppers, it's all in there.

ATLANTIC LOBSTER BURGER

Flavor 19, Sydney, NS

The patty's the thing here: lobster meat, mashed Yukon Golds, diced veggies, and panko. Covered with mango salsa, it's a mind-boggler and mouth-buzzer of the highest order.

JERK CHICKEN BURGER

Boogie's Burgers, Calgary, AB

Oh yeah, it's hot. But Boogie's jerk chicken is so much more, and one of the best things ever slapped on a bun. Fill your water first.

THE RELIGIOUS HYPOCRITE

The Burger's Priest, Toronto, ON

Vegetarian? Not quite. Portobello mushroom caps are stuffed with a secret cheese blend before being breaded and deep-fried. Top with bacon . . . hypocritical, indeed.

THE BLACK & BLUE BURGER

The Bungalow, London, ON

A juicy beef patty is wrapped in a crispy coat of Cajun spices, then topped with blue cheese and a crispy onion ring. Insane? Maybe.

AUTOSTRADA BURGER

Motor Burger, Windsor, ON

Got a hankerin' for a sausage and a burger? You've come to the right place: a chipotle-rubbed sausage patty is topped with goat cheese, Motor Sauce, and apple-fennel slaw. Yum.

Chewies Steam & Oyster Bar

EST. 2011
2201 WEST 1ST AVENUE
VANCOUVER, BC · V6K 3E6
604-558-4448
WWW.CHEWIES.CA

Vancouver may not be known as a hotbed of authentic Creole cooking, but that's about to change. Chewies is not only the place to come ogle hot male waiters (I mean . . . the women tell me they're hot), it's also making a name for itself by serving up a bevy of bayou classics that even the most hard-core Cajuns adore.

Grab a seat at Chewies's counter and your eyes will be as delighted as your taste buds, as the crew moves with eerie synchrony in tight quarters.

Chewies gets its name from owner Richard "Chewie" Chew, a veteran of the Vancouver restaurant industry who longed to bring two of his great culinary loves—oysters and Creole cooking—together. When a friend introduced Richard to chef Tyrell Brandvold, Chewie had his man. Tyrell started cooking his way across the US as a teenager, and ended up in New Orleans, where he perfected his Creole craft. His Canadian wife lured him north of the border, and now Tyrell has the chance to explore New Orleans cuisine all over again, this time in one of the funkiest neighbourhoods Canada has to offer.

Chewies is an all-day eatery, but its brunch has become the stuff of legend in Vancouver's Kitsilano neighbourhood.

Tyrell's Braised Short Rib Hash is one of the best breakfast dishes I've ever eaten. The highlight of this masterpiece is the short ribs, which are seared at high heat to lock in flavour, then braised overnight with vegetables, herbs, red wine, and tomato paste. When the hash hits your table, it's a multi-layered delight that makes you happy to be alive: deep-fried Cajun home fries are the foundation, followed by a homemade black-eyed pea ragout. Then comes smoked Gouda, the pulled short ribs, and two perfectly poached eggs. This is one *serious* meal, people, so settle in.

N'awlins spice meets West Coast groove in Chewies's Southern Crab Cake Benny, which starts with an English muffin spread with avocado and chive oil. Then comes the party, meaning two red rock crab cakes spiked with jalapeños, lemon juice, Creole spices, and panko. Add a poached egg atop each and drizzle with Tyrell's special Cajun hollandaise sauce, and it's just like me: sweet but hot!

The brunch party at Chewies continues with the Breakfast Po' Boy (bacon, fried egg, lettuce, tomato, avocado, and Creole remoulade), Southern Fried Chicken and Waffles (buttermilk fried Creole chicken drizzled in honey butter on homemade waffles), French Quarter French Toast (coated with crushed roasted pecans), and Mushroom Benny (delicious mushroom ragout instead of ham). But make sure you leave space for Tyrell's traditional French Quarter Beignets, square doughnuts sprinkled with icing sugar and served with a side of chicory-infused caramel glaze.

Dinner is an equally authentic affair at Chewies. From starters like Creole Garlic Prawns to Coconut & Jalapeño Mussel Steamers, rest assured your taste buds will be tickled. Po' boys come in several variations. Gumbo and Jambalaya are a trip down South . . . without the humidity. Of course, there are always freshly shucked oysters to be had, if you're looking for an aphrodisiac.

That might be a bit dangerous with all these good-looking male waiters wandering around, so just focus on the food, ladies. Focus on the food.

Chewies's French Quarter Beignets are modelled after the traditional beignets that New Orleans' legendary Café du Monde has been serving for over 150 years.

This breakfast meal is as traditional as it gets, and is also the first grits dish I've ever eaten. For the uninitiated, Chewies' grits start out as coarsely ground white corn simmered in water for 20 minutes before being loaded up with butter, white Cheddar, and Parmesan cheese. Topped with poached eggs, it's a symphony of flavours, and the grits are perfect for soaking up all the delicious juices.

Grits

2 cups grits
½ cup grated Parmesan cheese
¼ cup shredded white Cheddar cheese
¼ cup butter
Salt

BBQ Shrimp

1 cup finely diced yellow onion
1 cup finely diced celery
¼ cup minced garlic
¼ cup chopped fresh rosemary
1 cup beer
1 cup shrimp stock
½ cup Creole tomato sauce
¼ cup Worcestershire sauce
1 pound large shrimp, peeled and deveined
Zest and juice of 1 lemon
2 tablespoons cold butter
Salt and pepper
Creole seasoning

Poached Eggs

Vinegar or seasoning of your choice (optional)
8 eggs

Assembly

3 to 4 green onions, sliced (optional)

Grits

In a saucepan over medium-high heat, combine the grits and 8 cups water and bring to a boil. Reduce heat and simmer for 20 minutes, or until the grits are soft. Stir in the cheeses and butter. Season with salt to taste. Remove from heat and set aside.

BBQ Shrimp

In a large greased skillet over medium heat, cook the onions, celery, and garlic, stirring occasionally, until the onions are translucent. Stir in the rosemary, then the beer, and simmer for 3 to 5 minutes, until the alcohol has been cooked off. Add the shrimp stock, tomato sauce, and Worcestershire sauce and simmer for 15 minutes. Add the shrimp and simmer for 3 to 4 minutes, or until cooked through. Add the lemon zest and juice. Stir in the butter. Season to taste with salt, pepper, and Creole seasoning. Remove from heat and set aside.

BBQ Shrimp & Grits with Poached Eggs

Makes: 4 servings

Poached Eggs

Bring a saucepan of water to a boil over medium heat. Add the vinegar or seasoning (if using) to taste. One at a time, crack 2 to 4 eggs into the water (poaching eggs can be tricky, so only cook as many eggs at one time as you comfortably can) and simmer over medium-low heat for 2 to 4 minutes (depending on desired softness of yolk). Using a slotted spoon, transfer the eggs to a plate lined in paper towel. Repeat with remaining eggs.

Assembly

Divide the grits evenly among individual serving plates. Spoon the shrimp with sauce over top. Arrange 2 poached eggs on each serving and sprinkle with the green onions.

The Dish Bistro and the Runaway Spoon

EST. 1996

12417 STONY PLAIN ROAD NORTHWEST

EDMONTON, AB · T5N 3N3

780-488-6641

WWW.THEDISHANDSPOON.COM

Two things run deep in my blood: love of food and love of music. Both come home to roost at The Dish Bistro and the Runaway Spoon, where accomplished musician and chef Michael Verchomin creates delicious old-school comfort dishes with the flair of a maestro. Couple Michael's genius with owner Carole Amerongen's life-long love of everything foodie, and you've got the score for a restaurant that leaves its customers singing its praises.

The Dish and Spoon ("The Dish" is the café portion of the business; "The Runaway Spoon" the catering division) got its start back in the mid-1990s, when Carole caught wind of a favourite deli closing its doors and plunged fork-first into her dream of owning a restaurant. Edmonton native Michael joined the fold a few years later, and the two have been making beautiful music ever since. And if you happen to hear the occasional jazz riff ringing out of the kitchen, fear not: that's just Michael's way of celebrating *his* two great loves.

Michael started me off with his Cherry

Hey, a fella's gotta make a living, right? Busking with Michael Verchomin isn't just for fun . . . it's profitable to boot!

Balsamic Short Ribs, which are so tender, hearty, and flavourful that I almost swore. The Alberta beef ribs are hand-selected by Michael and cut to his exacting specifications, then seared in their own fat to retain flavour. Then the ribs are braised for hours in beef stock spiked with sour cherries, ginger, garlic, fennel, and balsamic vinegar, and left overnight to soak up a stupid amount of flavour, then served with garlic mashed potatoes and fresh sautéed seasonal vegetables. You'll love the combination of almost-crispy exterior and fall-off-the-bone tenderness.

Comfort food gets an unexpected twist with Michael's Deep Dish Sweet Potato Shepherd's Pie, which starts with a sautéed blend of ground beef, vegetables, herbs, spices, and portobello mushroom fins (which add a rich, earthy flavour) in The Dish's signature beef stock. This rich foundation is covered with a piped blend of white and sweet mashed potatoes, then baked and topped with fried sweet potato chips and purple yam chips. Like most of Michael's creations, it's a symphony of flavours, one that will leave you savouring every bite.

Michael hits the high notes with every item on The Dish's menu, including the Gourmet Mac & Cheese (a locals' favourite overflowing with Asiago, Cheddar, and Gouda cheeses), Wild Mushroom & Feta Pasta (chunks of portobello mushrooms and crumbled feta in rosemary cream sauce), and Swiss Shrimp Melt (served open-faced on a soft German bun bubbling with Swiss cheese). The Mango Curry Chicken Wrap is lunch with an Indian flair, combining grilled chicken with curried mango chutney, spinach, and tomatoes in a fresh tomato wrap. Pear & Cambozola Triangles are hand-held bites of indulgence, where flaky flatbread is topped with pears, caramelized onions, fresh thyme, and Asiago and Cambozola cheeses.

This kind of culinary inventiveness is a *du jour* affair at The Dish, and helps create an environment as inviting as it is fun. The energy is warm, the food is great, and the music is free. Sounds like a little slice of heaven to me.

Encore, maestro! Michael delivers a stunning performance with his Rustic Lamb Stew, which locals say is as hearty as it is flavourful.

Cherry Balsamic Short Ribs

Makes: 4 to 6 servings

Damn. If making people swear is your thing, try these stupidly delicious ribs. The secret is in the searing, which creates a crispy outside, the perfect complement to the tender goodness waiting beneath.

4½ pounds untrimmed beef short ribs

1 cup all-purpose flour

2 tablespoons canola oil

⅓ cup balsamic vinegar

1 small fennel bulb, diced

½ cup red wine

¼ cup pitted cherries

1 tablespoon honey

4 cups beef stock

2 garlic cloves

1 small onion, diced

½ teaspoon fennel seeds

1 bay leaf

Preheat oven to 325°F.

Trim any excess fat from the ribs. Dust the ribs with flour.

In a large heavy-bottomed pot over medium-high heat, heat the oil. Sear the ribs on all sides until browned. Add the vinegar, fennel, wine, cherries, honey, stock, garlic, onion, fennel seeds, and bay leaf and stir to combine. Bring to a boil, then transfer to the oven and cook for 3 hours.

Remove the pot from the oven and transfer the ribs to a plate. Strain the sauce through a fine-mesh sieve (discard solids). Return the sauce to the pot and cook over medium heat until reduced by half.

To serve, divide the ribs among the serving plates and top with the sauce.

Hearty Lamb Stew

Makes: 6 to 8 servings

Scoring high on the hearty scale is The Dish's lamb stew, a classic built around cubes of rich lamb that have been browned with fresh rosemary, then braised in beef stock. Add onions, tomatoes, and chunks of sweet and white potatoes, and you've got a rich blend perfect for warming your innards on a blustery Edmonton afternoon.

2 pounds leg of lamb, trimmed and cubed
¼ cup olive oil
1 tablespoon minced garlic
1 tablespoon chopped fresh rosemary
Salt and pepper
1 small onion, cut into ½-inch dice
1 carrot, roughly chopped
1 can (28 ounces) crushed tomatoes, with juice
½ cup white wine
4 cups beef stock
1 potato, cut into 1-inch dice
1 sweet potato, cut into 1-inch dice

Preheat oven to 325°F.

In a large bowl, toss the lamb with the oil, garlic, rosemary, and salt and pepper.

In a large oven-safe pot over medium heat, brown the seasoned lamb on all sides. Add the onions and carrots and sauté until the onions have browned. Add the crushed tomatoes and wine and cook, stirring occasionally, until reduced by half. Stir in the beef stock. Cover, transfer the pot to preheated oven, and cook for 1 hour.

Add both kinds of potatoes and cook until the lamb and potatoes are tender, an additional 1 to 1½ hours.

Serve stew with warm, crusty bread.

EE Burritos

EST. 2003
102 AVENUE P S
SASKATOON, SK · S7M 2W1
306-343-6264

Saskatoon is known for many things, but you can bet your bottom burrito that Salvadoran food is not one of them. Until now, that is. Because it only takes one trip to EE Burrito to be converted to the Central American side of life, thanks to chefs and owners Kathleen Lipinski and Manrique Medrano, who are committed to homemade freshness and serving up tamales so big that customers have dubbed them a "lunch box in a banana leaf."

Opened by a husband-and-wife team back in 2003, EE was purchased by Kathleen and Manrique, who have been slowly phasing out the Tex-Mex elements of the menu and introducing more traditional preparations for their ever-growing customer base. Eager diners flock here for a Latin American twist on comfort food in a lively and welcoming atmosphere, where everyone feels like part of *la familia*.

A haven of Salvadoran delights in the middle of our great country, EE Burritos is an integral part of Saskatoon's cultural menu.

And nothing says Salvadoran deliciousness more than Kathleen's pupusas, a ridiculously authentic dish of moist and tender cornmeal pancakes stuffed with a variety of delicious fillings and fried on the flattop. The Mixed Pupusa Platter features pupusas filled with cheese, refried beans, and chicharrón, which is ground pork sautéed with veggies. The Loroco Pupusas are filled with creamy cheese and loroco, a Central American herb reminiscent of green pepper. All pupusas are served with pupusa salsa, and cortido, a Salvadoran coleslaw. You'll love the soft warm cakes, which manage to walk the fine line between soft and crispy.

All in the family! Manrique and Kathleen are committed to pleasing their ever-growing customer base, and do so with a tantalizing variety of Central American tongue-pleasers.

Manrique showed me the fine art of tamale cooking, and what an art it is. His tamales start out as masa, a starchy corn-based dough laid out inside a banana leaf. (Sure, banana trees might seem like they're hard to come by in Saskatchewan, but not if you know where to look.) Then Manrique spoons in piles of tender chicken chunks that have been sautéed in homemade tomato sauce, followed by olives, chickpeas, vegetables, and hard-boiled egg. The giant log is then rolled in the banana leaf, wrapped in aluminum foil, and steamed. When finished, the leaf is peeled apart, and the tamale sliced open and covered in homemade salsa. *Dios mio!* I had no idea a banana leaf could be so flavourful, a perfect complement to the rich delights hiding inside.

For more Latin American happiness, try EE's Salvadoran Steak (a 10-ouncer topped with creamy cheese and pepper sauce) or Lemon-Tortilla Soup (served with freshly fried tortilla chips and a sprinkling of parsley). Mexican menu items include Mexican Shrimp (sautéed shrimp with jalapeños and a shot of tequila), Nachos Grandes (buried in shredded beef, chicken, or pork; melted cheese; tomatoes; chirimol salsa; black olives; and sour cream), and Tacos served on either soft or crisp corn tortillas with several meat fillings (pork marinated in bitter orange juice, beef in lizano salsa, and chicken in cumin and seasoned salt).

Saskatoon and El Salvador. North and south. Hot and not-so-hot. But in the end, they're not really that far apart, are they?

Pozole Rojo

Makes: 4 to 6 generous portions

Now, you might not think that a country with an average annual temperature of 73°F would need a hearty soup to warm the soul, but the Pozole Rojo does just that . . . and is perfect for a cold Saskatchewan afternoon. The soup starts with a homemade pork stock, to which Kathleen adds chunks of tasty pork, onions, garlic, herbs and spices, and meaty kernels of white hominy corn. Finished with shredded lettuce, sliced radish, onion, avocado, and a generous squeeze of lime, the Pozole is as tasty as it is rich in colour.

Pork

4 quarts pork stock (substitute chicken
   stock if needed)
3½ pounds pork (pork butt is best), cubed
12 large garlic cloves, finely chopped
2 medium onions, diced
5 sprigs fresh cilantro, chopped
2 bay leaves
2 tablespoons dried oregano
8 guajillo chilies
6 pasilla chilies
1 ancho chili
1 can (10 ounces) hominy corn
Salt and pepper

Garnishes

6 radishes, finely sliced
3 limes, halved
3 avocados, diced (optional)
1 head iceberg lettuce, finely sliced
1 medium onion, finely diced
Oregano (optional)

In a large pot over medium-high heat, combine the stock, pork, garlic, onions, cilantro, bay leaves, and oregano and bring to a boil. Reduce heat to medium and simmer for about 45 minutes, or until the meat is tender and cooked through (be careful not to overcook).

Meanwhile, place the chilies in a saucepan and add just enough water to cover them. Cook over high heat until the chilies soften. Remove from heat, strain the chilies (reserve cooking liquid), and set aside until cool enough to handle. Once the chilies have cooled slightly, remove and discard the seeds and stems (you might want to wear gloves). Transfer the chilies to a blender and add the cooking liquid. Blend on high speed until the mixture forms a smooth paste.

Once the meat is tender, stir in the prepared chili paste, corn, and salt and pepper to taste and bring to a boil. Boil for an additional 15 minutes, until heated through.

Ladle into serving bowls and top with your garnishes of choice. (If you have the patience, your soup will be more flavourful if you let it cool and then cover and refrigerate it overnight before reheating.)

El Camino's

EST. 2010

3250 MAIN STREET

VANCOUVER, BC · V5V 3M5

604-875-6246

WWW.ELCAMINOS.CA

Chef Jason Carr loves Latin American food, and couldn't be happier than when he's running El Camino's kitchen.

There was a time when feasting on delicious Latin American food meant long, expensive journeys to exotic locales. Since 2010, though, Vancouverites have had it easy. El Camino's brings Latin American street food to Vancouver in a lively, loud, and friendly environment that celebrates the simple-yet-delicious fare that makes the region famous. But be sure to leave your sombrero at the door, amigo. El Camino's is no stereotype, but a retro-funk joint that combines casual and hip without a sniff of pretense.

El Camino's is the brainchild of five partners who recognized that for all of Vancouver's culinary offerings, there was still a gap when it came to Latin American food. Now head chef Jason Carr is busy introducing a new generation of restaurant-goers to an entirely new food vocabulary, including such tongue-tempting delights as arepas, empanadas, and bocadillos.

Jason started me off with an arepa, the corn-flour-based love child of a pita and a pancake. These soft, warm pockets of love are South America's answer to takeout pizza, and are traditionally offered in countless varieties.

Also filling your hands at El Camino's are the bocadillo creations. Spanish for "small bite," bocadillos are sandwiches traditionally served on baguette-style bread, but you don't make a reputation for ingenuity by doing what everyone else does, now do ya? Here the bocadillos are served up on Asian bánh mì buns, which offer a thick, crunchy crust with a delightfully soft interior.

I had the Carne Guisada Bocadillo, which might mean "beef short rib sandwich" but sounds like the language of love to me. The sandwich begins with a massive hunk of beef that's rubbed, fried for texture, then braised with peppers, tomatoes, and in-house pilsner for as long as 6 hours. After the meat is pulled, it's topped with sweet caramelized onions, chimichurri sauce, arugula, and torched Spanish Manchego cheese. The beef is so tender it's almost illegal, and the chimichurri sauce adds a brightness and freshness that leaves your tongue longing for more.

Comfort food comes in all shapes and sizes, and El Camino's Lomo Saltado has a unique Peruvian twist. The dish is anchored by slices of marinated flat iron steak that are stir-fried at very high heat with peppers, onions, tomatoes, and garlic, then bathed in a lime juice– and soy-infused lomo sauce. Served either atop a bed of crispy, twice-fried french fries (Peruvian poutine!), or a mound of jasmine rice, the Saltado is a complex combination of juicy meat and crispy vegetables, and the lime kicks you right where you need it.

Other traditional offerings at El Camino's include empanadas, pastry turnovers available in meat or vegetarian options. Tacos are served on soft white corn tortillas in several varieties. The Pescado Taco is filled with fried Baja cod, tangy pickled red onion, smoked chili slaw, and chipotle crema. The Pollo Taco may look and sound simple, but the hunks of buttermilk roasted chicken, pico de gallo, chimichurri aïoli, and lettuce are mysteriously delicious.

So cancel that ticket to Lima, my friends . . . assuming you're just going for the food, that is. Come to think of it, there's no Machu Picchu in Vancouver, but El Camino's is just as memorable.

One of chef Jason's menu favourites, the Lomo Saltado, is Peruvian poutine, without the cheese. You'll love the tangy zip of the lime.

Gambas Arepas

Makes: 5 servings

At El Camino's, the Gambas Arepas are Fan Fave *numero uno*. They start with a ball of arepa dough flattened and fried on the flattop grill before being charbroiled for a few seconds, then surgically sliced to reveal its delicate interior. Into this pocket chef Jason Carr stuffs a generous portion of shrimp fried with paprika and homemade red salsa, along with fresh arugula and smoked paprika mayo. This crispy, creamy corn pillow left me wanting more.

Salsa

½ cup canned diced tomatoes, with juice
1 tablespoon chopped fresh cilantro
¼ teaspoon lime juice
¼ teaspoon minced garlic
¼ teaspoon sugar
Pinch of ground cumin
Pinch of chipotle powder
Pinch of anchovy powder
Pinch of smoked paprika
Salt and pepper

Smoked Paprika Mayonnaise

⅓ cup mayonnaise
½ teaspoon smoked paprika

Arepas

2 cups white corn flour
Pinch of salt
2 tablespoons olive oil, divided
½ pound shrimp
1 bunch of arugula

Salsa

In a bowl, combine the tomatoes, cilantro, lime juice, garlic, and sugar. Add the cumin, chipotle powder, anchovy powder, and paprika. Season with salt and pepper to taste. Set aside.

Smoked Paprika Mayonnaise

In a bowl, combine the mayonnaise and smoked paprika. Set aside.

Arepas

Preheat oven to 400°F.

Place the corn flour in a bowl. Add a pinch of salt and 1½ cups water. Using your hands, mix until a dough forms.

Roll the dough into 5 even balls. Using your hands, form arepas by flattening each ball into the shape of a hamburger patty.

In a skillet over medium heat, heat 1 teaspoon oil. Fry 1 or 2 arepas at a time, flipping once, until golden brown on both sides. Remove from heat and transfer arepas to a baking sheet. Bake arepas in preheated oven for 12 minutes. Remove from oven and set aside.

Add the remaining oil to the skillet and heat over medium heat. Sauté shrimp until they turn pink and are cooked through. Stir in prepared salsa and heat through. Remove from heat.

Using a butter knife, cut a small pocket in the middle of each arepa. Spread prepared mayonnaise inside to taste. Stuff each arepa with shrimp mixture and arugula. Serve.

Fiesta Mexicana Restaurante y Cantina

EST. 2011

793 NOTRE DAME DRIVE

KAMLOOPS, BC · V2C 5N8

250-374-3960

Mexico might be the #1 tourist attraction among British Columbians, but once-yearly trips at Spring Break don't always satisfy hunger pangs that occur much more frequently. Luckily for Kamloopsers (Kamloopsites? Kamloopsians?), there's Fiesta Mexicana, which brings the taste of Mexico home, thanks to owners Rodd Cruikshank and Liz Lujan, and wacky chef Alberto "Beto" Vazquez, who is as fun-loving as he is talented.

As delicious as it is, Fiesta Mexicana owes its existence to a bit of serendipity. In 2001, Rodd and Liz were all set to move to Liz's native Mexico, when a deal to sell their tapas bar fell through. The two decided that if they couldn't go to Mexico, they would bring Mexico to Kamloops. A few months of renovations later, Fiesta Mexicana was born: a light, friendly, and fun place to enjoy authentic south-of-the-border cuisine. From the bright colours, adobe accents, and Mexican music, the place has the feel of an authentic Mexican cantina.

If Rodd and Liz are the creative minds behind Fiesta Mexicana, then chef Beto is its lifeblood. Originally from Guadalajara, Beto is a seasoned restaurateur, having opened his own hot dog and burger joint in Mexico at the ripe ol' age of 16. His experience and passion are evident in every dish he creates, especially his world-class Enchiladas Poblanas. This complex taste sensation starts with three corn tortillas stuffed with chicken and buried under Jack cheese. Then comes the complex part, the Mole Poblano Sauce, which contains dozens of ingredients, including chili peppers and melted chocolate. Served alongside Mexican rice and

"Beto" Vazquez is a patient man, enduring the occasional outburst from overzealous TV show hosts who can't help but break into song after eating his food.

homemade pico de gallo, the enchiladas are mysteriously delicious. I love how the sweetness/bitterness of the chocolate accents the rest of the dish's flavours.

Asada Zacatecas is also served with corn tortillas, but don't let Beto see you try to fill them with the hefty meat-and-veggie creation on your plate. This is no taco! Instead, the tortilla is meant to be eaten alongside the mound of fried homemade chorizo, tender slices of steak, and grilled onions intermingled with Beto's secret blend of spices. Heck, you can even use the tortilla to scoop your refried beans, mixed greens, pico de gallo, or guacamole. Just don't fill it!

Fiesta Mexicana's menu is a tribute to classic Mexican favourites of all shapes and sizes. Tacos are a-plenty. Try the California Fish Tacos, three flour tortillas filled with grilled shrimp or tilapia and topped with lettuce and cheese and served with rice, pico de gallo, and creamy chipotle sauce. They've also got quesadillas, of which the Tocino-Pollo (grilled chicken and bacon) is a personal favourite. Fajitas are represented, too, including the notable Aire, Tierra, y Mar Fajitas, a sizzling enterprise of chicken, steak, and shrimp. If you're daring, still hungry, or just plain adventurous, end your meal with Deep-fried Ice Cream. It's a classic way to finish off a visit to Mexico . . . even if you never left Kamloops.

Enchiladas Poblanas are a bestseller at Fiesta Mexicana, and the Mole Poblano Sauce is a complex blend of more than three dozen ingredients.

Burrito Guadalajara

Makes: 4 burritos

Chef Beto Vazquez wants to fill up plates and stomachs, and he wants to fill you. And if anything fits the bill on both fronts, it's the Burrito Guadalajara, which stuffs the biggest flour tortilla I've ever seen with grilled chicken, homemade chorizo, Mexican rice, and refried beans. Beto covers it all in a warm blanket of cheese sauce and fresh pico de gallo. If this is how people in Guadalajara eat all the time, someone call a doctor!

Pico de Gallo

6 tomatoes, finely chopped
2 red onions, chopped
Leaves from 1 bunch of fresh cilantro, finely chopped
2 teaspoons salt
1 teaspoon garlic powder

Cheese Sauce

4 cups milk
5 cups shredded Monterey Jack cheese
¼ cup canned jalapeño, drained
½ teaspoon garlic powder
½ teaspoon salt

Burrito Filling

1 tablespoon oil
¾ cup sliced chicken
¾ cup chorizo sausage

Assembly

4 flour tortillas (12 inch)
4 cups cooked rice
4 cups refried beans

Pico de Gallo

In a bowl, combine the tomatoes, onions, cilantro, salt, and garlic powder. Set aside.

Cheese Sauce

In a small saucepan, bring the milk just to boiling. Slowly stir in the cheese until melted and well combined.

In a bowl, combine the jalapeño, garlic powder, and salt. Add the jalapeño mixture to the cheese sauce and mix well.

Burrito Filling

In a skillet over medium-high heat, heat the oil. Cook the chicken and sausage until both are well done. Add ¼ cup of pico de gallo and cook, stirring occasionally, for 5 minutes.

Assembly

Lay the tortilla on a flat work surface. Mound 1 cup of rice and 1 cup of refried beans along centre and top with the chicken and sausage mixture and pico de gallo to taste. Fold up the burrito (bottom first, then fold in sides, overlapping) and warm in a 350°F oven for 5 minutes. Transfer the burrito to a serving plate and pour ¾ cup of cheese sauce over each, followed by the remaining pico de gallo.

Highlevel Diner

EST. 1982

10912 88 AVENUE NORTHWEST

EDMONTON, AB · T6G 0Z1

780-433-0993

WWW.HIGHLEVELDINER.COM

t was the year *Thriller* was released. The Commodore 64, too. Prince William was born, Olivia Newton-John's *Physical* rocked the charts, and The Great One still wore Oilers orange and blue. Well, in addition to all these cultural landmarks, 1982 was special for one other reason: it's the year Edmonton's Highlevel Diner was born. And though lots has changed in the world in the past three decades, there's one thing you can count on: the Highlevel's world-class cinnamon buns are true to their original recipe . . . and taste as good as ever.

Started by a group of young, enthusiastic people who worked together at a local eatery and believed in the idea of giving Edmontonians great comfort food at fair prices, the Highlevel Diner has never veered from its founders' ideals. Even the building's exterior and dining room are virtually unchanged from the way they appeared more than 30 years ago, proof that some things do get better with age.

Just ask Kim Franklin. Kim is the only original owner still left, and knows that homemade diner food never goes out of style. That's why she's happy to have chef Debbie Parker running the kitchen. Almost always found with a smile on her face, Debbie is as passionate about food as she is about loving life. Debbie started her food career in her early 20s, eventually landing at the Highlevel, where her passion for delicious comfort food melded perfectly with the Highlevel's ideals.

And what a relationship it's been! I love all of Debbie's creations, especially her Spinach Pie (spanakopita), which weighs in at more than a pound per piece! Debbie says the key to good spinach pie is working fast with the phyllo, but the piles of spinach, feta, herbs, and spices have something to do with it, too! An item on the Highlevel menu since Day 1, the spanakopita is crispy, buttery, and packed with Mediterranean flavours.

When Edmontonians vote for their favourite food, the Highlevel is always at or near the top of the list, thanks to the inspiration of Debbie Parker . . . and her underage assistants.

Like any good diner, the High-level does burgers well, and there are several options for eager customers. Debbie whipped up a Ural Burger for me, which comes with its own legend. Apparently, the recipe comes from the grandmother of one of the original owners, who carried it across the Ural Mountains into Bulgaria. When the extended family immigrated to Canada, the recipe came too. Tales or not, the Ural is delicious, a blend of ground beef, onions, bread crumbs, eggs, olive oil, hot pepper sauce, vinegar, and red pepper. Served with the Highlevel's homemade ketchup, it's delicately seasoned and huge on flavour. And the homemade ketchup is off the hook.

The Highlevel's interior is virtually unchanged since it opened its doors more than three decades ago, with hanging stained-glass decorations that send splashes of colour across the room.

Ready for dessert? If you're like any of the thousands of customers who bang on the High-level's doors on a regular basis, you'll be looking for the Cinnamon Buns, which devotees say outstrip every other cinnamon bun on the planet by sheer girth alone. The buns start as 8-ounce discs of dough that are rolled into thick ropes, dipped in melted butter, then rolled in a blend of brown sugar and cinnamon. These buns are truly miraculous: sweet but not overly so, with a warm, chewy centre that makes any morning better. The Bread Pudding is also a local favourite, no doubt due to the fact that they use cinnamon buns in place of bread.

The Highlevel does its diner heritage proud with a huge and varied menu, which includes its many themed daily specials. Mondays are for Fish & Chips; Tuesdays for Turkey, and Sundays for Prime Rib. But the most popular night of all here in Edmonton is Ukrainian Thursdays, where the Ukrainian Platter is king. Thanks to the heritage of other chef Adam Stoyko, this plate features a host of authentic dishes, including homemade perogies, sweet or sour cabbage rolls, garlic sausage, and a bowl of mouth-watering borscht with dill sour cream.

Classic. Authentic. Old school. Delicious. It's all the vocabulary of the Highlevel Diner, a time-less classic that doesn't need gimmicks to impress.

Black Bean Chili

Makes: 4 to 6 servings

This is the heartiest vegetarian chili you'll ever lay your taste buds on. Black beans are mixed with a special paste that packs in the heat, then served with homemade cornbread, to wow everyone at the table.

2 cups dried or canned black beans
1 dried ancho chili
1 dried chipotle chili (or more to taste)
4 tablespoons ground cumin
2 tablespoons dried oregano
2 tablespoons sea salt
2 tablespoons black pepper
3 garlic cloves
½ cup olive oil
1 cup diced onion (¼-inch dice)
2 cans (14 ounces each) diced tomatoes, with juice
1 can (14 ounces) crushed tomatoes, with juice
Guacamole
Cheddar cheese
Sour cream

If using dried beans, place the black beans in a bowl and cover with water. Set aside to soak overnight. Drain the beans and rinse under cool running water. In a saucepan of boiling water, cook the beans until tender, 30 to 45 minutes. Drain and set aside.

If using canned beans, rinse under cool running water and drain. Set aside.

To reconstitute the ancho and chipotle chilies, place in a bowl and cover with boiling water. Set aside to soak until soft and plump. Drain. Remove the stems and most of the seeds from the peppers (you might want to wear gloves when handling the chipotle).

In a food processor fitted with a metal blade, blend the prepared chilies, cumin, oregano, sea salt, black pepper, and garlic. With the motor running, slowly add the oil to make a thick paste.

In a medium heavy-bottomed pot over medium heat, combine the onions, prepared chili paste, tomatoes, and prepared black beans and simmer until the onions are soft.

Serve with cornbread or bread for dipping, and guacamole, Cheddar cheese, and sour cream.

Sandwich Substitutes

Hey, I love a good *sandgweech.* From po' boys to cheesesteaks, hoagies to grilled cheese, I'm an out-and-out sandwich guy. But sometimes you just gotta put the bread aside and fill your hands with something a little different. Luckily, there are tons of options out there, thanks to the ingenious folks at these joints.

HALIBUT FRITTERS

Smitty's Oyster House,
Lower Gibsons, BC

How is it that these bite-size poppers disappear so damn quickly? Must be the fish. Or the beer-tempura batter. Wait, maybe it's the homemade malt syrup and tartar sauce.

CANDY APPLE POGOS

Murray Street, Ottawa, ON

This ain't no carnival food, people. Homemade sausage wrapped in cornmeal batter, deep-fried, and topped with homemade apple jelly. Fun food on a stick!

GRANDMA'S FRIED CHICKEN

The Wallflower Modern
Diner, Vancouver, BC

I love you, Grandma. And your fried chicken, too. Crispy, moist, and drizzled with chicken gravy. Damn good.

SAUSAGE ROLLS

Rocket Bakery and Fresh
Food, St. John's, NL

Like no sausage roll you've ever had before. Ever.

LAMB POPSICLE ROGAN JOSH

The Smokin' Buddha, Port
Colborne, ON

OK, so you probably gotta eat the rice with a fork, but the grilled lamb chops are finger food of the finest order, especially when surrounded by rogan josh sauce.

LOBSTER BURRITO

Icehouse, Montreal, PQ

Icehouse stuffs this burrito with a heap of lobster sautéed in a medley of exotic ingredients topped with corn, grilled onions, shredded cheese, and even some potato chips. Big. Good.

TACOS

La Taqueria Pinche Taco
Shop, Vancouver, BC

Twelve fillings, each more delicious than the last, and one of four salsas on two soft corn tortillas. You'll never go back to a fast-food joint again.

REGGAE WRAP

Soulyve, Orangeville, ON

Fill a crispy-yet-soft roti with shredded jerk chicken, tropical salsa, Cajun mayo, and a mound of traditional fixings, and you're smiling . . . Jamaican-style.

Hilltop Diner Cafe

EST. 1946

23904 FRASER HIGHWAY

LANGLEY, BC · V2Z 2K8

604-514-9424

WWW.FACEBOOK.COM/HILLTOPDINERCAFE

WWW.HILLTOPDINER.CA

When I think old-school diner, I think three things: homemade desserts, hefty portions, and a fun-loving family behind it all. Well, that's exactly what you get at the Hilltop Diner, a Langley institution that has been keeping people smiling for more than 70 years. Whether it's the gravy-drenched open-faced meat loaf sandwich, the creamy Flapper Pie, or the loving banter between the owners and their children, the Hilltop is a classic in every sense of the word.

Family comes first at the Hilltop. Sisters Sandie Parley and Andrea Zaiser-Hearty own the joint, but that's not where it ends. Sandie's son Kris is the creative and generous head chef, while Andrea's daughter Jami works as the Hilltop's second cook. The result of such deep connections is a diner that doles out the love as generously as it does its portions. Pull up a stool at the counter or take a seat at a cozy table. Trucker or movie star (the Hilltop's also served as a movie set), grandparent or teen, you're going to feel at home.

And what better way to say "welcome" than with the Hilltop's massive Open-Face Meat Loaf Sandwich, a stupidly delicious mountain of toast, meat, mashed potatoes, and gravy that made me feel warm all over. I've eaten meat loaf that tasted like it was made out of particle board, but Kris's is a tribute to everything moist and tender in the world.

Everyone plays their part at the Hilltop. Andrea's daughter Jami Zaiser-Hearty is the diner's second cook and a master of meat loaf.

Not sure what his secret is, but the beer gravy sure didn't hurt. As one fan said, the gravy is so good, you could pour it on a shoe and eat it!

Kris is a genius in the kitchen, as his Grilled Apple Fritter breakfast sandwich attests to. Part dessert, part breakfast of champions, the open-faced sandwich replaces the tired ol' notion of a bun with a deep-fried apple fritter as its foundation. Buttered (!) and grilled on the flattop, the fritter is piled high with a homemade pork sausage patty, fried egg, and Cheddar cheese. Heck, let's make it a dessert and drizzle some sweet glaze all over it. Served with a mound of potato hash, it's a Catucci way to start your day.

The Hilltop's culinary inspiration certainly doesn't end with Kris. Sandie is a gifted baker and, as the sign says, the Hilltop is famous for its pies. Sandie has a slice to suit every visitor, and her pie know-how knows no bounds. The Pecan Pie is served with a scoop of ice cream, a bit of classic diner heaven. The Sour Cream Raisin Pie boasts an old-school mélange of raisins and sour cream at its custardy heart. Oh, and in case there's any space left after a massive meal, the pieces are, um, *gigantic* (you thought, perhaps, they wouldn't be?).

Like any good diner, the Hilltop's menu has burgers and sandwiches galore. The Monte Cristo Sandwich has been served for decades at the Hilltop, a mountain of roasted ham and turkey under gooey mozzarella cheese between three slices of French toast. The Anarchist Burger is a heart-pounding combination of two beef patties, a thick slice of ham, fried egg, cheese, and three onion rings . . . all smothered in a meaty bath of homemade chili. The Chicken and Swiss Avocado Burger sounds healthier, but certainly isn't short on size or taste.

It's all just another day at the diner at the top of the hill, where old school comes home.

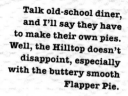

Talk old-school diner, and I'll say they have to make their own pies. Well, the Hilltop doesn't disappoint, especially with the buttery smooth Flapper Pie.

Sour Cream Raisin Pie

Makes: One 10-inch pie

Co-owner Sandie Parley is a master pie maker, and her expertise spans every type imaginable, from the traditional tart-yet-sweet combination of the Sour Cream Raisin Pie to the Flapper Pie, a Canadian prairie classic.

Crust

1 10-inch pie crust

Filling

6 eggs, separated
3 cups raisins
2 cups sour cream
¾ cup sugar
1½ teaspoons ground cinnamon
1 teaspoon salt
1 teaspoon baking soda

Meringue

¼ teaspoon cream of tartar
5 egg whites (from filling)
¼ cup sugar

Filling

Crack eggs over one medium bowl, carefully separating the egg yolks from the whites and placing yolks in separate medium bowl. Set aside.

In a saucepan over medium heat, combine the egg yolks, raisins, sour cream, sugar, cinnamon, and salt and bring to a boil. Cook, stirring constantly, for about 5 minutes, until thickened (it should be the consistency of pudding). Remove from heat and stir in the baking soda. Pour the mixture into the pie crust. Refrigerate for 1 hour.

Meringue

Using a stand or hand mixer on medium speed, sprinkle the cream of tartar over the reserved egg whites and beat until frothy. Increase the speed to high and slowly pour in the sugar. Continue mixing until stiff peaks form.

Assembly

Preheat oven to 400°F.

Spread the meringue over top of the pie filling. Bake in preheated oven for 7 to 10 minutes, or until the meringue is lightly browned. Remove the pie from the oven and serve immediately.

Crust

1¼ cups graham crumbs + extra for topping

⅓ cup margarine, melted

Filling

5 cups 2% milk, divided

4 tablespoons cornstarch

5 eggs, separated

¼ cup sugar

2 tablespoons margarine, melted

1 teaspoon vanilla extract

Meringue

¼ teaspoon cream
of tartar

5 egg whites (from filling)

¼ cup sugar

Flapper Pie

Makes: One 10-inch pie

Crust

Preheat oven to 350°F.

In a bowl, combine the graham crumbs and margarine. Pour the mixture into a 10-inch pie plate and, using a spatula, press the mixture over the bottom and sides of plate to form an even crust. Bake in preheated oven for 10 minutes, or until the crust starts to brown. Remove from oven and set aside to cool.

Filling

In a bowl, combine 1 cup milk and the cornstarch (make sure there are no lumps). Set aside. Crack eggs over one medium bowl, carefully separating the egg yolks from the whites and placing yolks in separate medium bowl. To bowl with egg yolks, add the margarine and vanilla and whisk until combined. Set aside.

In a large saucepan over medium heat, combine the remaining 4 cups milk and the sugar and cook, stirring frequently, so milk doesn't burn. Stir in the cornstarch mixture and cook, stirring constantly, for 5 minutes, until thickened. Whisking constantly, bring mixture to a boil (it should thicken). Remove from heat and pour filling into prepared pie crust. Set aside.

Meringue

Using a stand or hand mixer on medium speed, sprinkle cream of tartar over the reserved egg whites and mix until frothy. Increase the speed to high and slowly pour in the sugar. Continue mixing until stiff peaks form.

Assembly

Preheat oven to 350°F.

Spread meringue over top of the pie filling. Crumble remaining graham crumbs over top. Bake in preheated oven for about 15 minutes, or until the meringue is lightly browned. Remove from the oven and set aside until cooled completely, then refrigerate for at least 2 to 3 hours before serving.

Holy Grill

EST. 2003
827 10 AVENUE SOUTHWEST
CALGARY, AB · T2R 0A9
403-261-9759
WWW.HOLYGRILL.CA

I n my world, a restaurant is really, really good if I take the opportunity to visit it every time I'm in town. This is the Holy Grill, one of my fave eateries in Canada, where delicious and inventive food is made even better by the trio of fun-loving brothers that run the place. Nick, John, and Andrew Yee are a self-proclaimed "food-slinging octopus," one that keeps Calgarians happy with wildly popular breakfasts and panini lunch specialties.

Though the Yee boys now have more than a decade of experience under their collective belts, it wasn't always that way. Back in 2003, 23-year-old Nick and 25-year-old John took a leap of faith and opened Holy Grill; baby brother Andrew joined the team a few years later. Sure, early patrons were sometimes confused by their unique name (is it a restaurant or house of worship?), but once word spread about the heavenly dishes being created inside, a legend was born. Now the Holy Grill is a gathering place, one where customers genuinely feel at home.

Breakfast comes in many forms at the HG, but one of my favourites is the South Beach Benny with Bacon and Smash-browns: English muffins topped with Roma tomatoes, poached eggs, thick-cut bacon, a hefty dose of homemade hollandaise sauce, and slices of avocado. Nick will tell you the avocado and tomatoes will keep you lean for those days on South Beach; I say the avocado adds a creamy experience you won't soon forget.

But what makes the South Beach a truly mind-blowing experience is the Smash-browns, crispy pieces of local potato love that are blanched in the deep-fryer before

I love these guys! Andrew (left), Nick (middle), and John (right) move with a synchronicity in the Holy Grill's kitchen that borders on precognition.

being seasoned with salt and pepper, then shoved in a bag where they're unceremoniously beaten with a tenderizing mallet. Then it's back into the fryer again before being served piping hot. How good are they? Stupid good! Other breakfast offerings at the HG are the Pacific Benedict (smoked salmon eggs Benedict) and Farm House Panino (that's right, paninO . . . as in *one*), which melds bacon, eggs, Cheddar cheese, and fresh tomatoes together in gooey harmony on fresh flatbread from a local Lebanese bakery.

We interrupt this chapter for an impromptu Italian lesson: one paninO, two paninI. That's right, people, there's actually no such word (in Italian, anyway) as paniniS. Arcane matters of language notwithstanding, the Yee boys are renowned for their panini, which come in many a form at the Holy Grill. Fill it with fish, fowl, pork, or veggies; no matter what, you're in for a tasty treat.

John stuffed me silly with the appropriately named Italian Panino, which sees sundried tomato cream cheese smeared on a flatbread, then filled with a bounty of meats from my homeland, including capicollo, calabrese, and Genoa salami. Follow this with thick slices of provolone cheese and Roma tomatoes, then grill it all together in the panini press and you've got everything that's good in the world right in your hands. I could eat this crispy-yet-gooey delight all day!

If Italian's not your thing (and I can't imagine why it wouldn't be, but I digress), don't despair: panini come in many forms at the Holy Grill. The Mr. Chicken features 8 ounces of bird, three cheeses, creamy avocado, and homemade roasted red pepper mayonnaise. The Pacific is a delicious alternative to bagels, piling a mountain of smoked salmon, cream cheese, spinach, red onions, artichoke hearts, and capers on the mammoth bread.

Like any good joint, the Yee boys don't overlook the side dishes. All of the Holy Grill's panini and burgers are served with hand-chipped fries, golden sweet potato chips, or, my personal favourite, the beet root chips. I love the earthy taste of beets any time, but deep-fry them, season them, and serve them up with homemade garlic, chili, and sour cream sauce and you've made a friend for life, baby! Why can't all veggies be deep-fried?

That's a question I'll leave to the Yee brothers. After all, when three men can feed hundreds of eager customers quickly and deliciously and still keep a smile on their faces, it's obvious that they know what they're doing. See ya soon, boys!

Hot Chick Panino

Makes: 1 panino

Did someone say sprawling? At a whopping 12 inches, Holy Grill's Hot Chick Panino is stuffed with two eggs, capicollo, provolone, tomato, and spicy hot peppers. Don't forget to press and grill to a golden crisp.

Special equipment: panini grill

2 large eggs
5 to 6 slices capicollo
1 pita (12 inch)
1 tablespoon soft cream cheese (optional)
4 slices provolone cheese
2 tablespoons banana pepper rings
1 Roma tomato, sliced
Salt and pepper
Spinach leaves (optional)
Hot sauce (optional)

In a greased skillet over medium heat, fry the eggs until the yolks are mostly cooked (over medium to hard). Set aside.

In a greased skillet over medium heat, fry the capicollo for 1 minute per side. Set aside.

Place the pita on a clean work surface. Spread with cream cheese (if using) and arrange a row of provolone cheese slices across the centre. Top with the banana peppers and then the slices of fried capicollo. Arrange the cooked eggs on top. Add 5 to 6 slices of Roma tomato and season with salt and pepper to taste. Top with the spinach and/or a drizzle of hot sauce (if using).

Fold the left and right edges of the pita about 2 inches toward the centre. Using both thumbs, fold the bottom lip of the pita up to cover the top of the ingredients in the middle. Fold once more to close the top.

Heat panini grill to 420°F.

Place the folded pita on the grill and press down firmly. Grill for 4 to 5 minutes. Remove the panino from the grill and, using a sharp knife, cut diagonally lengthwise.

Kawaii Crepe

EST. 2009
201-99 OSBORNE STREET
WINNIPEG, MB · R3L 2R4
204-415-2833
WWW.KAWAIICREPE.CA

You gotta hand it to the crêpe. I mean, there are few other food items so dang versatile that they work equally well at breakfast, lunch, dinner, *and* dessert. What, you want *more* surprises from this deliciously thin yet surprisingly hearty pancake? Here's one: they're not just from France! In fact, Kawaii Crepe specializes in *kurēpu*, a Japanese take on a classic European dish. And with enough fillings to satisfy every taste from Tokyo to Brittany to, well, Winnipeg, it's easy to see why the place has become the city's go-to crêpe destination.

But it's not just the food that draws the droves to Kawaii Crepe. The place is funky and fun, and more reminiscent of Japanese anime than a traditional Canadian café. The brightly painted walls are lined with red leather couches to offset the modern white tables and red-and-white chairs opposite them; a giant bulletin board—Love Notes & Sweet Thoughts—allows customers to share random positive thoughts with their fellow crêpe devotees.

All this love is the brainchild of owners Candy Lam and Phil Salazar, who became huge fans of Japanese crêpe shops on their many trips overseas. Sensing a gap in the local food scene (really, there isn't an overabundance of Japanese crêpe shops in Winnipeg?), they took a leap of faith despite the fact that neither had any restaurant experience.

Experience schmexperience . . . this place rocks! Head artista RJ Kowalchuk might have a degree in computer science, but he's Kawaii's resident crêpe

RJ Kowalchuk is a fun-loving and carefree guy who doesn't take himself too seriously . . . unless you're talking about his *kurēpu*, that is.

master. And master them he does, beginning with the Pump Up the Yam, a crispy-yet-tender creation stuffed with moist hunks of seasoned chicken, chunks of baked yam, caramelized onions,

Change of clothes not provided. A sure sign that someone has just demolished a Big Feast crêpe is a shirt stained with house-made barbeque sauce.

and peppercorn mayo, then drizzled with maple syrup. It's a mind-blowing combo of sweet and savoury at the same time—yummy!

Other savoury offerings include the Big Feast, a Kawaii classic that fills the crêpe with a hefty portion of pulled pork alongside a mound of crunchy homemade coleslaw. I love the combination of the soft, savoury meat and the vinegary punch of the crispy slaw. Good? Stupid good! The Ninja Crêpe is a stealthy amalgam of juicy chicken, red peppers, cilantro, and house-made peanut sauce. The ninja part? The chili sauce hidden among the other fillings, ready to judo chop your taste buds. The Popeye is strong to the finish, with spinach, feta, and pesto. The Chickplease smears a generous schmear (see what I did there?) of homemade hummus on the crêpe, followed by red peppers and alfalfa sprouts.

If it's sugar you crave, buckle up, people. It's-a-Smore is a sweet sensation oozing with toasted marshmallows, chocolate-hazelnut spread, and graham cracker chunks . . . it's like camping, only without the tent. Or the mosquitoes. Or the sleeping-on-the-ground part. As with all Kawaii's creations, it comes in a convenient stand designed to hold the crêpe upright when your mouth needs a rest between bites. The Cheesecake Crêpe is filled with lemon cream cheese filling, mixed berry coulis, and graham wafers. Fans of creaminess and crunchiness will love the many textures of the Peanut Butter Cream Cheesecake Crêpe, which blends peanut butter cream cheese, house-made chocolate fudge, and cookie crumble into a ridiculously tasty mountain of hand-held goodness.

But be warned: with enough menu items to keep you going from dawn 'til dusk, Kawaii Crepe is one of those places you might find hard to leave. Having your gut filled with a ton of food won't help the situation either. But, hey, with so many cool vibes flowing, why would you wanna go anywhere else?

Uptown Crêpes

Makes: 4 to 6 servings

Kawaii's Uptown Crêpes pack a surprise punch that will leave your taste buds intrigued. Here, seasoned chicken breasts are topped with avocado and a house-made citrus-and-chipotle mayonnaise. For big-time appetites, the Big Feast Crêpes are guaranteed to fill even the emptiest of stomachs.

Chipotle Citrus Mayo

¾ cup mayonnaise

2 tablespoons concentrated frozen orange juice, thawed

1 tablespoon lemon juice

½ teaspoon lemon pepper

Chicken

6 large skinless, boneless chicken breasts

Salt and pepper

Crêpes

4 eggs

1 cup all-purpose flour

½ cup milk

2 tablespoons melted butter

Assemby

3 avocados, peeled, pitted, and sliced

Chipotle Citrus Mayo

In a blender on medium-high speed, blend all of the ingredients until smooth. Set aside.

Chicken

Season the chicken with salt and pepper to taste.

In a skillet over medium-high heat, pan-fry the chicken, turning occasionally, until cooked through. Remove from heat and set aside to cool slightly, then slice.

Crêpes

Combine all of the ingredients in a large bowl and stir well.

Heat a lightly oiled skillet over medium-high heat. Pour ½ cup batter into the skillet and tilt pan to coat evenly. Cook the crêpe for about 2 minutes, until the bottom is light brown. Loosen with a spatula, flip, and cook until the bottom is light brown. Transfer the crêpe to a plate, keeping warm. Repeat with remaining batter.

Assembly

Place a crêpe on a serving plate. Top with some avocado, then sliced chicken. Drizzle with sauce to taste. Fold crêpe over. Repeat with remaining crêpes, and serve.

Big Feast Crêpes

Makes: 8 to 10 servings

Special equipment: slow cooker

Timing note: pork needs 10 to 12 hours to cook

Pulled Pork

3 to 4 pounds pork butt, trimmed of fat

Salt and pepper

¾ cup apple cider vinegar

1 to 1½ cups barbeque sauce

Mustard Vinegar Coleslaw

7 cups finely shredded green cabbage
  (about 1 head)

1 cup finely sliced red onion

1 cup grated carrot

¼ cup white wine vinegar

2 tablespoons sugar

2 tablespoons whole-grain mustard

2 tablespoons mayonnaise

⅛ teaspoon salt

⅛ teaspoon black pepper

⅛ teaspoon cayenne pepper

Crêpes

4 eggs

1 cup all-purpose flour

½ cup milk

2 tablespoons melted butter

Pulled Pork

Season the pork with salt and pepper. Place in a slow cooker. Pour the vinegar over the meat. Cook on low for 10 to 12 hours, until tender. Transfer the pork to a plate and discard the liquid. Using two forks, shred the pork into small pieces. Return the shredded pork to the slow cooker. Add the barbeque sauce and stir well. Heat through.

Mustard Vinegar Coleslaw

In a large bowl, combine the cabbage, onion, and carrots.

In a small bowl, combine the vinegar, sugar, mustard, mayonnaise, salt, black pepper, and cayenne and stir well. Add the vinegar mixture to the cabbage mixture and toss until the vegetables are evenly coated. Cover and refrigerate for 20 minutes. Stir before serving.

Crêpes

Combine all of the ingredients in a large bowl and stir well.

Heat a lightly oiled skillet over medium-high heat. Pour ½ cup batter into the skillet and tilt the pan to coat evenly. Cook the crêpe for about 2 minutes, until the bottom is light brown. Loosen with a spatula, flip, and cook until the bottom is light brown. Transfer the crêpe to a plate, keeping warm. Repeat with the remaining batter.

Assembly

Place a crêpe on a serving plate. Top with some coleslaw, then pulled pork. Drizzle with barbeque sauce. Fold crêpe over. Repeat with remaining crêpes and serve.

Kekuli Café

EST. 2009
505-3041 LOUIE DRIVE
WEST KELOWNA, BC · V4T 3E2
250-768-3555
WWW.KEKULICAFE.COM

As gonzo as we Canadians may be for doughnuts, fried bread has been part of our national appetite for much longer. Enter bannock, long a staple for First Nations Canadians, and the cornerstone of the menu at Kekuli Café. Not satisfied with resting on the laurels of tradition, though, Kekuli ushers an ancient dish into the 21st century, courtesy of owner and self-taught chef Sharon Bond, whose passion for good food is as deeply rooted as her love of tradition. As the Kekuli boasts to its guests, "Don't panic . . . We have bannock!"

A proud member of the Nooaitch First Nation, Sharon learned to value fresh food and honed her creative cooking skills under the guidance of her father, a hunter and fisherman, and mother, a gardener and kind-hearted baker who often gave away much of what she baked. Yet as big as bannock was during Sharon's upbringing, she was hard-pressed to find it in restaurants. A loan from Aboriginal Business Canada and some considerable sweat equity later, the Kekuli Café was born. A decade later, the Kekuli is a community hub that offers delicious breakfasts and lunches, all centred on the traditional aboriginal bread in all its forms.

On the morning side of the menu is one of Sharon's most popular dishes, the Breakfast Bannock. This classic big-bite sandwich takes ham, bacon, or sausage, melted Cheddar cheese, and a fried egg and stuffs them between two pieces of freshly fried bannock. Bye-bye bagels!

When the lunch crowd hits, Kekuli Café is more than ready, taking traditional dishes and spinning them into exotic creations. The Buffalo Bannock Burger sandwiches a perfectly grilled quarter-pound buffalo patty between

If you need a bannock fix and feel the pangs of distress welling up inside your gut, fear not. You've come to the right place.

two deliciously crispy pieces of bannock and a mound of fixings. But what makes this dish so bright and imaginative is the homemade Saskatoon berry barbeque sauce that Sharon blankets it in.

Want some Mexican with your bannock? Then go for the Indian Taco, a classic aboriginal comfort food that Sharon and her friends grew up enjoying at area pow wows. Hard-to-find no more, the Indian Taco features a plate-size piece of fried bannock smothered with homemade chili, shredded iceberg lettuce, fresh homemade salsa, shredded Cheddar cheese, and a large dollop of sour cream.

Italy meets First Nations in the Bannock Indian Supremo Pizza, which starts with an 8-inch round of fried bannock as its crust, followed by tomato paste, homemade chicken or beef chili, a choice of fresh vegetables, and a generous smattering of shredded cheese. Yet unlike traditional pizza, the Supremo never sees the inside of an oven. Instead, it's grilled on a flattop until the cheese is melted and gooey.

So put your Boston creams away, people, and get traditional! Fried or baked, for breakfast or lunch, sweet or savoury, bannock is the answer to all your doughy needs. And if you find yourself too stuffed to finish off one of Sharon's miraculous creations, don't panic . . . Just call me!

Sharon Bond describes herself as ready for anything. I say she's warm and bubbly, a natural hostess and ambassador for the Nooaitch First Nation.

Berry Bannock Bread Pudding

Makes: One 8-inch pudding

Finish off your bannock fix with a heaping portion of Berry Bannock Bread Pudding, which combines the chewy delight of baked bannock with the creamy taste of homemade pudding and a stew of berries. Serve it with ice cream and chocolate sauce for a perfect marriage of hot and cold, creamy, and crunchy.

Berry Mixture

4 cups frozen mixed berries
¼ cup white sugar
2 cups fresh mixed berries

Bannock

4 cups all-purpose flour
1 cup whole milk
1 egg
1 tablespoon white sugar
1 teaspoon vanilla extract
½ teaspoon ground cinnamon
½ teaspoon ground nutmeg
3 egg whites
½ teaspoon cream of tartar
Turbinado, raw, or brown sugar
Dash of nutmeg
Ice cream
Chocolate sauce

Berry Mixture

In a large saucepan over medium heat, combine the frozen berries and sugar. Cook until the berries have thawed and sugar has melted. Stir in the fresh berries and heat until warmed through.

Bannock

In a large bowl, combine the flour, milk, egg, sugar, vanilla, cinnamon, and nutmeg. Set aside. Using a stand or hand mixer on high speed, beat the egg whites until frothy. Sprinkle in the cream of tartar and beat until stiff peaks form. Gently fold the egg mixture into the flour mixture until just incorporated.

Assembly

Preheat oven to 350°F.
Pour the berry mixture into an 8- × 8-inch cake pan and dollop the bannock mixture over top. Sprinkle with the turbinado sugar and a dash of nutmeg. Bake in preheated oven for 20 to 25 minutes, until golden brown. Serve with ice cream and chocolate sauce.

Buffalo Beef Stew

Makes: 4 to 6 servings

If you're lucky enough to hit Kekuli Café on a "wild Wednesday," warm your heart with owner Sharon Bond's ridiculously tasty Buffalo Beef Stew, which combines tender chunks of slow-cooked buffalo with a host of potatoes and vegetables.

¼ cup canola oil or olive oil
¼ cup butter
2 pounds buffalo stewing meat, cubed
Splash of red wine
2 onions, roughly chopped
2 garlic cloves, minced
4 cups beef stock
1 tablespoon Worcestershire sauce
2 tablespoons steak spice
A few sprigs fresh thyme and rosemary

1 bay leaf
4 medium carrots, sliced crosswise
4 medium potatoes, peeled and cut into chunks
4 celery stalks, diced
2 cups corn kernels (fresh or frozen)
2 cups peas (fresh or frozen)
Salt and pepper
2 tablespoons cornstarch

In a large skillet over medium-high heat, heat the oil and butter. Add the buffalo meat and cook, stirring occasionally, until browned on all sides. Add the red wine, onions, and garlic, and cook while stirring until the onions are translucent. Stir in the beef stock, Worcestershire sauce, steak spice, thyme and rosemary, and bay leaf and bring to a boil. Add the carrots, potatoes, celery, corn, and peas. Reduce heat and simmer until the vegetables are tender, 1 to 2 hours. Discard bay leaf. Season with salt and pepper to taste.

In a small bowl, whisk together the cornstarch and ¼ cup of water. While stirring, slowly drizzle into the stew, then continue to stir until desired thickness is reached.

Serve with freshly baked bannock or buns of your choice!

La Taqueria Pinche Taco Shop

EST. 2009
322 WEST HASTINGS STREET
VANCOUVER, BC · V8B 1K6
604-568-4406
WWW.LATAQUERIA.CA

There was a time in my life when salsa was salsa: the chunky stuff that came from a jar and tasted like ketchup. Luckily, there are guys like Marcelo Ramirez Romero and restaurants like La Taqueria to set me straight. Here I learned the subtle differences between authentic Mexican salsas, and that you don't need to bury tacos in mounds of fixings to make them *muy rico*.

Marcelo knows salsa . . . and not just because of his nationality. His family owns more than 20 eateries in Mexico, and he grew

Ambitious and personable, owner Marcelo Romero is on a mission to bring the best of Mexican street food to the people of Vancouver.

up working in them. When he moved to Vancouver in 2006, it didn't take long for him to see an opportunity: there were loads of Tex-Mex options, but few served the authentic cuisine he knew so well.

But La Taqueria doesn't just *taste* like the real Mexico, it looks the part, too. You can't help but be struck by the colourful mural of the Virgin Mary adorning the outside wall, or the turquoise counter covered in Mexican skeleton figurines celebrating the Dia De Los Muertos. So sidle up and place your order, then wait for your name to be called and your mouth to be wowed.

Décor aside, the beauty of La Taqueria is in its simplicity. Marcelo offers 12 fillings, served in a taco or a quesadilla (stuffed with creamy queso, authentic Mexican cheese). I started off with the De Cachete (braised beef cheeks), a Mexican street classic. Marcelo braises the cheeks for a few hours in a pot with water, white vinegar, and lots of herbs and spices. Then the beef is shredded so fine that it seems to melt into the two corn tortillas that serve as each taco's foundation. Why two tortillas? Marcelo says that on the streets of Mexico, the heat will sometimes cause one to crack; the second one is your backup.

Once your taco is ready, the salsa is up to you. Marcelo's salsa station serves up four varieties, but I opted for the mild salsa verde. The key to this deliciously fine brew is tangy tomatillos, which are blended with avocado, cilantro, garlic, jalapeños, salt, and lime juice. The salsa lends a light, bright bite (hey, that rhymes!) to the tender beef.

Pork tacos are also very popular in Mexico, perhaps none more so than the carnitas, which are native to Marcelo's hometown of Guadalajara. The pork is chopped into chunks and cooked in lard until golden brown. For added flavour (as if pork cooked in its own lard needs *anything* for added flavour), Marcelo tosses in pork skin and a caramel sauce for colour. When done, the pork gets the hand-shredder treatment, and is topped with home-made pickled red onions.

Native to Marcelo's hometown of Michoacan, Mexico, carnitas are a savoury delight accented perfectly by the tangy bite of the pickled red onions.

Salsa, you ask? For this baby, Marcelo tried to kill me with the Salsa de Chile de Árbol. But once I got past the fire in my mouth, I was able to appreciate the flavours of the salsa, not to mention the rich, juicy pork and tangy onions.

Vegetarians have their day at La Taqueria, and the Rajas con Crema is so good you'll never miss the meat. The foundation of this taco is charbroiled poblano peppers and corn, which get chopped and sautéed with onions and sour cream. Served on a taco covered with a layer of fresh queso, this handful of love is so creamy it needs no salsa. Which may be a good thing, since one of the two salsas left in Marcelo's armoury is a super-spicy habanero version that I wasn't going near (the other is a medium smoky chipotle that sounds *way* more manageable). Another meatless delight is the De Picadillo, which features sautéed ground tofu in a secret tomato-based sauce, originally made by Marcelo's great-grandmother, spiked with green and black beans, olives, capers, onion, and garlic.

Want more? Got more! Fillings, that is: Pollo con Mole (chicken with chocolate mole sauce), De Lengua (braised beef tongue), Pescado (grilled seasonal fish with pico de gallo), and Al Pastor (pork marinated in achiote chili and pineapple) offer enough variety to keep you coming back for a long, long time.

Which is exactly what you'll do.

Vegetarian alert! La Taqueria's Rajas com Crema is known to make meat-eaters drool, and no wonder. Smoky poblano peppers, corn, sour cream, and fresh queso pack a full-bodied flavour punch.

Asada

Makes: 5 to 6 servings

Who says the love of meat is just a Canadian thing? La Taqueria's Asada starts as a hunk of AAA flank steak. Grilled to perfection, it's served with chopped onion and cilantro.

Olive oil
Lime juice
½ onion, minced
1 garlic clove, minced
Ground cumin
Black pepper
1 flank steak (2 pounds)
½ onion, diced
Fresh cilantro, finely chopped
20 corn tortillas (6 inch)

In a small bowl, whisk together equal parts oil and lime juice. Add the minced onion, garlic, cumin, and pepper and whisk to combine.

In an airtight container or resealable bag, combine the prepared marinade. Add the steak and turn to coat well. Cover or seal and refrigerate for at least 30 minutes.

In a small bowl, combine the cilantro and diced onion. Set aside.

Preheat a barbeque or grill pan to medium high.

Grill the marinated meat (discard marinade) for 3 to 4 minutes per side. Using a sharp knife, cut the steak into thin slices. Set aside.

Warm the tortillas in a flat griddle, skillet, or "comal" (cast-iron plate). (You can speed up the process if you soak the tortillas in a vegetable oil and water mix.)

To serve, top four tortillas per person with grilled beef and cilantro and onion mixture.

Louisiana Purchase

EST. 1989
10320-111 STREET NORTHWEST
EDMONTON, AB · T5K 1L2
780-420-6779
WWW.LOUISIANAPURCHASE.CA

Edmonton might seem like the North Pole to people from New Orleans, but there's some fine southern cookin' being served up here in Alberta's capital . . . even if the bayou is about 4,000 kilometres away! From spicy jambalaya to crispy fried alligator, Louisiana Purchase is a Creole-lover's delight, and one that's been feeding locals, tourists, and rock legends like The Rolling Stones alike for more than two decades. Who says you can't get no satisfaction?

The roots of Louisiana Purchase stretch back to the early 1980s, when Dennis Vermette opened a Cajun-inspired restaurant in the West Edmonton Mall called Café Orleans. When people started lining up to get a taste of the Deep South, Dennis knew he was on to something, and Louisiana Purchase became a reality in the city's downtown core. Dennis set his sights on retirement in 2011, but he knew his baby was in good hands with the Halabi family, the new owners who have respected the restaurant's storied past while putting their own thumbprint on it.

That thumbprint includes Louisiana Purchase's Alligator Kebabs, a wildly popular dish that is forever etched into my cranium as another Catucci first. Coming straight from the South Saskatchewan River, the gator is cut into chunks, then marinated for several hours before being floured, deep-fried, and coated in co-owner and chef Rajaa Berro's sweet and spicy glaze. (That was a joke, people. There are no alligators in the South Saskatchewan River. Just piranhas.) Served on a skewer atop homemade Black Bean Mango Salsa, the gator tastes just like chicken. Only not really. Wait, maybe it does . . . Nope, no it doesn't. Aww, hell . . . it's good!

Who said I was just another pretty face? Rajaa Berro may be an expert in the world of Creole cooking, but he's met his match in Catucci when it comes to kebab-ery.

While the gator is a new-found delight, one of Louisiana Purchase's most popular old-time favourites is the Satisfaction Plate. This dish used to be called the Combo Plate, but when the Rolling Stones ordered it to go (happens all the time in Edmonton!) and raved about it, The Satisfaction it became. The Satisfaction starts with a massive mound of Jambalaya (local pork sausage, chicken chunks, cubes of ham, onions, and peppers tossed together with Rajaa's "tomato rice" and loads of Cajun seasonings), which itself is enough to fill most mortals. Serve it with a portion of Traditional Red Beans (a Cajun staple spiked with garlic sausage) and Shrimp Creole, and there's enough food and flavour there to keep the whole band happy.

The Louisiana Purchase is an exercise in the unique, and every dish is a taste of something you can't get anywhere else. The Flank Steak Po' Boy features blackened flank steak topped with fixings on a toasted bun, while the Salmon-Shrimp-Crawfish Boudin is a homemade sausage stuffed with sweet crawfish, tender salmon, tasty shrimp, and saffron-infused rice, then topped with a peppercorn cream sauce. Bouillabaisse is a Creole classic seafood soup brimming with crab, mussels, scallops, and shrimp.

Brimming. It's a good way to describe almost everything about Louisiana Purchase. Brimming with fun. Brimming with flavour. Brimming with famous musicians. And given the line-ups outside the joint on weekend, brimming with success, too.

It's survival of the fittest at Louisiana Purchase . . . and gators everywhere are scared.
Alligator Kebabs are tasty and tender, and definitely don't taste like chicken.

Blackened Blues Catfish

Makes: 4 servings

Bluesman Buddy Guy is a big fan of the Blackened Blues Catfish at Louisianna Purchase. And why wouldn't he be? Chef Rajaa Berro and crew bring in the freshest Louisiana catfish, then coat the fillets in a blackening spice mix before frying in butter. I love how thick and crispy the coating becomes, and the spice mix adds a bit of smokiness to the five-alarm blaze in my mouth. The fish is flaky and moist, and served with a touch of Creole sauce.

Cajun Blackening Spice

1½ teaspoons black pepper
1½ teaspoons garlic powder
1½ teaspoons paprika
1½ teaspoons dry mustard
1 teaspoon cayenne pepper
1 teaspoon onion powder
1 teaspoon white pepper
1 teaspoon salt
½ teaspoon ground cumin

½ teaspoon sweet paprika
½ teaspoon ground thyme
½ teaspoon dried basil
½ teaspoon ground oregano
¼ teaspoon cayenne pepper
1½ cups vegetable stock
1 can (26 ounces) diced tomatoes,
    with juice
1 can (14 ounces) crushed tomatoes,
    with juice

Creole Tomato Sauce

2 tablespoons vegetable oil
1 cup chopped sweet red pepper
½ cup chopped onion
¼ cup diced celery
1 tablespoon minced garlic

Catfish

4 boneless, skinless catfish fillets (6 to 8
    ounces each)
3 tablespoons butter

Cajun Blackening Spice

In a bowl, combine all of the ingredients and stir well.

Creole Tomato Sauce

In a saucepan over medium heat, heat the oil. Sauté the red pepper, onion, celery, and garlic for 4 minutes, until the onions are translucent. Add the paprika, thyme, basil, oregano, and cayenne and sauté for 2 minutes or until fragrant. Add the stock and diced and crushed tomatoes and bring to a boil. Reduce heat and simmer for 20 to 30 minutes, stirring occasionally. Set aside.

Catfish

Liberally coat both sides of the catfish fillets with the Cajun blackening spice.
Heat a large, heavy skillet over medium-high heat. Melt the butter, then carefully add the catfish fillets to the pan, being careful not to splash butter or burn your fingers. Cook the catfish for 6 to 8 minutes per side (use a metal spatula to gently flip), until the catfish is opaque.

Assembly

To serve, ladle the Creole tomato sauce onto serving plates, then arrange 1 catfish fillet on top of each plate. Serve with vegetables and potatoes.

Miura Waffle Milk Bar

EST. 2010
2521 MAIN STREET
VANCOUVER, BC · V5T 3E5
604-687-2909
WWW.MIURAWAFFLEMILKBAR.CA

Reader . . . meet waffle. Waffle . . . meet reader. What, you think introductions are unnecessary when it comes to the ever-popular waffle? Well, if you're expecting *this* waffle to be dripping in maple syrup, you've come to the wrong place. Here at the Miura Waffle Milk Bar, owners and chefs Dennis Miura and Jenny Kim-Miura are serving up waffle sandwiches—or "sandos," as they call them—of the most savoury and ingenious kinds, where the meat is baked right into the batter!

Jenny Kim-Miura and husband Dennis Miura have built a reputation on turning the everyday waffle into an ingenious work of culinary art.

Inviting, relaxing, and charming, Miura reflects the attitude and relationship of Jenny and Dennis, one of the nicest couples I've ever met. The joint was Jenny's idea; Dennis created the Asian-inspired menu. From the simple to the ridiculous, these two are turning heads and appetites to a food that's not just for breakfast anymore.

I mean, I guess you *could* eat the Bulgogi for breakfast, if chowing down on marinated barbequed beef at the crack of dawn is your thing. This Bulgogi Sando starts with Dennis's signature buttermilk waffle batter, which is piled high with the beef before being blanketed in another layer of batter. Once cooked, the waffle is cut in half, then filled with homemade kimchi, egg salad, and bulgogi sauce. This is a unique symphony of tastes that works together beautifully well, which explains why it's Miura's best seller.

Equally ambitious is the Wasabi Salmon Sando, house-cured salmon inside a waffle blanket. After cutting, the hefty halves (say *that* 10 times fast!) are stuffed with lettuce, fresh herbs, and in-house wasabi ranch sauce. You could call this creation fresh and light, but I'm not that restrained: I call it *freakin' delicious*! Thanks, Dennis, you've reinvented the waffle for those of us who thought it was only a breakfast food.

Fresh cured salmon is delicious enough on its own. Bake it in a waffle and serve with fixings and wasabi ranch sauce, and you're taking things to a whole new level.

Other savoury offerings at Miura include the Hoisin, anchored by hoisin pork sausage and filled with cilantro, cucumber, pickled radish, and carrots. The Kachan is Miura's spin on chicken and waffles, featuring ginger- and soy-marinated fried chicken, Asian slaw, and Thousand Island dressing.

Miura is a stay-all-day kinda place, so after feasting on your main, why not finish it off with more waffles, this time in the form of dessert? The Fruits & Cream is a sweet tooth's delight, where a layer of homemade pastry cream is slathered on a fresh waffle (Dennis's mom's idea), followed by seasonal fruit. The Banana Caramel features bananas, whipped cream, cookie crumbs, and caramel sauce. And if you're wondering where the milk bar comes in, it's a tribute to Dennis's flavoured milk addiction. From the Choco-Wasa Shake (dark chocolate with a hint of wasabi) to Mango Passionfruit Yoggy Milk (yogurt milk), there's something for all the cow-lovers in the audience.

Now, if you and your waffle need some time alone, I understand. After all, that waffle is a complex creature, and those tired old lines you try out on those *other* waffles ain't gonna work here, pal.

Want chocolate sauce on your waffle? Forget it. Owners and chefs Dennis Miura and Jenny Kim-Miura surprise with a homemade teriyaki sauce, followed by a mound of ice cream. And while it may strike many of us as strange to put teriyaki sauce on dessert, the two flavours work gorgeously together, not to mention the warmth of the waffle wrapped around the cool ice cream.

Special equipment: ice-cream maker
Timing note: ice cream must chill overnight

Vanilla Ice-Cream Base

1 cup half and half (18%) cream
1 cup heavy or whipping (35%) cream
5 egg yolks
¼ cup sugar
1 tablespoon vanilla extract

Teriyaki Sauce

½ cup sugar
½ cup mirin
2 tablespoons soy sauce

Assembly

4 to 6 waffles of your choice

Vanilla Ice-Cream Base

Prepare an ice bath (ice in a large bowl) and rest a smaller bowl on top.

In a small, heavy saucepan over medium heat, heat the half and half and heavy creams until bubbles form around the edges.

Meanwhile, in a small bowl, whisk together the egg yolks, sugar, and vanilla until smooth. Slowly add ½ cup of the cream mixture, whisking constantly so the eggs don't curdle. Gradually add the egg mixture to the remaining cream mixture, whisking constantly. Cook, stirring constantly, until the mixture coats the back of a wooden spoon. Remove from heat and pour into the bowl set on top of the ice bath. Cover and let chill overnight in the fridge.

Transfer the chilled ice-cream base to the chilled container of your ice-cream maker and process according to the manufacturer's instructions.

Transfer the ice cream to a chilled container and store in the freezer.

Teriyaki Sauce

Combine all of the ingredients in a small, heavy-bottomed saucepan. Simmer over medium heat for 10 to 12 minutes, until syrup-like in consistency. Remove from heat, transfer to an airtight container, and set aside to cool at room temperature.

Assembly

Place 2 scoops of homemade vanilla ice cream on one side of a waffle. Drizzle with teriyaki sauce and garnish with whipped cream. Cut waffle in half and sandwich together.

The Reef Restaurant

EST. 1999
4172 MAIN STREET
VANCOUVER, BC · V5V 3P7
604-874-5375
WWW.THEREEFRESTAURANT.COM

Here in fast-paced Canada we rarely enjoy the ultra-relaxed benefits of Island Time. But the Caribbean way of life (and dining) is alive and well at The Reef Restaurant, where you get dishes as deep and flavourful as Jamaican days are long, even when the thermometer dips below zero outside. Grab a seat, groove slowly to the funky reggae vibe, and chill with good eats, good peeps, and good times.

Good times are guaranteed when friendship is the foundation, and The Reef's owners Liz da Mata and Simon Cotton have been buddies since their teenage years. Both also have extensive restaurant experience, so when Liz decided to open her own restaurant, it only made sense that Simon would be at her side. Choosing the cuisine was a bit more challenging, but given Simon's family forays to Barbados as a youth and Liz's Brazilian and Portuguese heritage, the menu soon became clear. Add Ms.

The vibe of the Caribbean is alive and kicking at The Reef, where the walls are covered in beachy colours, brick, and metal siding.

Paulette (head chef Paulette Wedderburn) to the mix, and you've got the recipe for down-home deliciousness that Vancouverites have embraced with open arms.

Ms. Paulette's Curry Chicken Roti is an explosion of neatly wrapped island flavour. Boneless chicken thighs are soaked for 24 hours in a rich marinade highlighted by fresh thyme and jalapeños, then slow-cooked with a slew of spices and potatoes. The hearty stew makes a delicious meal on its own, but rolled in a soft and flaky roti, it's melt-in-your-mouth yumminess in every bite. Hot? A bit. But the richness of flavours is *so* worth the burn.

The Reef brings the best of North-meets-South with its Jerk Chicken Poutine. OK, so let's be honest here: *anything* tastes good when you serve it with fries, cheese, and gravy, but The Reef's jerk chicken is as rich, mysterious, and flavourful a topping as you'll find anywhere. The meat's marinated for like a hundred years before being baked, hand-shredded, and piled on the fries. Top with jerk gravy, and you'll wonder why nobody ever thought of doing this before.

The Reef makes variety an art form, and every dish on the menu is a tribute to the marriage between Liz and Simon's vision and Paulette's skill. Ackee & Saltfish is the national dish of Jamaica, and a Ms. Paulette favourite. The rich stew, an intriguing salty-sweet blend served with rice and homemade coleslaw, is brimming with hunks of salted cod, tomatoes, onions, jalapeños, and ackee fruit. Features change regularly, so you might be lucky enough to wander by when Dominica Beef (marinated and seared beef tenderloin topped with salsa verde) is on the menu. Or try the Mo-Ca Burger (covered in jerk gravy, grilled pineapple, and provolone cheese), Maracas Bay Mahi (zesty curry-lime fish with island chayote and apple slaw), or St. Bart's Lamb Shank (served in red coconut curry sauce) for a quick trip to the Caribbean.

And if you're surprised at the relaxed groove slowly washing over you as the scents of the Caribbean waft across your nostrils, settle in . . . you'll get used to it. Like so many regulars at The Reef, you may find yourself lingering for hours after your meal is done.

Ackee & Saltfish is the dish Ms. Paulette ate while growing up in Jamaica, and she's proud to bring it to The Reef. Take one taste of this classic Caribbean comfort dish and you'll be glad she did.

Island Thyme Chicken

Makes: 6 servings

Island Time meets fresh thyme in The Reef's Island Thyme Chicken, a super-marinated concoction bursting with the flavour of fresh thyme and oven-cooked in rich coconut milk. The chicken is served on a mound of creamy mashed potatoes alongside fresh vegetables, but I say anything cooked in coconut milk tastes like sunshine. That's Caribbean comfort, my friends!

Timing note: chicken needs to marinate for 24 hours

5 to 6 sprigs of fresh thyme
1 onion, sliced
3 garlic cloves, finely chopped
2 tablespoons grated fresh ginger
2 tablespoons honey
1 teaspoon seasoning salt (or to taste)
6 bone-in, skin-on chicken breasts
2 cans (14 ounces each) 18% coconut milk or coconut cream

In a resealable bag, combine the thyme, onion, garlic, ginger, honey, and seasoning salt. Add the chicken, seal, and turn to coat well. Refrigerate for 24 hours.

Preheat oven to 350°F.

Transfer the chicken (discard marinade) to a roasting pan. Pour over the coconut milk. Cover with aluminum foil and cook in preheated oven for 45 minutes to 1 hour, or until the internal temperature of the chicken registers 350°F on a meat thermometer.

Transfer the cooked chicken to a plate and cover, keeping warm. Pour the pan juices into a heavy-bottomed saucepan and cook over medium heat, whisking periodically, until it turns a cappuccino colour and is thick enough to coat the back of a spoon.

Pour the sauce over the chicken and serve with mashed potatoes and your favourite vegetables.

Breakfasts & Brunches to Boggle the Buds

Just because you're rubbing the sleep outta your eyes doesn't mean you can't get creative. After all, some of the world's greatest innovations were invented in the wee hours of the morning. Just don't ask me what they are. Either way, creativity is the calling card of these breakfasts, which will leave your taste buds deliciously confused.

PORK BELLY DUTCH BABY

Edgar, Gatineau, QC

Serve some rich pork belly in a pancake bowl, sprinkle with sugar and cinnamon, and top with homemade applesauce, aged Cheddar, and a river of maple syrup. Damn yummy, I say!

HANGOVER WAFFLE

Pressed, Ottawa, ON

OK, so I don't usually top my waffles with smoked beef brisket, Quebec cheese curds, and brown gravy. But after this . . . I just might.

PEROGY BENNY

Shine Café, Victoria, BC

Is it dinner or breakfast? Beats me, but a base of perogies topped with caramelized onions, candied bacon, sour cream, poached eggs, and chive hollandaise is so good you won't care.

SUCRÉ-SALÉ-CROUSTILLANT

L'Avenue, Montreal, QC

Say it in any language you want. This daring blend of panko-crusted brioche French toast, Jarlsberg-blanketed ham, poached eggs, and hollandaise sauce is a mind-blower.

GREEN EGG & HAM

Pie, Barrie, ON

What, you don't eat pizza for breakfast? Try smothering it with pesto, fresh mozzarella, roasted potatoes, bacon, spinach, and an egg. See?

BARQUE BENEDICT

Barque Smokehouse, Toronto, ON

Poached eggs on smoked brisket on cornbread, bathed in barbeque hollandaise sauce. Say what?

THE LOBOTOMIZER

Memphis Fire, Winona, ON

What? Bacon and Cheddar cooked in the pancake batter? I'm game, but only if you cover it with three over-easy eggs, more Cheddar, and hot sauce.

Shine Café

EST. 2004
1548 FORT STREET
VICTORIA, BC · V8S 5J2
250-595-2133
WWW.SHINECAFE.CA

People come and people go, but some make an impression on your heart that lasts forever. That's Barry Thomson, one of my favourite chefs, favourite restaurant owners, and favourite people in this great country of ours. Yeah, he's an amazing chef, whipping up adventurous brunch dishes that people line up for. But what makes Barry truly extraordinary is the love he puts into his food, his restaurant, and his life.

Shine Café is born of Barry and wife Lauren's love of breakfast. The couple had long made a habit of going out for their morning meal when they realized that they could do it better. They had years of restaurant experience, so when the right space became available, Barry and Lauren dove in and have never looked back. Now Shine boasts two locations in Victoria; Barry flits between the two and Lauren helps out while also tending to their growing brood at home.

Scottish mechanic-turned-restaurateur Barry Thomson is one of the warmest humans I've ever had the pleasure of meeting. LOVE that guy!

Shine is a benny lover's dream, in large part due to Barry's inventive take on hollandaise sauce (Shine has seven different kinds!). These sauces complement Barry's ingenious breakfast creations. And speaking of ingenious, eggs Benedict meets Thanksgiving dinner and fast food in the OOO Benny. This whirlwind of creative genius sees an English muffin topped with a couple slices of house-roasted turkey, followed by a blanket of a mashed roasted yam, onion rings (yes, onion rings), and maple hollandaise sauce. This is one of those dishes that has so many flavours going on, you need a moment to tease them all apart. For me, it tasted a little like Thanksgiving dinner, which always makes me smile.

Eggs Benedict is an art form at Shine, and the variety of choices is mind-boggling. One of the most stupidly delicious combinations is the Perogy Benny, which is an occasional visitor to

Barry's menus. No English muffin here, the PB uses four perogies as its foundation, followed by caramelized onions, candied bacon, and sour cream. This bed is topped with poached eggs and a loving blanket of chive hollandaise. The Tuscan Benny slaps local sausage atop an English muffin, then grilled tomatoes, melted Cheddar, a poached egg, and sundried tomato hollandaise.

If your world begins and ends with bennies, stop reading. The more adventurous among you will learn that Shine offers other breakfast fare, sandwiches, omelettes, salads and soups, and even burgers. Victoria is brunch-crazy, though, and it's these dishes that are begged for day after day. Robin's Hash (also named after a long-time Shine customer) is a scramble of eggs, Cumberland sausage, tomatoes, caramelized onions, and spinach served atop roasted potato hunks and sprinkled with feta cheese. The Scottish Breakfast (served at Barry's father's insistence) comprises two eggs, two slices of bacon, grilled tomato, Scottish black pudding, and potato scones.

If it's sweet you crave, there's always the Blueberry Pancakes, a simple recipe that customers rave about. The Eiffel Tower is a more involved affair, where French toast is piled high and layered with yogurt, fresh fruit, banana, and crunchy granola. That exotic taste you're detecting in your breakfast is the vanilla chai each slice of bread is dipped in.

That's how they roll at Shine Café, where sweetness is served up daily on the plate and in the heart, and inventiveness is always on the menu. If you don't believe me, just ask for Barry.

One customer was so loyal, he had a dish named after him—Robin's Hash.

Beckett's Benny (named after a former employee and life-long fan of Shine) starts with an English muffin, then gets sassy with sliced avocado followed by diced chicken that's been fried with red onions, roasted garlic, Cheddar cheese, and salsa. This gooey mess is topped with delicately poached eggs and a generous helping of chipotle hollandaise sauce. As if that weren't enough, Shine Café tacks on four wedges of delicious potato scones, which are warm, crisp, and unbelievably comforting.

Hollandaise Sauce

8 egg yolks
3 teaspoons lemon juice
Pinch of salt and pepper
2 cups unsalted butter, melted
¼ 7-ounce can chipotle peppers
⅓ cup brown sugar

Topping

1 teaspoon butter
4 cups diced roast chicken
½ red onion, thinly sliced
1½ cups salsa
2 teaspoons roasted garlic
2 cups shredded Cheddar cheese

Poached Eggs

2 tablespoons vinegar
8 eggs

Assembly

4 English muffins
Butter
1 avocado, peeled, pitted, quartered, and sliced

Hollandaise Sauce

In a medium glass bowl, whisk together the egg yolks and lemon juice until smooth.

Fill a saucepan with 2 inches of water and bring to a simmer. Set the bowl with the yolk mixture on top of the pan to create a double boiler, making sure that the water does not touch the bottom of the bowl. Whisk the egg mixture until the sauce is slightly thickened and doubled in volume (don't let it get too hot or the eggs will scramble).

Remove from heat and place the bowl on a rolled-up kitchen towel or other non-slip surface. Season with salt and pepper to taste. Whisking constantly, pour the melted butter into the egg mixture in a thin stream and whisk until it reaches a smooth, silky consistency. Keep warm until ready to serve. In a blender or using a mortar and pestle, blend chipotle peppers with brown sugar. In a medium bowl, combine 1 teaspoon of the chipotle purée and 2 cups of the hollandaise. Set aside.

Topping

In a large skillet over medium heat, melt the butter. Add the red onion and then chicken, and sauté for 2 minutes. Add the salsa and roasted garlic, then the Cheddar, and cook, stirring occasionally, until heated through and the cheese is melted. Keep warm over low heat.

Beckett's Benny

Makes: 4 servings

Poached Eggs

Fill a large saucepan three-quarters full of water. Add 2 tablespoons vinegar and bring to a full rolling boil over high heat. Reduce heat to medium-high and, using a slotted spoon, stir water in a circular motion. Gently crack the eggs into the middle of the saucepan and simmer until eggs are cooked to your liking. (For 8 eggs at a time, cook for 5 minutes for soft poached. Increase time for harder yolks.) Using the slotted spoon, transfer to a plate lined in paper towel.

Assembly

Split the English muffins in half, then toast and butter them. Place two English muffin halves on each serving plate. Divide the avocado evenly among the split English muffins. Top each with ½ cup of the chicken topping and 1 poached egg. Spoon over the chipotle hollandaise. Serve with potato scones (optional).

Skinnytato

EST. 2011
615 JOHNSON STREET
VICTORIA, BC · V8W 1M4
250-590-6550
WWW.SKINNYTATO.COM

I f love is the primary ingredient for a good meal, then Skinnytato has everything necessary to keep even the most discerning customers happy. Here Katherina Koper and her husband, Greg, serve up a host of heart-warming Polish-inspired dishes, each seasoned with the sweet flavours of two people who feel truly blessed to be living their dream.

Katherina and Greg left Poland in the early 1980s, settling in Edmonton in 1986. Though the couple longed to own their own restaurant, the right opportunity never presented itself. It wasn't until Greg made an impromptu trip to Victoria that their dream started taking shape. Katherina soon followed, and it wasn't long before Skinnytato was born. The place may be tiny—its six tables accommodate a whopping 17 customers—but it's big on taste, love, style, and comfort. What more do you need?

Glad you asked! When it comes to food at Skinnytato, I definitely, positively, absolutely need more of Katherina's insanely delicious Potato Pancakes. This quintessential eastern European fave starts with mounds of grated potatoes, fried on the flattop grill until they're addictively crispy. Wait! There's more: Katherina folds the giant pancake in half like an omelette, but not before she stuffs it to overflowing with Hungarian goulash, sauerkraut and Polish sausage; sauerkraut and mushrooms; or spinach and feta cheese. Served with four side salads, the dish will warm your heart on the coldest day. Hey, does it even get cold in Victoria?

Sweet and joyful Katherina Koper knows I carry my own fork, but her passion for feeding people was just too powerful to resist. And who am I to argue?

Potato Pancakes put Skinnytato on the map, and the dish doesn't disappoint. Get it with red cabbage salad, potato salad, coleslaw, and beet salad, and you've got the full Polish experience.

Tradition is also represented in Skinnytato's stupidly popular Perogies, which customers say taste unlike anything they've ever had. Katherina swears the secret is the freshness. I say it's the fillings, which range from traditional potato and bacon to blueberries. I was also lucky enough to fill my innards with the Polish Hunter's Stew, a hearty medley of sauerkraut and sweet white cabbage peppered liberally with hunks of cubed beef, pork, and Polish bacon. Served with a side of three potato pancakes, it's enough to make me start reciting famous Polish sayings: A good appetite needs no sauce . . . *Na zdrowie!*

Soup is a Skinnytato specialty, and it doesn't get any more traditional than Borscht, a tantalizingly simple mixture of puréed beets and onions that's served with a side of sour cream. Katherina's Pickle Soup is also in high demand; just don't ask her to reveal the secret of her recipe.

Want sweet? Got sweet! The Polish Apple Cake is a homemade apple cake topped with tangy Skinnytato plum sauce and a dollop of whipped cream. The Coconut Crêpes are also homemade, and topped with pineapples, ice cream, Skinnytato plum sauce, and whipped cream.

And if that ain't enough to stick to your ribs, my friends, then you need to see a doctor: there's something seriously wrong with your ribs.

Cabbage Rolls
Makes: 6 servings

If you're looking for a plateful of love (but wrapped in cabbage), then you've gotta try restaurateur Katherina Koper's Cabbage Rolls, which keep the good vibes going. Mounds of ground pork are sautéed with bacon, then mixed with cooked rice and sautéed onions before being rolled carefully in a boiled cabbage leaf. Covered in homemade tomato sauce and baked to perfection, the rolls are tender, but with a deliciously surprising bite.

1¼ cups rice
1 large head cabbage
1 tablespoon oil
2 large onions, chopped
½ pound ground bacon
½ pound ground pork
Salt and pepper
Tomato sauce or mushroom sauce

In a medium saucepan over medium-high heat, bring the rice and 3 cups water to a boil. Reduce heat, cover, and cook for 20 minutes, or until all of the water has been absorbed. Set aside.

Meanwhile, preheat oven to 350°F. Fill a large pot with water and bring to a boil over high heat.

Using a sharp knife, carefully cut the core out of the cabbage head (discard core). Place the cabbage head in the boiling water and cook for 3 minutes or until the leaves are easily pulled from the cabbage head, being careful not to overcook. Remove the pot from the heat, drain the cabbage, and set the cabbage aside for a few minutes to cool.

Carefully separate the cabbage leaves from the head. Using a sharp knife, remove the thick centre rib from each leaf. Transfer the prepared cabbage leaves to a cutting board or clean work surface.

In a skillet over medium heat, heat the oil. Sauté the onions until translucent. Remove from heat and set aside to cool.

In a mixing bowl, combine the cooled onions, bacon, pork, and cooked rice. Season with a pinch of salt and pepper. Using your hands, mix until well combined.

Lay 1 cabbage leaf flat on a clean work surface. Place a handful of the meat and rice mixture in the centre of the leaf. Fold one end up, fold the sides over the filling, and then roll the whole thing away from you to encase the meat filling. Place in a casserole dish or Dutch oven, seam-side down. Repeat with the remaining cabbage leaves and filling.

Cook in preheated oven for 1 hour or until the cabbage is tender and meat is cooked through.

Serve topped with warm tomato sauce or mushroom sauce.

Slickity Jim's Chat 'N' Chew

EST. 1997
3475 MAIN STREET
VANCOUVER, BC · V5V 3M9
604-873-6760
WWW.SLICKITYJIMS.COM

What is it with Vancouver and cool, funky eateries whose personalities are as big as their menus? Coincidence or not, this is one city to visit if you've got time on your hands, a hole in your leg, and a smile on your face. And for all the joints here that warm your heart, Slickity Jim's Chat 'N' Chew is the granddaddy of them all. A neighbourhood institution since 1997, Jim's is so well-loved that when the building burnt down in 2010, locals threw a benefit concert to kick-start its renaissance. The restaurant reopened less than a year later to an even greater flood of customers than the first time around.

Despite its name, there's no slick Jim waiting for you at Slickity's. Instead, the heart and soul of this place is Mike Zalman, a punkadelic dude who left Toronto and a purple mohawk behind with one thing on his mind: Vancouver. It didn't take long for Mike to make his mark in the food biz, delivering homemade soup to local restaurants. Business took off, and Mike realized that his destiny lay in something bigger. Firmly ensconced in the big city, Slickity Jim's pays homage to Mike's love of small-town diners, places where people come together for good company and even better food.

So you can't decide what to start with? No problem. Just order the Abstract Notion, a mood-dependent dish described as follows in Mike's menu:

The idea here is that the chef slings together a meal: a brash combination of myriad colours, flavours, textures, tastes, and varying degrees of what some may call the mad prophecies of the spiritually ridiculous.

With a décor that marries classic American diner with Old West saloon, Slickity Jim's is the kind of place people visit even if they're *not* hungry.

As funky as he is fun, owner and chef Mike Zalman is a beautiful guy whose positive energy can be tasted in every meal he makes.

Uh . . . I'll take one!

That's right, the Abstract Notion changes according to Mike's gourmet-inspired and slightly maniacal whims. For me, it was fresh salmon, bacon, garlic, white beans, jalapeño butter, fresh herbs, and a fig reduction sauce, all accompanied by a side of charbroiled asparagus. Abstract? Yep. Freakin' delicious? Oh, yeah! This is one abstract notion I can actually understand.

If you're one of those types who needs a little more predictability in your life, you can't get more concrete than the Double Belly Buster Pork Platter, a combo of tastes so varied that you won't know whether to focus on the main or the sides. Carnivore that I am, this guy went straight for the pulled pork, a pile of shredded glory that's marinated for *two days* before being smoked for half a day, pulled, then simmered to order in Slickity Jim's homemade Kansas City BBQ Sauce. Use the house-made cornbread to soak up the juices, and cool your mouth with a mound of tangy coleslaw.

But what made the DBBPP (quick . . . figure out what that stands for!) a one-of-a-kind experience was its Jalapeño Butter Beans: white beans cooked in white wine and drenched in jalapeño butter. I've never had beans like that: crispy on the outside, warm and soft on the inside, they are an official member of John Catucci's All-Time Favourite Side Dishes. In other words, when you make a *side dish* that good, you're doing something right!

Of course, there's lots going right in Mike's kitchen, which is why his joint is a *You Gotta Eat Here!* Fan Favourite. The Louisiana Gumbo (featuring Andouille sausage) is flavourful and spicy, but not blow-your-face-off hot. Chicken Pot Pie is as comforting as food gets . . . and it's served in a cast-iron pot! The Gobble Gobble Hey Hey is a smoked turkey sandwich served with caramelized onions and Asiago cheese, and melted together on focaccia. Gobble Gobble? That's the turkey. Hey Hey? That's the party in your head!

And OK, so there's a party going on in your head. Don't get self-conscious. Remember that Mike is a deliciously quirky guy, everybody is welcome, and fun is always on the menu.

The Louisiana Gumbo, a tribute to Mike's travels through the southern US, is a complex, slow-cooked treat that starts with a roux, okra, garlic, and ends with rich slices of Andouille sausage and diced chicken. Seasoned with cayenne pepper, thyme, and Worcestershire sauce, the mixture is then doused with diced tomatoes and simmered for at least 2 hours. Sassy!

Note: When cooking gumbo, keep in mind that there are no absolute formulas. If you like it spicier, add more spice. If you like it meatier, add more meat. The only element that the dish will fail without is time. The slow simmer is imperative to infuse the stew with flavour. Be patient, give it some love, and the results will be worth it. If you can't find Andouille sausage, substitute chorizo (but you didn't hear it from me).

¼ cup butter

¼ cup all-purpose flour

1 can (32 ounces) diced tomatoes, with juice

Vegetable oil

½ pound boneless, skinless chicken thighs, cut into ¼-inch dice

1 Andouille sausage (about 4 ounces), sliced

¼ pound fresh okra, cut into coins

1 sweet green pepper, chopped

1 stalk celery, chopped

1 medium onion, chopped

2 garlic cloves, finely chopped

1 teaspoon dried thyme

1 teaspoon sweet paprika

Dash of Worcestershire sauce

Dash of cayenne pepper

Dash of hot pepper sauce

1 bay leaf

Salt and pepper

Rice, cooked

Green onions, chopped

In a saucepan over medium heat, melt the butter. Add the flour and cook, stirring constantly, until the paste turns a light brown. Stir in the tomatoes and set aside.

Cover the bottom of a large pot with oil and heat over medium heat. Sear the chicken until lightly browned. Add the sausage and the okra, green pepper, celery, onion, and garlic. Cook, stirring occasionally, until the vegetables begin to brown. Add ¼ cup of cold water, tomato and roux mixture, thyme, paprika, Worcestershire, cayenne, hot pepper sauce, and bay leaf and simmer over medium heat for at least 2 hours.

Most important: taste, consider, and adjust the seasonings. Salt and pepper will brighten the flavour. Add slowly and cautiously.

Serve over steamed rice and garnish with green onions.

Smitty's Oyster House

EST. 2007
643 SCHOOL ROAD WHARF
LOWER GIBSONS, BC · VON 1V0
604-886-4665
WWW.SMITTYSOYSTERHOUSE.COM

For a Toronto guy like me, fresh seafood is something that comes by plane, train, or automobile. Right off the boat? That's the stuff of legend . . . or Smitty's Oyster House, that is. This is the place where you can quite literally watch the menu being loaded off the trawlers docked a stone's throw from your table, and where the word "fresh" takes on a meaning all its own. What else would you expect from a seafood joint situated in the same town where *The Beachcombers* was filmed?

Smitty's comes to us courtesy of Stafford Lumley, who moved to Gibsons with his family after a lengthy stint running Rodney's Oyster House in Vancouver. Though Stafford hadn't necessarily planned on continuing in the restaurant biz after the relocation, some things never leave our blood. So when he noticed a vacant building on the town's historic wharf, it wasn't long before he had teamed up with friend and co-owner Shawn Divers, and Smitty's sprung to life.

Here you'll find the seafood joint that all others want to be when they grow up. Though Smitty's is relatively young, the building dates to the 1940s, giving it a rustic feel few restaurants can match. High ceilings, massive timbers, and exposed brick serve as the perfect setting for chef Conor Lowe's marvellous creations, including the Oyster Po' Boy, a sandwich as massive as it is messy.

The Po' Boy starts with the biggest freshly shucked BC oysters you've ever laid eyes upon, which are panko-breaded and pan-fried before being stuffed inside a steamed bun on a bed of lettuce and thinly sliced Roma tomatoes. Topped with Conor's spicy remoulade and served with sweet potato fries, they're a spicy, crunchy, creamy bit of seafood heaven. Equally blissful is the Crab and Prosciutto Spaghettini, a summery delight brimming with crab-stuffed pouches of prosciutto in a light tomato basil sauce spiked with a goat cheese.

Dining becomes a spectator sport at Smitty's, where you not only get waterfront views, you also get to watch local fishermen and crabbers ply their trade.

Don't be fooled by the face of fear. I *love* lobster, but I prefer it served up as Lobster Roll Sliders or alongside Dungeness crab, just like they do it at Smitty's.

Fish-and-chips lovers will go wild for Conor's take on this classic with his Halibut Fritters: bite-size bits of crunchy goodness coated with a beer-tempura batter fried just long enough to crisp up the outside while leaving the inside soft and warm. The fritters arrive at your table atop a pile of fries, but it's the homemade malt syrup and tartar sauce that will leave your taste buds clamouring for more. These things pop so easily into your mouth, you'll be amazed at how quickly you plough through a plate of them.

The Chili Lime Prawns may be an appetizer, but customers love them so much, they order two and eat them as a main. Ahi Tuna Tartare is a zesty and fresh blend of tuna, avocado, and crispy fried shallots served with wasabi dressing. Crab Soup is the perfect alternative for people who've had their share of chowders. Goat Cheese Baked Oysters are drizzled with butter, shallots, lime juice, and sambal sauce, which give the dish a tangy zip with a little afterburner thrown in for good measure.

And OK, so the only way into Gibsons is by boat or plane. The best things in life aren't always the easiest to reach, and Smitty's Oyster House is *so* worth the trip.

Mussel and Chorizo Pappardelle

Makes: 4 servings

For a taste of nirvana, you've gotta try one of chef Conor Lowe's pasta dishes. I had the Mussel and Chorizo Pappardelle, which features spicy chorizo and the most gigantic mussels imaginable in a rich cream sauce.

Note: A pasta roller is required to make fresh pappardelle. Store-bought dried pappardelle can be substituted for fresh pappardelle.

Fresh Pappardelle (Optional)

2 large eggs
2 cups all-purpose flour
½ teaspoon sea salt
Olive oil

Mussel and Chorizo Sauce

2 pounds fresh mussels
1 teaspoon olive oil
3 to 4 raw chorizo sausages
¼ cup minced garlic
3 tablespoons minced shallot
¼ cup tomato paste
1¼ cups dry white wine, divided
1 handful of fresh basil leaves
⅓ handful of fresh tarragon leaves
2 to 3 cups heavy or whipping (35%) cream
   (depending on desired consistency)
½ cup chicken stock, warmed (optional)
Sea salt
Freshly cracked black pepper

Fresh Pappardelle

In a small bowl, whisk together the eggs and 1 tablespoon of water.

In a large bowl, sift together the flour and salt. Form a well in the centre and pour the whisked eggs into it. Using a wooden spoon, slowly combine the wet and dry ingredients to form a soft dough.

Sprinkle flour over a clean work surface. Turn the dough out of the bowl and, using your hands, knead for about 10 minutes, until smooth and elastic. (If the dough begins to tear, sprinkle with more flour.) Form a ball and wrap tightly in plastic wrap. Refrigerate for 1 hour to allow dough to rest.

Unwrap the dough and divide into 2 even pieces. Working with 1 piece at a time, begin to roll the dough through the pasta machine on widest setting. After rolling the dough through the machine once, fold it over widthwise and reroll it through the machine. Repeat this process, gradually reducing the setting on your pasta machine, until your dough is smooth and $\frac{1}{16}$ inch thick. Set the dough aside on a lightly floured surface as you are working.

Once all the dough is prepared, cut it into 10- to 12-inch-long strips. Using a rolling pin, roll the strips and recut so that they are 1¼ inches wide. Your dough is now fresh pappardelle.

Either hang to dry at room temperature overnight, then store in airtight container in a cool, dry cupboard, or cook for same-day use.

To cook, bring a large pot of salted water to a boil. Cook the pappardelle for 5 minutes, until almost al dente. Using a colander, drain the noodles. Immediately rinse under cold running water. Allow the noodles to drip dry for 1 minute and then toss with olive oil to coat. Set aside.

Mussel and Chorizo Sauce

Debeard the mussels and rinse under cold running water. Discard any that do not close when tapped. Set aside.

In a skillet over medium-high heat, heat the oil. Remove the casings from the sausage and crumble the meat into the pan. Cook, stirring often, until the meat is nearly cooked through. Add the garlic and shallots and cook, stirring frequently, until the garlic is fragrant, brown, and sticks to the pan. Add the tomato paste and stir to combine. Pour in 1 cup wine, using a wooden spoon to stir and scrape up any brown bits from the bottom of the pan. Tear the basil and tarragon leaves into pan and continue to cook, stirring often, until the alcohol has cooked off. Stir in the heavy cream and blanched pappardelle. Cook for 1 to 2 minutes, allowing the pappardelle to absorb the liquid in the pan.

Remove the pan from the heat. Add the chicken stock to thin sauce, if desired. Taste the sauce and season with salt and pepper to taste. When you are satisfied with the sauce, divide the sauced pappardelle noodles among the serving plates.

Return the pan to the stove and bring the sauce to a simmer over high heat. Add the mussels and remaining ¼ cup white wine. Stir, cover, and cook for 3 to 4 minutes, until mussels have opened (discard any that haven't). Remove the pan from heat and set aside, covered, for 2 minutes.

Divide mussels and sauce among the plates and serve immediately.

Smokin' George's BBQ

EST. 2010
UNIT #5, 4131 MOSTAR ROAD
NANAIMO, BC · V9T 6A6
250-585-2258
WWW.SMOKINGEORGESBBQ.COM

Quick, how do you know you've visited a great barbeque joint? Sure, it may be the mess all over your face, but for me it's the smell of smoke that permeates every fibre of your clothes. And that's exactly what I got with Smokin' George's. My suitcase was my own personal smokehouse for days after I visited the joint, and every time I opened it, I was reminded of the mind-blowing meals George Kulai serves up on a daily basis. Hey, Nanaimo . . . you've arrived!

Like most barbeque aficionados, George lives to smoke . . . meat, that is. You probably wouldn't guess that this is a guy who spent three decades in high-end cuisine before opting for the stability of a government job. But George and his wife, Lea Ortner, yearned for something more down to earth, and Smokin' George's was the answer. At this joint, food and good times play centre stage, and all pretense is checked at the door.

Happiness is served up every day at Smokin' George's, where Nanaimoites can sit back and be themselves in an unpretentious setting that makes everyone feel like family.

Smokin' George's looks every bit as casual as it sounds. Located in an industrial part of Nanaimo, it sports grey concrete floors, high ceilings, and exposed pipe work, all part of the couple's plan to make things as casual as possible. As for George, you'll never see him sporting one of those chef jackets he had to wear during his fancy-pants days. Now he rolls up his sleeves and gets down and dirty with smokin' twists on traditional comfort food.

And nothing spins those two realities like George's Loaded Baked Potato with Brisket, a teetering tower of deliciousness. The dish is built upon halved potatoes that are baked then deep-fried for a crispy-yet-tender texture. The potatoes are fork-fluffed, then doused in George's signature house barbeque sauce and buried under a mound of tender beef brisket that's been smoked for 12 hours. Add more barbeque sauce, some caramelized onions, and a three-cheese blend, and you've got a mountain of goodness that few baked potatoes can rival.

George's Crispy Chicken Soft Tacos also feature smoked goodness, but not necessarily where you'd expect it. The flour tortillas are filled with crispy fried chicken chunks that have soaked in buttermilk for a full 48 hours, making them just about the most tender things you've ever shoved in your face. Things get über-tasty with the Smoked Corn Salsa, a zesty mélange featuring hunks of smoked corn and lime. Throw in a mustard-based barbeque sauce (George's take on Carolina Gold Sauce), and you've got one great taco.

Come to think of it, almost everything at George's is mind-blowingly good, from Deep-Fried Dill Pickles to Mom's Smokin' Pit Beans. BBQ Ribs are massive side ribs big enough to feed a family of cave people; Crispy Mac Cheese features deep-fried balls of comfort goodness. Or go totally off the wall with George's Pulled Pork Poutine, and you'll see why people get addicted to this place after only one visit.

Just don't try to keep your addiction a secret, OK? Your clothes will tell the tale of where you've been.

George never set out to serve tacos at his barbeque joint, but customer demand pushed him to create this masterpiece of crispy fried chicken on a fresh tortilla.

Pulled Pork Lasagna

Makes: 6 servings

Pulled pork and barbeque sauce . . . in lasagna? Sorry, Nonna, but I have to admit, this is terrific! I mean, pulled pork on anything is delicious, but sandwich it between lasagna noodles, tomato sauce, and a three-cheese blend, and it's a taste combination that'll blow you away.

Timing note: pork needs to roast for 12 hours

Pulled Pork

⅓ cup sweet paprika

2 tablespoons white sugar

2 tablespoons brown sugar

1½ tablespoons fine sea salt

1 tablespoon chili powder

1 tablespoon hot pepper flakes

1 tablespoon cayenne pepper

1 tablespoon garlic power

1 tablespoon dry mustard

1 tablespoon onion powder

1 tablespoon black pepper

1 teaspoon ground cumin

1 teaspoon dried oregano

3 to 4 pounds pork butt (bone-in)

Tomato Sauce

2 tablespoons oil

1 onion, finely chopped

½ cup tomato paste

2 teaspoons puréed or finely minced roasted garlic

2 teaspoons dried basil

2 teaspoons dried oregano

1 teaspoon black pepper

1½ cups tomato juice

1 cup diced tomatoes

Salt

Lasagna

12 cooked lasagna sheets

Tomato Sauce

Pulled Pork

3 cups shredded Asiago, white Cheddar, and mozzarella cheese mix

Pulled Pork

Preheat oven to 225°F.

In a small bowl, combine all of the ingredients—except the pork—to create a spice rub.

Rub the spices all over the pork. Transfer the pork to a roasting pan, cover the pan tightly with aluminum foil, and roast in preheated oven for 12 hours. The meat should be tender and falling off the bone.

Remove from the oven and set aside to cool slightly. Once cool enough to handle, using your hands, pull the pork apart into shreds. Set aside until ready to use.

Tomato Sauce

In a skillet over low heat, heat the oil. Cook the onion, stirring occasionally, until translucent, about 10 minutes. Stir in the tomato paste and cook, stirring occasionally, for 2 minutes (be careful not to burn the onion). Stir in the garlic, basil, oregano, and black pepper and cook for 3 minutes. Stir in the tomato juice and tomatoes and cook, stirring occasionally, for 15 to 20 minutes. Check for seasoning and add salt to taste, if needed. Remove from heat, keeping warm.

Lasagna

Preheat oven to 350°F.

Grease a 12- × 9-inch and 4-inch-deep baking pan with oil. Arrange 4 of the cooked lasagna noodles in a single layer on the bottom of the pan. Cover with one-third of the tomato sauce. Top with half of the pulled pork. Cover with one-third of the cheese mixture. Repeat the 4 layers. Cover with the remaining lasagna noodles. Top with a little tomato sauce (be sure to reserve some of the tomato sauce) and the remaining cheese. Cover the pan with nonstick aluminum foil and bake in preheated oven for 1½ hours.

Remove the foil and cook for an additional 15 minutes, until top is slightly browned.

Remove the pan from the oven and set aside, uncovered, for about 30 minutes to allow the lasagna to set before serving.

Assembly

In a small saucepan, heat the remaining tomato sauce.

Place a ladleful of sauce on each serving plate and top with a slice of lasagna.

Sofra

EST. 2006
10345 106TH STREET NORTHWEST
EDMONTON, AB · T5J 0J2
780-423-3044

You'd think with all the chowing down I've done that I would have eaten in a Turkish restaurant once or twice. Well, Sofra was my maiden voyage to the spicy world of Turkish cuisine, and it made me lament that I've waited this long. Had I known there were Turkish delights like Yuksel Gultekin's to be had, I would have sought them out long ago. Then again, Yuksel is a one-in-a-million kinda guy, so finding this type of dedication to culinary craft isn't all that easy . . . unless you're in Edmonton, that is!

Sofra owes its beginnings to Yuksel's adventurous and enterprising spirit. He earned his chops in restaurants across his native Turkey, but then hit the high seas on luxury cruise ships. Five years later he found himself in Edmonton visiting a friend, and was so smitten with the place he never left. It wasn't long before Yuksel and his incredibly supportive wife, Chandra, recognized the city's lack of Turkish cuisine, and, in 2006, Sofra was born. Now the restaurant is abuzz with the constant flow of customers who appreciate Yuksel's heart-warming spirit as much as his belly-warming creations.

Yuksel warmed my belly and my mouth with his Adana Kebab, a meal that's cooked the way a burly man like me really wants his food prepared: on a sword! The Adana starts with tender, hand-chopped AAA Alberta beef that's loaded with a mind-boggling array of spices, then carefully hand-moulded around an imposing blade that's propped a few inches over a hot grill. When done to perfection, the kebab is pulled off the blade (sorry, no sword-fighting allowed!) and served alongside grilled seasonal

If Yuksel Gultekin looks the least bit concerned, it's because he knows that entrusting me to stick meat onto a sword is risky business.

vegetables, salad, and a heaping scoop of whole-wheat bulgur, a popular Mediterranean grain. I loved the smoky chorizo-like flavour of the kebab, though I'm not sure I needed it in the 35°C heatwave Edmonton happened to have when I visited!

Yuksel handcrafts every item on his menu, and it shows. The Ispanakli Pideler (Turkish pizza) is a dish that was chosen one of the 25 best things to eat in Edmonton by *Avenue* magazine. Shaped much like a canoe, the dough can be topped with a variety of items, including spinach and mozzarella; chicken, tomato, and green pepper; or ground beef, onion, tomato, and green pepper. The Sultan's Sofrasi is a monstrous meat platter that feeds two or more with generous portions of chicken kebab, lamb kebab, beef meatballs, and succulent rack of lamb. Make sure you don't overlook the Yaprak Sarma (stuffed grape leaves) along the way!

Dessert is equally exotic, and highlighted by Yuksel's Baklava, a Mediterranean classic that sandwiches ground pistachio and walnuts between layers of delicate, buttered phyllo. Baked and then doused in warm honey syrup, it's a sinfully rich but surprisingly light dessert that drips down your chin for good measure. I'm not sure if the Peynirli Kayisi are meant to be a dessert or an appetizer, but my taste buds don't care. I mean, when you're stuffing apricots with herbs, garlic, chili pepper, and parsley-infused feta cheese, it doesn't matter, does it?

Break out of your shell, Canada! Sofra might be small and off the radar, but Yuksel's dedication to quality and his ridiculously tasty creations are world-class. And don't be surprised if you find yourself booking a trip to Istanbul soon after your meal. You won't be the first.

You can count me among the countless patrons who can't resist Sofra's Baklava, a Middle Eastern classic dessert that drips with the sweet taste of honey.

Coban Kavurma
(Turkish Lamb Casserole)

Makes: 4 servings

Comforting and subtly spicy, Sofra's Coban Kavurma is a Turkish shepherd's pie. Unlike the original incarnation, this one doesn't use potatoes. Instead it combines chunks of pan-fried lamb with heaps of vegetables in a delicious red wine gravy. Topped with handfuls of mozzarella (hey, it's Turkish and Italian all in one!) and baked in ramekins, the Coban Kavurma is rich in flavour, a perfect blend of meat, veggies and herbs.

Timing note: lamb must marinate overnight

2 pounds lamb meat (preferably from the leg), cut into ½-inch cubes
6 tablespoons olive oil, divided
Salt and pepper
1 cup red wine
1 sweet green pepper, diced
1 small zucchini, diced
2 tomatoes, diced
16 white mushrooms, sliced
1 tablespoon dried oregano
¼ teaspoon salt
¼ teaspoon black pepper
1 cup shredded mozzarella

Place the lamb in a resealable bag and drizzle with 2 tablespoons oil to coat the meat. Season to taste with salt and pepper. Seal the bag, turn the meat to coat, and refrigerate for 8 hours. Preheat oven to 350°F.

In a large skillet over medium heat, heat the remaining 4 tablespoons oil. Add the lamb and cook, stirring occasionally, for 10 minutes. Add the wine and cook while stirring until the wine has reduced completely, about 2 to 3 minutes. Add the green pepper and zucchini and cook for 2 minutes. Stir in the tomatoes, mushrooms, oregano, salt, and pepper and cook for 2 more minutes. Remove from heat.

Divide the mixture among 4 ramekins or small casserole dishes and top each with ¼ cup mozzarella. Bake in preheated oven for 5 minutes or until cheese is melted.

Tibetan Kitchen

EST. 2008
680 BROUGHTON STREET
VICTORIA, BC · V8W 2C9
250-383-5664
WWW.TIBETANKITCHEN.COM

They say the world is a much smaller place than it used to be, and after a trip to Victoria's Tibetan Kitchen, I'm beginning to believe it. How else can you explain a restaurant owned by a woman born in India to Tibetan parents, who met her Canadian husband on a cruise ship in international waters and settled in Victoria? Now those are the ingredients for one spicy curry!

That's the multifaceted life of Pemba Bhatia, a spunky and free-spirited woman whose Tibetan refugee parents fled to northeast India, where they started their family. This is where Pemba first learned to cook, combining Chinese-inspired meals with Indian flair. While working on a cruise ship years later,

Pemba Bhatia's Victoria restaurant career started as a takeout joint in Market Square, but overwhelming response led to the birth of the Tibetan Kitchen.

Pemba met her Canadian soon-to-be husband, ship captain William Frowd. When the couple settled in Victoria, the stage was set for Pemba to pick up her culinary roots. Given the rave reviews her Kitchen's received, she's right on track.

Pemba's hallmark is the blending of culinary influences, and her Shepta is a prime example. At first glance, the dish resembles a classic chow mein stir-fry, but one taste tells a different story. Yes, it has egg noodles covered in a heap of tender sautéed slices of beef and lots of different vegetables, but what separates Pemba's Shepta is its rich curry flavours. The dish warmed my heart, though getting through the massive pile of food is no small feat . . . even for a pro like me.

Worlds collide exotically in the Tibetan Kitchen's Samosas, which Pemba served to me with her Curried Onion Rings. A dish she's been making since she was a girl at her mom's side, the samosas start with homemade dough pockets filled with sautéed potatoes, yams, and lots of spices. For a little West Coast surprise, Pemba adds dried cranberries, which add a sweet sensation to the flavourful bites. The onion rings are coated in homemade chickpea batter spiked with more eastern spices, which gives them a taste I've never experienced before. Who knew Tibetans were such champions of deep-fried goodness?

I could wax poetic for hours about the endless array of Tibetan Kitchen offerings. The Tibetan Pan-Fried Momos are hand-rolled dumpling delicacies stuffed with a kaleidoscope of fillings, like vegetables, pork, and beef, or even chocolate-and-blueberry stuffing for those of you with a sweet tooth. Sha-Palei is a ground beef–filled pita pocket with veggies, secret "Pemba spices," and shredded Cheddar cheese. Beef Thukpa is what your Tibetan grandmother feeds you when you've got the sniffles: a heaping bowl of chicken broth filled with beef and vegetables in Pemba's signature flavours.

Come to think of it, Pemba could easily be your Tibetan-Indian-Canadian grandmother. OK, so that means you might not know which flavour will be coming at you at any given moment, but when the world's this small, a little surprise doesn't hurt, now does it?

Momos are a staple of the Tibetan diet. First steamed and then pan-fried, they are served piping hot with a delicious cilantro-mint dipping sauce.

Wild Salmon Curry

Makes: 4 servings

This dish is anchored by a piece of fresh, pan-seared salmon that's been coated in exotic spices, on top of which lies a blanket of homemade cashew curry sauce. Served at the restaurnt alongside a mound of brown rice and Thai wild rice, homemade lentil soup, and homemade puris (deep-fried puffed bread) or rotis (pan-fried flatbread), the salmon curry is flaky, tender, and smooth. I was amazed at how creamy the curry sauce was, even though there wasn't a drop of cream in it. Tibetan hugs all around!

2 cups vegetable oil, divided
1 onion, finely chopped
1 teaspoon grated fresh ginger
1 teaspoon grated garlic
2 teaspoons curry powder
2 teaspoons garam masala
2 cups tomato paste
2 cups unsalted raw cashews
Salt
4 boneless, skin-on salmon fillets (6 ounces)
2 teaspoons roughly ground mustard seeds
Rice
Cilantro

In a skillet over medium heat, heat the oil. Add the onion and cook, stirring often, until golden brown. Add the ginger, garlic, curry powder, garam masala, tomato paste, cashews, and salt to taste, and cook, stirring occasionally, for 5 minutes. Set aside to cool.

Transfer the cooled mixture to a food processor fitted with the metal blade and purée until smooth.

Preheat oven to 350°F.

Rub the salmon fillets with the curry mixture and season with salt to taste.

In a clean skillet over medium-high heat, heat 1 tablespoon of oil. Sear the salmon for about 40 seconds each side. Transfer the salmon to an oven-safe dish and set aside, reserving the pan.

To the same skillet, add 2 cups of water, mustard seeds, and cashew purée and bring to a simmer over medium heat. Pour over the salmon and bake in preheated oven for 2 minutes, or until the salmon is cooked through and no longer pink in the middle.

Serve the salmon with its sauce over white or brown basmati rice and garnish with chopped fresh cilantro, if desired.

Via Tevere Pizzeria

EST. 2012
1190 VICTORIA DRIVE
VANCOUVER, BC · V5L 4G5
604-336-1803
WWW.VIATEVEREPIZZERIA.COM

Generally speaking, obsessions are considered unhealthy propositions. Clothes . . . doughnuts . . . cute little elves wearing pink tutus—all vices that are best served in moderation. Just don't tell that to brothers Frank and Dominic Morra. Because when it comes to food, the Morra men have one thing on their minds—Neapolitan pizza—and the culinary world is a better place for it.

Want proof? Got proof: Via Tevere was one of the *first* restaurants in Canada to be certified by the (feel free to use your best Godfather accent here) Associazione Verace Pizza Napoletana, an organization charged with safeguarding the cultural heritage of Italy's most famous export. Want more proof? The place is named after the street in Naples where Frank and Dom's dad grew up. Still skeptical? Via Tevere's wood-burning oven is imported directly from Naples! So trust me when I say that eating here is like a trip to the old country, right in downtown Vancouver.

There's a real family feeling at Via Tevere, where customers feel like they've walked straight into an Italian kitchen serving up the family's best meals.

True to their roots, the Morra men know that the heart and soul of any good Neapolitan pizza is its crust. Gorgeous in its simplicity, the dough starts in the mixer and is then rolled, kneaded, and stretched by hand with the love and attention any good pizza deserves. The dough is *never* touched by a rolling pin, *never* leaves the marble slab it's being kneaded on, and *never, ever* gets tossed in the air. Hey, those Associazione Verace Pizza Napoletana boys don' mess aroun'. Capish?

Frank and Dom's crust is the perfect foundation for an array of pizzas as delicious as they are simple. And none is simpler than the Margherita, the original Neapolitan creation where the dough is lovingly brushed with hand-milled San Marzano tomato sauce (another association requirement!) before being topped with fresh basil and fior di latte (flower of milk) mozzarella. Not to make it seem like these

Like brother Dom, chef Frank is proud to serve authentic Neapolitan pizza. Ever jovial but always demanding, he personally checks each pizza before sending it to the table.

guys abide by a strict set of rules or anything, but the pizza is then placed in the wood-fired oven for exactly 90 seconds—not 89, not 91, but 90.

And that's all the Margherita needs to cook to a deliciously charred, golden brown, smoky, chewy delight that hints of a torrid love story between the basil, sauce, and creamy mozzarella, but never really shows you what's going on behind closed doors. Sorry. Neapolitan pizza brings out the romantic in me.

Looking for a little more adventure in your mouth? You can't go wrong with the Salsiccia e Rapini, a Via Tevere signature dish that centres on Frank's uncanny ability to hand-pick the best rapini (broccoli rabe) leaves and sear them in olive oil until they're tender but mysteriously bitter. From there it's onto the dough alongside the authentic Italian sausage that gives this pizza its hearty personality, along with delicate mounds of fior di latte. I like to describe the taste the way my Italian brothers and sisters would: ridiculous! In a good way, that is.

If sauce isn't your thing (and I have *no* idea why Via Tevere's sauce *wouldn't* be your thing!), then go for the Filetto, a so-called "white pizza" that gingerly lays slices of San Marzano tomatoes on its olive oil base. Garnished with basil and roasted garlic and topped with fior di latte, this masterpiece only needs 60 seconds in the oven before hitting your taste buds. Bite into it and you've officially hit Italian nirvana as the tomato slices pop in your mouth, bathing it in warm, sweet tomato juice.

Want more? Got more! The Capricciosa Pizza is garnished with prosciutto cotto (Italian cooked ham), salami, mushrooms, artichokes, olives, and fior di latte. The Vesuvio Pizza is a spicy delight that features spicy salami picante and capicollo. Desserts come in varied forms, and range from classic Tiramisu to Neapolitan Graffe, a deep-fried fritter dusted with sugar and cinnamon and drizzled with melted Nutella.

If there's any question as to how Vancouverites have taken to this little piece of Naples, just visit the place. Seems obsessions are contagious.

Capricciosa Pizza

Makes: 1 pizza

Via Tevere's Capricciosa Pizza is a Neapolitan Pizza with a twist. The salami and olives are the perfect salty complement to one another, and the artichoke enhances its other extraordinary flavours. Eat it with a knife and fork if you want, but Frank encourages the traditional style of folding a slice in half (resulting in a "libretto") to truly grasp the taste of old Italy.

Timing note: dough needs 3 to 4 hours to rise and 3 hours to sit

Dough

4 cups flour (preferably Italian OO white flour)
3 teaspoons kosher salt
2 teaspoons instant dry yeast

Pizza

½ cup canned San Marzano tomatoes, blended
¾ cup chopped fresh mozzarella (preferably fior di latte)
1 to 2 fresh basil leaves, torn
1 to 2 cremini mushrooms, sliced
6 whole pitted black olives, sliced
5 artichoke hearts, quartered
6 to 7 slices mild salami, torn into bite-size pieces
1 slice prosciutto cotto, torn into bite-size pieces
Sprinkle of grated Parmesan cheese
Drizzle of olive oil

Dough

In a large bowl, whisk together the flour, salt, and yeast. Add 2 cups of water and, using your hands or a wooden spoon, stir until a ragged dough forms. Turn out onto a lightly floured surface and knead until smooth and elastic. Cover the bowl with plastic wrap and set aside at room temperature for 3 to 4 hours to rise.

On a lightly floured surface, divide the dough into 4 even balls. Cover one ball with plastic wrap and set aside for an additional 3 hours before use. Transfer the remaining 3 balls to individual freezer bags and freeze for use another time.

Pizza

Preheat oven to 500°F.

Roll the dough into an 8-inch circle on a piece of parchment paper. Spread the blended tomatoes evenly over the top of the dough. Sprinkle with an even layer of mozzarella. Top with the basil, mushrooms, olives, artichoke hearts, salami, and prosciutto. Sprinkle with the Parmesan and drizzle with the olive oil. Slide the parchment onto a pizza stone or baking sheet and cook for about 15 minutes, until golden.

The Wallflower Modern Diner

EST. 2009

2420 MAIN STREET

VANCOUVER, BC · V5T 3E2

604-568-7554

WWW.THEWALLFLOWERMODERNDINER.COM

When she gave The Wallflower Modern Diner its unique moniker, owner and chef Lisa Skelton definitely didn't name it after herself. Just visit the place and you'll see what I'm talking about. Lisa? No wallflower here. In fact, she's the one in the Hello Kitty short shorts and go-go boots doing rad '80s dances while she cooks up an array of eats sure to please all the peeps in your party.

Lisa is one of those huge, bright, and fun personalities that makes a mark wherever she goes, and The Wallflower certainly exudes her charm. Sometimes called "a place where cool kids take their parents," the diner was born of Lisa's realization that few Vancouver eateries could feed all of her eclectic friends' dietary needs. When a local restaurant closed its doors, Lisa saw the space, chewed her proverbial cud for a few hours, then wrote a cheque. On January 2, 2009, The Wallflower opened its doors . . . to rave reviews.

Today the diner serves up old-school comfort classics with a modern twist, and there are buckets of options for those looking for vegetarian, vegan, and gluten-free goodness. But as yummy as the food is, the best part of The Wallflower may be its vibe. This is a joint that brings people together. Sit at the bar with a stranger and you may just walk out with a friend. No wonder the place is a *You Gotta Eat Here!* Fan Fave.

It wouldn't hurt if that soon-to-be-friend ordered Lisa's Meat Loaf Wellington, a "crazy awesome" dish that takes a shot at ritzy-schmitzy restaurants where fun is definitely, positively *not* allowed. The beef-and-pork dish combines everything you love about your mom's meat loaf, then wraps it in puff pastry with bacon, mushrooms, and onions and covers it in gravy. The unexpected comes in the form of chopped pickles, which add

Hip and cool Lisa Skelton was drawn to the restaurant industry at a young age. Even when working as a waitress, she volunteered in the kitchen on her days off.

a surprising brightness to the dish. Why do pickles go in meat loaf, you ask? Because Lisa says they do!

Lisa's Beef Stroganoff is a hearty take on a traditional continental dish that starts with a massive roast that's slow-cooked for 6 hours. In another pot, a pile of macaroni is sautéed in a gravy-and-sour cream bath, to which Lisa adds beef and more chopped pickle surprise. (Don't argue: Super Fans *love* those pickles!). After the whole creamy mess boils, it makes its way into a bowl, is topped with Swiss cheese, and baked until bubbly brown. Top with a slice of dill pickle and a dollop of sour cream and you've got a heart-warming meal.

Like I said, it's not all meat at The Wallflower, and the menu has an extensive vegan selection, including Cajun Tofu: fried fingers of tofu tossed with fiery Cajun spice and served with The Wallflower's homemade creamy peanut sauce. Thunder Fries are nachos on veggie steroids, where mounds of crispy fries are topped with handfuls of nacho cheese, vegetarian chili, sliced olives, jalapeño peppers, and a massive dollop of sour cream.

And if those folks at the next table lean over and ask you what you've ordered, hand them the plate. It's all part of being something bigger at The Wallflower, where everyone's a member of one big, quirky, and totally awesome family.

Grandma's Fried Chicken

Makes: 4 servings

For a trip down memory lane, try Grandma's Fried Chicken, one of The Wallflower's most popular dishes . . . for obvious reasons. The bone-in, skin-on thighs are dredged in corn flour and Grannie's secret seasonings (salt and pepper . . . *shh*), then pan-fried to crisp golden brown before being finished in the oven, then perched atop mashed potatoes and smothered in homemade gravy.

Fried Chicken

1 cup corn flour
1 teaspoon salt
1 teaspoon black pepper
4 bone-in, skin-on chicken thighs
1 cup canola oil

Gravy

1 medium onion, chopped
2 cups chicken stock
2 tablespoons cornstarch

Mashed Potatoes

6 russet potatoes, peeled and sliced
½ cup milk
2 tablespoons butter
Salt and pepper

Fried Chicken

Preheat oven to 450°F.

In a shallow bowl, combine the corn flour, salt, and pepper.

Pat the chicken dry with paper towel. Dredge both sides of the chicken in the flour mixture to coat evenly. Set chicken aside.

In a skillet over medium heat, heat the oil. Cook the chicken thighs for 3 to 4 minutes per side, until browned. Transfer the chicken to a baking dish and cook in preheated oven for 30 minutes or until the chicken registers an internal temperature of 180°F on a meat thermometer.

Mashed Potatoes

Meanwhile, in a large saucepan of boiling salted water, cook the potatoes until tender, about 20 minutes. Drain well. Add the milk, butter, and salt and pepper to taste. Mash or whip to desired texture. Set aside, keeping warm.

Gravy

Transfer the chicken drippings to a small saucepan and heat over medium heat. Add the onion and sauté until soft.

In a bowl, whisk together the chicken stock and cornstarch. Add to the onion and cook, whisking constantly, until the gravy reaches desired thickness.

Assembly

Divide the chicken among serving plates and serve with a generous helpings of mashed potatoes topped with ladlefuls of gravy.

Wildside Grill

EST. 2008
1180 PACIFIC RIM HIGHWAY
TOFINO, BC · V0R 2Z0
250-725-9453
WWW.WILDSIDEGRILL.COM

here are tacos . . . and then there are *tacos*. There are fish tacos . . . and then there are *FISH TACOS!* (Can you scream it, my brothers and sisters?) Well, nestled in the hip surf town of Tofino, BC, is the Wildside Grill, home of some of the best fish tacos you've ever wrapped your lips around. So much more than a one-dish joint, the Wildside is a seafood-lover's dream, where co-owner Jeff Mikus is a fisherman who plies his trade on local seas all day long. Then he hands his catch off to fellow co-owner Jesse Blake, the master of the Wildside's kitchen, who turns it into some of the freshest, most creative offerings you've ever eaten at a place with no indoor seating. Yeah . . . it's all wild at the Wildside.

It was no accident that got Jeff and Jesse together. The two have been friends for years, Jeff working the seas while Jesse was a chef at upscale restaurants around town. Yet when a local fish shack hit the market, the two saw an opportunity and jumped on it. For Jesse, the Wildside was a chance to revisit his surfer roots and offer up food that all of Tofino's residents could enjoy. And judging by the line-ups outside the joint—including the daring locals who do so in the dead of winter—they're on the right track.

Yet as exotic as the flavours on the plate may be, there's nothing pretentious about Wildside Grill. A lone takeout window is framed by a chalkboard menu and seating comprises a handful of wooden picnic tables around the rustic wooden building. If the gods are smiling, you might even land a seat under the cedar gazebo, a handy shelter in case a legendary Tofino squall rolls in. Either way, you're very likely to share your table with surfer dudes and dudettes, who will no doubt regale you with stories of the day's triumphs.

As fresh as it gets. No, not co-owner Jeff Mikus, but the seafood he hauls in every day, which is the foundation of Wildside's insanely fresh menu.

If the classic club sandwich took a West Coast surfing trip, this is what it would become! The Cod Club is a symphony of seafood and enough food to keep any landlubber happy.

For a taste of what these waters have to offer, go for the Cod Club Sandwich, a mouth-stuffer you've got to commit to because it's ending up on your shirt no matter what you do. The CC starts on a whole-wheat kaiser roll dressed in sweet chili mayonnaise, avotillo sauce, and bacon. On top of this Jesse perches a massive and unbelievably fresh hunk of deep-fried, panko-crusted cod. Not enough for you? Add some pink baby shrimp and a pile of fixings, and it's a sandwich you've got to hold to believe.

Equally unbelievable and every bit as delicious is the Wildside's West Coast Poutine, where comfort food meets Pacific funk. Sure, it's got deliciously crispy fries and mounds of cheese, but this bad boy hits the briny with Jesse's seafood gumbo, itself a tomatoey flavour-blast of chorizo sausage, generous chunks of fresh fish, okra, and loads of herbs and spices. Garnished with sour cream, it's soul food on fries.

Of course, there's boatloads (see what I did there?) more at the Wildside. The Oyster Burger is monstrous, with tempura-battered and panko-crusted balls of crunchy seafood heaven. The Salmon Burger is an exercise in grilled freshness and served with smoked tomato relish, corn relish, and avocado. And yes, the Fish & Chips are fried to crispy perfection. Hell, this place is so hip they even serve non-fish items!

Personally, I'd say you're crazy to break outside the seafood box when it's Wildside fresh, but they say the salt air does crazy things to people. Who is this landlubber to argue?

Built on warmed corn tortillas, these tacos start with a layer of Monterey Jack cheese, shredded cabbage, chipotle mayonnaise, and homemade "avotillo" sauce, a tempting blend of tomatillos, avocados, jalapeño, and spices. That alone would be enough, but Jesse steals the show with a mound of tempura-battered ling cod that's been fried to perfection. Topped with homemade tomato salsa, fresh cilantro, and lime juice, this is a hot-damn, finger-snappin', stupidly tasty taco.

Avotillo Sauce

1 tablespoon vegetable oil
1 small onion, finely chopped
1 jalapeño pepper, seeded and finely chopped
1 large garlic clove, finely chopped
1 teaspoon ground coriander
1 teaspoon ground cumin
6 medium tomatillos, finely chopped
2 tablespoons white vinegar
2 tablespoons lime juice
2 tablespoons sugar
2 avocados, peeled, pitted, and smashed
Salt and pepper

Chipotle Mayo

1 cup mayonnaise
2 tablespoons finely chopped fresh cilantro
1 tablespoon crushed chipotle peppers
1 tablespoon lime juice

Fresh Tomato Salsa

9 Roma tomatoes, finely chopped
1 jalapeño pepper, seeded and finely chopped
1 small onion, finely chopped
1 teaspoon minced garlic
2 tablespoons finely chopped fresh cilantro
2 tablespoons lime juice
2 teaspoons sugar
2 teaspoons sea salt

Fish

8 cups canola or vegetable oil
Tempura batter (store-bought or homemade)
18 fillets skinless, boneless fresh ling cod (1½ ounces each)

Assembly

18 fresh whole corn tortillas (6 inch)
1 cup shredded Monterey Jack cheese
½ head green cabbage, shredded
Fresh cilantro sprigs
6 lime wedges

Avotilla Sauce

In a large saucepan over low heat, heat the oil. Sauté the onion, jalapeño, and garlic until the onion is soft and translucent. Add the coriander and cumin and cook, stirring, for 30 seconds. Stir in the tomatillos, vinegar, lime juice, and sugar, and bring to a simmer. Cook, stirring occasionally, until the tomatillos are just softened. Remove from heat.

Add the avocados and, using an immersion blender, purée until smooth. Season with salt and pepper to taste. Cover and refrigerate until ready to use.

Chipotle Mayo

In a small bowl, whisk together all of the ingredients. Cover and refrigerate until ready to use.

Fresh Tomato Salsa

In a medium bowl, combine all of the ingredients. Cover and refrigerate until ready to use.

Fish

Pour the oil into a deep-fryer or large pot and heat until it registers 350°F on a cooking thermometer. (If you are using a pot, use enough oil to float the fish strips.)

Prepare tempura batter according to package directions (or your favourite recipe).

Working one fillet at a time, dip the fish into the tempura batter, coating both sides, then slowly add the coated fish to the hot oil to form a quick crust (be careful not to overcrowd the fish or the pieces will stick to the bottom of the pan or each other—cook only a few pieces of cod at a time). Once the outside crust is golden brown and the fish is floating, about 2 minutes, transfer the fish to a plate lined in paper towel or a metal rack placed over paper towel.

Assembly

In a hot skillet, warm the tortillas until lightly toasted and soft.

Fill the tortillas with cheese, cabbage, avotillo sauce, and chipotle mayo. Top with the tempura-fried fish and fresh tomato salsa. Garnish with fresh cilantro sprigs. Serve with a lime wedge alongside.

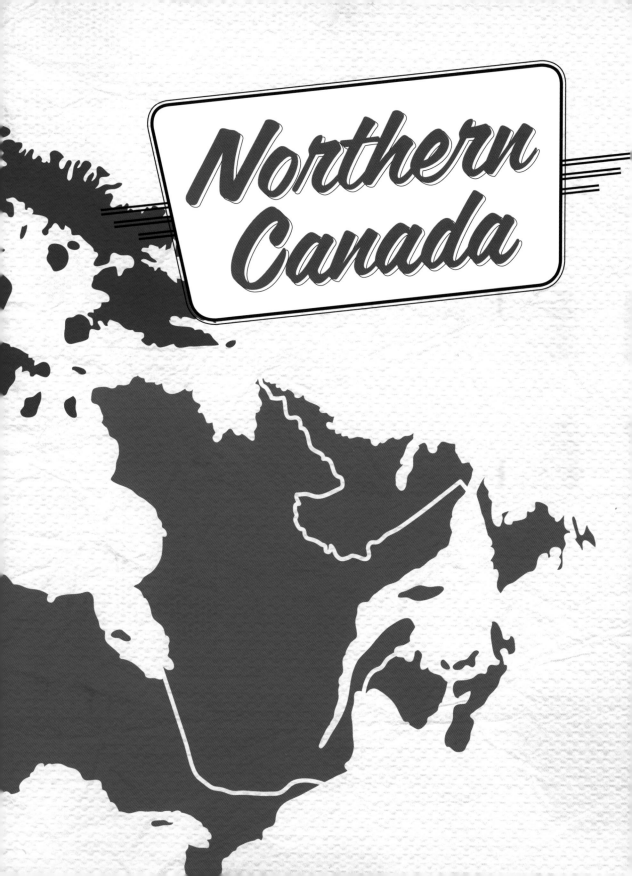

Antoinette's Food Cache

EST. 2008
4121 4TH AVENUE
WHITEHORSE, YT · Y1A 1H7
867-668-3505

People visit Whitehorse for lots of reasons. Midnight sun? Check. A taste of the gold rush? Check. Gateway to an untamed land where the caribou run free? Check. Caribbean home cooking? Wait a second . . .

But that's exactly what you get at Antoinette's, where one feisty woman's take on Caribbean comfort dishes has carved out a reputation that spans the territory. Here you get heaping, homemade Caribbean-inspired meals that warm the bellies of both devoted locals and the thousands of international tourists who visit this northern town every year.

And as odd as it may seem to travel north to get a taste of the Caribbean, there's nothing strange about Antoinette being at the helm of her own restaurant. Born on Tobago as the daughter of a cook and granddaughter of a baker, Antoinette's family emigrated to Toronto when she was just 11. She opened her first restaurant—to rave reviews—in Winnipeg in 2002. Years later, she started a version of Antoinette's in Dawson City, then took her successful brand with her when she moved to Whitehorse.

For cold Whitehorse winter days, nothing compares with Antoinette's Spicy Caribbean Pork, a combination plate featuring some of the tastiest delights this side of the Chilkoot Pass. As the name suggests, the dish features a heaping mound of pork shoulder that's been given the royal treatment: marinated in exotic spices, and braised. The juice-dripping meat is served alongside traditional rice and peas, oven-baked cinnamon yams, and a warm, chewy piece of Caribbean fried bread,

Though she was born on tropical Tobago, Antoinette GreenOliph hated the sun. So she followed her grandmother around the kitchen, learning the recipes that have made her eatery famous.

called "float." The meat is a sweet and spicy delight, and the float is the perfect way to scoop it all into your eagerly awaiting mouth. Top it off with the sweet, crunchy-on-the-outside-but-soft-on-the-inside yams, and you're ready for a good time.

Delicious combinations are an Antoinette specialty, and few are as tasty as the Squash and Lentil Sweet Chili Stew with Rack of Lamb. The lamb is dusted with a blend of secret spices, rubbed with Dijon mustard, and coated in panko before hitting the oven. Tender, crunchy, and stupidly flavourful, the lamb alone is a fantastic meal . . . but the fun has just begun. Joining the party on the plate is the stew, a flavourful marriage of kabocha squash, lentils, a dozen spices, tomatoes, and sweet Thai chili sauce. Spicy but not overpowering, the stew perfectly accompanies the rich flavours of the lamb.

For those of you who can't seem to leave Canadian cuisine behind, try Antoinette's Tocho, a Caribbean hybrid of nachos and poutine: fresh-cut french fries are smothered in a slow-cooked curry chicken gravy, then topped with shredded cheese for melting under the broiler and sprinkled with fresh diced tomatoes. Curry also plays a starring role in the Curry Lamb on Rainbow Rice, a local favourite that tops the flavour charts. The Baked Brie (sprinkled with caramelized brown sugar) is an irresistible appetizer. Dessert lovers get a taste of the exotic with the Tobagonian-Style Sweet Potato Pie, a traditional Caribbean meal-ender that's much more dense than our pumpkin pies but even yummier.

So go north, my people, to the town near the 60th parallel. The Caribbean awaits!

Antoinette's Squash and Lentil Sweet Chili Stew is so filling and popular that it's often ordered as a dish unto itself, with a side of Rainbow Rice.

Halibut TnT

Makes: 6 servings

Antoinette's is a focal point of the surprisingly sophisticated Whitehorse food scene, and it's easy to see why. Owner Antoinette's Halibut TnT (Trinidad and Tobago) combines a tender, flaky GreenOliph halibut steak with a light coconut curry and tomato sauce and serves it over her coucou, a creamy Caribbean cornmeal polenta made with okra and coconut milk. The dish is one of those rare finds that's light but filling, and the sauce's zing is fodder for pleasant memories.

TnT Sauce

3 tablespoons oil
2 tablespoons curry powder
3 garlic cloves, chopped
1 large onion, chopped
7 sprigs of fresh thyme, leaves only
3 sprigs of fresh basil, leaves only, chopped
Leaves and stems from ½ bunch of fresh
    cilantro, chopped
1 Scotch bonnet pepper, chopped (remove
    seeds for less heat, if desired)
2 tablespoons powdered chicken stock
3 cans (28 ounces each) tomatoes
2 cans (14 ounces each) coconut milk
Salt

Coucou

1 can (14 ounces) coconut milk
½ cup chopped fresh or frozen okra
1 cup cornmeal
Salt and pepper

Halibut

1 cup water
1 tablespoon butter
Pinch of salt
6 bone-in, skin-on halibut steaks
    (8 ounces each)

Assembly

Fresh spinach leaves
1 lime, cut into 6 thin wedges
Green onion, sliced lengthwise

TnT Sauce

In a saucepan over medium heat, heat the oil. Stir in the curry powder, then the garlic, onion, thyme, basil, cilantro, and Scotch bonnet pepper. Sauté until the vegetables are tender and fragrant, then stir in the stock and tomatoes. Cook for 2 to 3 minutes, stirring constantly. Stir in the coconut milk and season with salt to taste. Remove from heat and set aside until ready to use.

Coucou

In a medium saucepan, bring the coconut milk and okra to a boil. Remove from heat. While stirring, slowly add the cornmeal. Season with salt and pepper to taste. Return to low heat and stir until the mixture thickens. Remove from heat and pour into a greased 8- x 10-inch flat pan to cool completely.

Halibut

In a saucepan, bring water, butter, and salt to a boil. Reduce heat to medium-low and add one halibut steak. Cover the pan and poach for 7 minutes, or until the halibut is opaque. Set aside on a plate, keeping warm. Repeat with each halibut steak.

Assembly

Slice the cooled coucou into squares. Place one square in each serving bowl. Top with a handful of fresh spinach and top with prepared TnT sauce. Arrange a poached halibut steak on top and drizzle with more TnT sauce. Top with a fresh lime wedge and a slice of green onion.

Klondike Rib & Salmon

EST. 1994
2116 2ND AVENUE
WHITEHORSE, YT · Y1A 1B9
867-667-7554
WWW.KLONDIKERIB.COM

Everything is big in the Yukon. Exhibit A: Klondike Rib & Salmon, where the portions are massive and the personalities larger than life. Then again, when a joint is only open for a few fleeting months of light and warmth, you've gotta make up for lost time—and meals!

Making its home in the oldest operating building in Whitehorse, the Klondike is a step back in history, a tribute to the men and women who made the gold rush one of the most exciting times in Canadian history. And nobody says Big Personality quite like the lovely and adventurous Dona Novecosky, who stands as the undisputed heart and soul of the restaurant. Also the owner of a local backpackers' hostel, Dona is one of those people who makes everyone—both locals and visitors alike—feel like they're part of a bigger family.

And nothing says "Welcome to our Yukon clan" quite like Dona's Wild Elk Stroganoff, which takes the untamed flavour of elk and simmers it in a delicious bath spiked with copious amounts of red wine and a secret blend of Yukon herbs and spices. Hours later, Dona adds piles of mushrooms, pearl onions, a dense flour-and-butter roux, sour cream, and brandy. Served with a mound of garlic mashed potatoes and a warm slice of focaccia, it's insanely rich and creamy, with a hint of mystery from the elk meat. And yeah, so it was this guy's first time having elk, but it won't be the last.

The Klondike stays true to its wild and woolly roots by serving up its Alaskan Halibut, which is as amazingly fresh as it is ridiculously huge. At 8 to 10 ounces, the fillet is prepared simply—baked with salt, pepper, olive oil, and white wine—a tribute to the rich flavours of the fish itself, before being topped with a slice of creamy Brie cheese to contrast. Now Dona goes for the kill, topping the fish with her signature Yukon Jack Saskatoon Berry Sauce, which brings a surprising tartness to the party. Served with one of Dona's homemade bannock rolls, this is a hearty taste sensation that won't leave any room in your stomach for dessert. Unless you've got a gold miner's appetite, that is.

The Klondike's menu is a tribute to the wildness of the place Dona calls home, and offers enough items to keep you working long into the night. The King of the North Reindeer Stew is thick and hearty, and full of lentils, carrots, potato chunks, and onions. If yer looking for a slab

Gold rush, anyone? The Klondike is a step back in time, a destination for locals and tourists who want dang good eats in a rustic environment.

o' meat, the North American Bison is a 9-ounce rib-eye steak broiled to perfection and served with a side of wildberry sage reduction. The Alaskan Halibut Fish & Chips comes in one-, two-, or three-piece options and is served with Dona's "untouchable" tartar sauce. As the restaurant's name suggests, Ribs and Salmon are a house specialty: a half-rack of succulent pork ribs topped with two skewers of barbequed maple salmon. *Yee-haw!*

So pack your backpack and head north, young men and women. There's still gold in the Yukon, and it's being served up daily at Klondike Rib & Salmon.

Zany, energetic, and fun-loving, Dona Novecosky stumbled upon Whitehorse in the early 1990s and has called the romantic northern town home ever since.

Signature Sourdough
Bread Pudding

Makes: 8 to 10 servings

This bread pudding is big enough to stand as a meal on its own, never mind having it after a massive main course. But I suffered for the cause, my friends, gobbling down the entire portion, savouring the firm, crispy hunks of fresh sourdough bread. The bread pudding was served with vanilla ice cream, but the topping that sent me to *cheechako* (greenhorn) heaven was restaurateur Dona Novecosky's Yukon Gold caramel sauce, which is infused with a hefty helping of Yukon Jack whisky.

Sourdough Bread Pudding

8 eggs
3 cups white sugar
2 cups 2% milk
2 tablespoons vanilla extract
1½ tablespoons ground cinnamon
2 cups unsweetened flaked coconut
1½ cups raisins
1 loaf sourdough bread

Caramel Sauce

1 cup butter
4 cups icing sugar
2 cups heavy or whipping (35%) cream
½ cup Yukon Jack whisky

Assembly

Vanilla ice cream

Sourdough Bread Pudding

Preheat oven to 375°F. Grease a 9- x 11-inch baking pan.

In a large bowl, combine the eggs, sugar, milk, vanilla, and cinnamon. Stir in the coconut and raisins.

Rip the bread into bite-size pieces and add to the egg mixture. Stir to combine. Set aside for 10 minutes to soak.

Pour mixture evenly into prepared baking pan and bake in preheated oven for 45 minutes.

Caramel Sauce

In a large saucepan over medium heat, melt the butter. Add the icing sugar and heat until melted and colour changes to golden. Gradually whisk in the cream to avoid chunks. Cook for 2 to 3 minutes. Slowly stir in the whisky. Simmer for another 2 to 3 minutes, stirring constantly, until caramel reaches desired consistency. Remove from heat and set aside, keeping warm.

Assembly

Serve warm sourdough bread pudding with a scoop of ice cream drizzled with caramel sauce.

Acknowledgements

Many of you keep telling me what an amazing job I have. It's true, I do, but it takes a village for me to stuff my face with a burger, a poutine, and a strawberry shake. So I'd like to put down my fork and send some love to some amazing people.

Huge thanks to:

Michael Geddes, Sheldon Teicher, Rachel Horvath, Steven Mitchell, Sarah Nixey, Dila Velazquez, Matt Murray, Sarah Hewitt, Morgan Leech, Rachel Wagner, Michael Cammidge, Topher McFarlane, Bridget Lee, Sylvia van Helden, Margie Shields, Gabriela Skubincan, and everyone at Lone Eagle Entertainment. It's been an amazing ride.

Holly Gillanders, Leslie Merklinger, Emily Morgan, and everyone at Shaw Media and Food Network Canada for their constant support of the show.

Lorne Perlmutar, Morgan Flood, and Carolyn Sterling at Diamondfield Entertainment for having my back for over 15 years.

The incredible editors who keep finding the funny.

All the good folks at Fearless Post and VO2 Mix Audio Post.

The most amazing crew I've ever worked with—Jim Morrison, Monique Douek, Steve Lindsay, Scott Chappel, and Josh Henderson. You always bring such positive energy to the set, and I love you for it.

My co-writer and brother from another mother, Mike Vlessides. You make the writing process so much fun.

Brad Wilson and everyone at HarperCollins.

Mike Nahrgang, Josh Glover, John Calabrese, Anthony Ciardulli, and all of my friends whom I never see enough of.

My mom, Diana, my sisters, Marta and Rose, and their families: Kathy, Jay, Deanna, and Katherine. Thank you for always making sure I never let this show go to my head.

Finally, thanks to my wife, Shawne, and my daughters, Ruby and Claire. I know I'm away from home too much, but just know that you are always in my heart.

Oh yeah, and thanks to you, too.

Enjoy!

John Catucci

Brad Wilson at HarperCollins is not only one of the best guys I know, he's also one of the finest editors around. He adds more to a book like this than most people ever know, though he rarely gets his name in print. I'd like to put a stop to that, one book at time. Here's to you, Brad . . . in all your elegance!

And while Brad's skill may be in nurturing a book through its infantile stages, it's Kelly Hope who brings it to the finish line with aplomb and panache. Thanks, Kelly; you make things way too easy!

On the other end of the recognition scale is John Catucci, or Johnny C, as I like to call him. John's face is plastered all over this fine publication, with good reason. He is one of the hardest-working people I know, slogging countless hours on the road, away from his family at home in Toronto. How he manages to stay so upbeat and witty under such trying circumstances is utterly amazing to me.

The good folks at Lone Eagle Entertainment are the creative geniuses (geniuii?) behind *You Gotta Eat Here!* Michael, Rachel, and Sheldon, you are infinitely well prepared and incredibly easy to work with, traits that have made this project a joy to be associated with.

Finally, this book is for The Love Of My Life. Caroline Elizabeth, you mean everything to me. Everything. Sure, it might seem that I really like eating. Like . . . really. But I like you better. Way better. Nothing means anything to me unless you're attached to it.

Michael Vlessides

Lone Eagle Entertainment would like to thank all the people who have made *You Gotta Eat Here!* and this cookbook possible.

To our tireless production team, we appreciate all your hard work. Your dedication and passion is what makes the show great.

Great big thanks go out to our season two crew: Jim Morrison, Monique Douek, Steve Lindsay, Scott Chappel, and Josh Henderson.

To our funny man, John Catucci: we appreciate your endless appetite for making funny, delicious, and compelling television.

To Barbara Williams, Christine Shipton, Emily Morgan, Leslie Merklinger, Holly Gillanders, and our friends at Shaw Television and Food Network Canada: thank you for continuing to give us this opportunity to showcase North America's best food.

Thanks to Brad Wilson and the team at HarperCollins for helping us put together *You Gotta Eat Here Too!* and a big thanks to the rest of our book team: writer Mike Vlessides, photographers Josh Henderson and Geoff George, and book researcher Sarah Hewitt.

And a very special thank you to all of the inspirational restaurant owners and chefs across the country for greeting us with open arms and welcoming us into your kitchens to share your recipes and passions. We love what you are doing, so keep doing it right!

Finally, thanks to the viewers and readers who are fans of the show. Whether you're hopping in the car to visit one of our faves or taking on a *You Gotta Eat Here!* dish in your own kitchen, we appreciate your support!

Lone Eagle Entertainment

Recipe Index

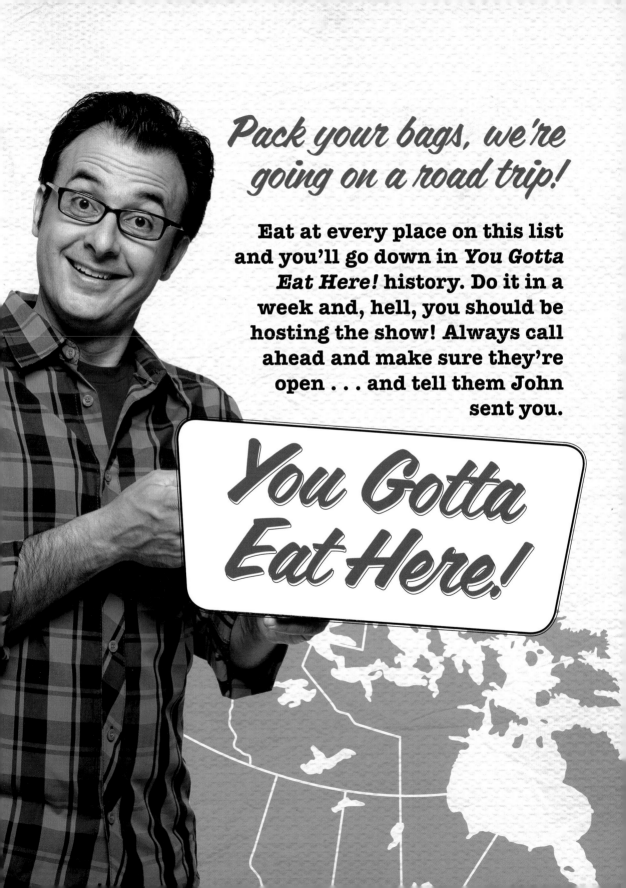

EASTERN CANADA

CHARLOTTETOWN
❑ *The Churchill Arms*
75 Queen Street
Charlottetown, PEI C1A 4A8
902-367-3450
www.churchillarms.ca

DARTMOUTH
❑ *Cheese Curds Gourmet Burgers and Poutinerie*
380 Pleasant Street
Dartmouth, NS B2Y 3S5
902-444-3446
www.cheesecurdsburgers.com

GLACE BAY, CAPE BRETON ISLAND
❑ *Colette's Place*
201 Brookside Street
Glace Bay, NS B1A 1L6
902-849-8430

HALIFAX
❑ *Tess*
5687 Charles Street
Halifax, NS B3K 1K5
902-406-3133
www.cheztess.ca

PETTY HARBOUR
❑ *Chafe's Landing*
11 Main Road, Petty Harbour
Petty Harbour, NL A0A 3H0
709-747-0802
www.chafeslanding.com

ST. JOHN'S
❑ *Rocket Bakery and Fresh Food*
272 Water Street
St. John's, NL A1C 1B7
709-738-2011
www.rocketfood.ca

SYDNEY
❑ *Flavor 19*
1225 Grand Lake Road
Lingan Golf Course
Sydney, NS B1M 1A2
905-562-2233
www.cbflavor.com/nineteen

CENTRAL CANADA

BARRIE
❑ *Pie*
31 Commerce Park Drive
Barrie, ON L4N 1XB
705-725-9663
www.eatmypie.ca

BRAMPTON
❑ *That Italian Place*
470 Chrysler Drive
Brampton, ON L6S 0C1
905-451-5552
www.thatitalianplace.ca

CALEDONIA
❑ *The Argyle Street Grill*
345 Argyle Street South
Caledonia, ON N3W 1K7
905-765-9622
www.theargylestreetgrill.com

VIVA
DOS

FLESHERTON
☐ *The Flying Spatula Diner*
125 Collingwood Street
Flesherton, ON N0C 1E0
519-924-2424

GATINEAU
☐ *Edgar*
60 rue Bégin
Gatineau, QC J9A 1C8
819-205-1110
www.chezedgar.ca

HAMILTON
☐ *Black Forest Inn*
255 King Street East
Hamilton, ON L8N 1B9
905-528-3538
www.blackforestinn.ca

☐ *Earth to Table Bread Bar*
258 Locke Street South
Hamilton, ON L8P 4B9
905-522-2999
www.breadbar.ca

LONDON
☐ *The Bungalow*
910 Waterloo Street
London, ON N6A 3W9
519-434-8797
www.bungalowhub.ca

☐ *The Early Bird*
355 Talbot Street
London, ON N6A 2R5
519-439-6483
www.theearlybird.ca

MISSISSAUGA
☐ *Mickey's Dragon Pizza*
1900 Lakeshore Road West
Mississauga, ON L5J 1J7
905-822-1411
www.feedyourdragon.com

MONTREAL
☐ *Icehouse*
51 Rue Roy Est
Montreal, QC H2W 2S3
514-439-6691

☐ *L'Avenue*
922 Avenue du Mont-Royal Est
Montréal, QC H2J 1X1
514-523-8780

NEWMARKET
☐ *Made in Mexico Restaurant and Cantina*
185 Main Street South
Newmarket, ON L3Y 3Y9
905-235-7722
www.madeinmexicorestaurant.com

NORTH YORK
☐ *Dr. Laffa*
401 Magnetic Drive
North York, ON M3J 3H9
416-739-7134
www.drlaffa.com

OHSWEKEN
☐ *Burger Barn*
3000 Fourth Line
Ohsweken, Six Nations of the Grand River
   Reserve, ON N0A 1M0
519-445-0088
www.burgerbarn.ca

ORANGEVILLE

❏ *Soulyve*

19 Mill Street

Orangeville, ON L9W 2M3

519-307-5983

www.soulyve.ca

OTTAWA

❏ *Murray Street Kitchen*

110 Murray Street

Ottawa, ON K1N 5M6

613-562-7244

www.murraystreet.ca

❏ *Pressed*

750 Gladstone Avenue

Ottawa, ON K1R 6X5

613-680-9294

www.pressed-ottawa.com

❏ *The SmoQue Shack*

129 York Street

Ottawa, ON K1N 5T4

613-789-4245

www.smoqueshack.com

PORT COLBORNE

❏ *The Smokin' Buddha*

Old Train Station

265 King Street East

Port Colborne, ON L3K 4G8

905-834-6000

www.thesmokinbuddha.com

PORT DOVER

❏ *The Crepe House*

2012 Park Street

Port Dover, ON N0A 1N0

519-583-9018

www.crepehouse.ca

TORONTO

❏ *Barque Smokehouse*

299 Roncesvalles Avenue

Toronto, ON M6R 2M3

416-532-7700

www.barque.ca

❏ *Black Skirt*

974 College Street

Toronto, ON M6G 1H4

416-532-7424

www.blackskirtrestaurant.com

❏ *The Burger's Priest*

3397 Yonge Street

Toronto, ON M4N 2M7

416-488-3510

www.theburgerspriest.com

❏ *Chino Locos*

4 Greenwood Avenue

Toronto, ON M4L 2P4

647-345-5626

368 Broadview Avenue

Toronto, ON M4M 2G9

647-349-3888

www.chinolocos.com

❏ *Fanny Chadwick's*

268 Howland Avenue

Toronto, ON M5R 3B6

416-944-1606

www.fannychadwicks.ca

❏ *The Hogtown Vegan*

1056 Bloor Street West

Toronto, ON M6H 1M3

416-901-9779

www.hogtownvegan.com

WINDSOR

❑ *Motor Burger*

888 Erie Street East

Windsor, ON N9A 3Y9

519-252-8004

www.motorburger.ca

❑ *Smoke & Spice Southern Barbeque*

7470 Tecumseh Road East

Windsor, ON N8T 1E9

519-252-4999

www.smokenspice.com

WINONA

❑ *Memphis Fire Barbeque Company*

1091 Highway 8

Winona, ON L8E 5H8

905-930-7675

www.memphisfirebbq.com

WESTERN CANADA

CALGARY

❑ *Big Fish*

1112 Edmonton Trail Northeast

Calgary, AB T2E 3K4

403-277-3403

www.big-fish.ca

❑ *Big T's BBQ & Smokehouse*

2138 Crowchild Trail Northwest

Calgary, AB T2M 3Y7

403-284-5959

www.bigtsbbq.com

❑ *Boogie's Burgers*

A-908 Edmonton Trail Northeast

Calgary, AB T2E 3K1

403-230-7070

www.boogiesburgers.com

❑ *Boxwood Café*

340 13th Avenue Southwest

Calgary, AB T2R 0W9

403-265-4006

www.boxwoodcafe.ca

❑ *Holy Grill*

827 10 Avenue Southwest

Calgary, AB T2R 0A9

403-261-9759

www.holygrill.ca

DRUMHELLER

❑ *Bernie & The Boys Bistro*

305 4th Street West

Drumheller, AB T0J 0Y0

403-823-3318

www.bernieandtheboys.com

EDMONTON

❑ *The Dish Bistro and the Runaway Spoon*

12417 Stony Plain Road Northwest

Edmonton, AB T5N 3N3

780-488-6641

www.thedishandspoon.com

❑ *Highlevel Diner*

10912 88 Avenue Northwest

Edmonton, AB T6G 0Z1

780-433-0993

www.highleveldiner.com

Louisiana Purchase
10320-111 Street Northwest
Edmonton, AB T5K 1L2
780-420-6779
www.louisianapurchase.ca

Sofra
10345 106th Street Northwest
Edmonton, AB T5J 0J2
780-423-3044

KAMLOOPS
Fiesta Mexicana Restaurant y Cantina
793 Notre Dame Drive
Kamloops, BC V2C 5N8
250-374-3960

LANGLEY
Hilltop Diner Cafe
23904 Fraser Highway
Langley, BC V2Z 2K8
604-514-9424
www.facebook.com/hilltopdinercafe

LOWER GIBSONS
Smitty's Oyster House
643 School Road Wharf
Lower Gibsons, BC V0N 1V0
604-886-4665
www.smittysoysterhouse.com

NANAIMO
Smokin' George's BBQ
Unit #5, 4131 Mostar Road
Nanaimo, BC V9T 6A6
250-585-2258
www.smokingeorgesbbq.com

PENTICTON
burger 55
84–52 Front Street
Penticton, BC V2A 1H7
778-476-5529
www.burger55.com

SASKATOON
EE Burritos
102 Avenue P S
Saskatoon, SK S7M 2W1
306-343-6264

TOFINO
Wildside Grill
1180 Pacific Rim Highway
Tofino, BC V0R 2Z0
250-725-9453
www.wildsidegrill.com

VANCOUVER
The American Cheesesteak Co.
781 Davie Street
Vancouver, BC V6Z 2S7
604-681-0130
www.americancheesesteak.com

Belgian Fries
1885 Commercial Drive
Vancouver, BC V5N 4A6
604-253-4220

Chewies Steam & Oyster Bar
2201 West 1st Avenue
Vancouver, BC V6K 3E6
604-558-4448
www.chewies.ca

❏ *El Camino's*
3250 Main Street
Vancouver, BC V5V 3M5
604-875-6246
www.elcaminos.ca

❏ *La Taqueria Pinche Taco Shop*
322 West Hastings Street
Vancouver, BC V0B 1K6
604-568-4406
www.lataqueria.ca

❏ *Miura Waffle Milk Bar*
2521 Main Street
Vancouver, BC V5T 3E5
604-687-2909
www.miurawafflemilkbar.ca

❏ *The Reef Restaurant*
4172 Main Street
Vancouver, BC B5V 3P7
604-874-5375
www.thereefrestaurant.com

❏ *Slickity Jim's Chat 'N' Chew*
3475 Main Street
Vancouver, BC V5V 3M9
604-873-6760
www.slickityjims.com

❏ *Via Tevere Pizzeria*
1190 Victoria Drive
Vancouver, BC V5L 4G5
604-336-1803
www.viateverepizzeria.com

❏ *The Wallflower Modern Diner*
2420 Main Street
Vancouver, BC V5T 3E2
604-568-7554
www.thewallflowermoderndiner.com

VICTORIA
❏ *Shine Café*
1548 Fort Street
Victoria, BC V8S 5J2
www.shinecafe.ca

❏ *Skinnytato*
615 Johnson Street
Victoria, BC V8W 1M4
250-590-6550
www.skinnytato.com

❏ *Tibetan Kitchen*
680 Broughton Street
Victoria, BC V8W 1C9
250-383-5664
www.tibetankitchen.com

WESTBANK
❏ *Kekuli Café*
505-3041 Louie Drive
Westbank, BC V4T 3E2
250-768-3555
www.kekulicafe.com

WINNIPEG
❏ *Kawaii Crepe*
201-99 Osborne Street
Winnipeg, MB R3L 2R4
204-415-2833
www.kawaiicrepe.ca

NORTHERN CANADA

WHITEHORSE

❏ *Antoinette's Food Cache*

4121 4th Avenue

Whitehorse, YT Y1A 1H7

867-668-3505

❏ *Klondike Rib & Salmon*

2116 2nd Avenue

Whitehorse, YT Y1A 1B9

867-667-7554

www.klondikerib.com

About the Authors

John Catucci is an actor, a comedian, an author, and the host of *You Gotta Eat Here!* He may not be a chef, but he knows a great burger when he eats one. John has also been a member of The Second City Touring Company, where he honed the improv skills he now displays in restaurant kitchens across Canada. He lives in Toronto, Ontario. Follow him on Twitter **@johncatucci** and **@yougottaeathere**.

Michael Vlessides is the bestselling author of *The Ice Pilots* and a freelance writer whose award-winning work has been published in magazines around the world. A graduate of New York University's School of Journalism, Michael lives in Canmore, Alberta, though he has been known to travel farther afield for a plate of poutine, a gourmet hot dog, or a maple bacon doughnut.